ABOUT THE AUTHOR

B ORN IN CRACOW, Poland, Jack Michalowski has lived in many places: Belgium, Canada, Hong Kong and Singapore and most recently in Bahrain in the Middle East. Originally trained as architect, he has worked for over twenty years in both energy and finance industries in senior executive positions. He currently works as managing director of a Dubai-based infrastructure fund sponsored by a subsidiary of the World Bank. Widely traveled, he speaks seven languages.

ACKNOWLEDGMENTS

I WOULD LIKE TO thank my wonderful first editor, James Morgan, for his major edit work in streamlining this book to make it, hopefully, accessible to a wide audience of readers. I would also like to thank my agent, Curtis Russell of P.S. Literary Agency, for his long and tireless work of promoting the book, even though we eventually had to end the agency contract. Also, I would like to thank my family and friends—my first readers—for their patience and their input during the time I was working on the book. Last but not least, I would like to thank people from Xlibris: my editor and co-ordinator, Joy Daniels, for her help and great patience, my marketing agent Rey Barnes and the website design co-ordinator, Yanie Cortes.

I would also like to acknowledge the works that have deeply influenced the creation of this book: the ground-breaking 1955 book 'Energy and Society' by Fred Cottrell, a study of the critical relationship between energy and the fate of civilizations; Equally ground-breaking 1988 book 'The Collapse of Complex Societies' by Dr. Joseph Tainter, demonstrating that complex societies tend to collapse once their overhead costs exceed what the underlying energy regime can support; The amazing 1976 book by Jean Gimpel about the Industrial Revolution of the Middle Ages, entitled 'The Medieval Machine'; Jeremy Rifkin's two excellent books, 'Entropy' and 'End of Work'; and finally, Eric Drexler's stunning nanotechnology predictions contained in his 1986 book, 'Engines of Creation'.

For sourcing of the historical part of this book, I would like to acknowledge Fernand Braudel's two monumental works: 'The Civilization and Capitalism' and 'The Mediterranean and The Mediterranean World in the Age of Philip II', each a storehouse of socio-economic insights about early modern Europe; George

Huppert's 'After the Black Death' and Carlo Cipolla's 'Before the Industrial Revolution', each a great social and economic study of the Renaissance and the Baroque era; David Hackett Fisher's 'The Great Wave', a source of superb economic analysis with a special focus on inflation and economic cyclicality; again, Jean Gimpel's 'Medieval Machine', as the primary source for the chapter about the medieval economy and technology; for the chapters referring to Renaissance and Baroque Spain, the primary sources were 'Spain 1469-1714' by Henry Kamen and 'Spain in America' by Charles Gibson; for the extensive insert outlining the decline of Late Roman Empire, the primary source was excellent book by Ramsey McMullen, 'Corruption and the Decline of Rome'.

I would like to also acknowledge authors Hohenberg and Lees for the material based on their excellent book 'The Making of Urban Europe'; J.R. Hale for his insightful study of the Renaissance in his book 'War and Society in Renaissance Europe'; J.K.J. Thomson for the material based on his book 'Decline in History'; and finally Paul Johnson's monumental 'History of the Modern World' for the material related to the 1917 Russian Revolution.

BAROQUE TOMORROW

*WHY INEQUALITY TRIUMPHS
AND PROGRESS FAILS?*

Jack Michalowski

Library of Congress Control Number: 2012922047
ISBN: Hardcover   978-1-4797-5365-9
                 Softcover   978-1-4797-5364-2
                 Ebook   978-1-4797-5366-6

To order additional copies of this book, contact:
Xlibris Corporation
1-800-618-969
www.Xlibris.com.au
Orders@Xlibris.com.au
502146

CONTENTS

PART THREE
NOW

PART FOUR
BEYOND

We live in a reality of rising inequality, impoverished middle class, declining real incomes, mounting debts. Real wages have not grown in a generation. High taxes, record high costs of housing, energy, food, medical care and education eat away most of our incomes. The 'post-industrial' nations stopped growing; many are so deep in debt, they are on the verge of bankruptcy. Wealth gap is the biggest in almost a hundred years. Half of all Americans are now classified as poor and near-poor. Middle class, shrunken, indebted and increasingly jobless, faces a grim future.

None of the futurists of a generation ago expected this kind of future. Yet, history shows us that exactly the same trends existed before. Oddly, they typically surfaced when progress, once broad, would narrow down mainly to information technology . . . .

This book will strip away some of our most cherished illusions: the mantra of accelerating technological progress; the concept of 'modern era'; dreams that instant access to information, abundance of information-processing gadgets or every kid having a college degree will somehow rescue us from our current predicament.

Welcome to a brand new world—a radically different view of our past, present and future.

To the Memory of my Mother

INTRODUCTION

"We will have man on Mars by 1984"
—US Vice President Spiro Agnew, 1970[1]

"A record number of Americans—nearly 1 in 2—have fallen into poverty or are scraping by on earnings that classify them as low income."
—US Conference of Mayors Survey, December 2011[2]

OUR WORLD IS in a state of crisis. In the developed countries, economies still have not truly recovered from their near-collapse in 2008. Financial problems of one sort or another are all over the news. In America, almost a fifth of all homeowners continue to risk foreclosure; poverty rates are the highest since the 1930s. In most once-rich countries, unemployment and underemployment rates are terrifying high. Average people in the U.S. and the UK are earning less and working harder and longer than ever in living memory. They are also feeling less secure than ever before. For the first time in America's history, the average American is less educated and poorer than his parents, with the past decade seeing the most dramatic rise in poverty in modern times. By some accounts, average U.S. income is now the same as in 1989—or, by other accounts, as in 1968. In the UK, the common belief is that real incomes and living standards are falling—eroded by escalating living costs—and that crime rates are rising. Western Europe and Japan have hardly grown for several decades and are in deep trouble. The long-term economic prospect for most developed, 'post-industrial' countries is uniformly grim.

With more than half of all young people in many post-industrial countries facing unemployment and masses of government employees facing job and salary cuts, riots and street protests accompany the massive crisis of confidence and hope in the future.

How did we get here? The 50s and the 60s, and even the 70s and the 80s were still the time of enthusiastic optimism about what lay ahead. We took for granted that the best was still ahead of us. We took for granted that the lives of our children—their incomes, their life spans, their living standards—would be much better than ours. We took for granted that the future would hold every promise imaginable, full of yet-undiscovered inventions and wonders.

The reality of the sixties—the halcyon era, the peak of mass prosperity and proof of success of the 'consumer' version of capitalism-cum-welfare system—underpinned these beliefs. The decade managed to combine the best of all worlds: record high GDP growth in what were still 'industrial' countries, record high productivity growth, record high real wages for ordinary people, and near full-employment. American 'consumer economics', copied into Europe and Japan after the war, turned these countries within a couple of decades into prosperous consumer kingdoms, copycat Americas. Exporting their goods into wide-open U.S. market, they were growing even faster than the U.S. itself. In 1960, the worst unemployment—below four percent—was in Denmark and Italy, two percent in Britain and Spain, and just one percent in Germany[3].

But this was supposed to be just the starting point. The promise of a better future was based not just on improvements of our existing inventions and machines, not on more efficient access to information or more efficient manufacturing but on the expected wave of dramatic technological innovations that would alter every facet of our daily lives. Within the following half a century, we expected to see a world completely transformed.

This book was born on the back of such expectations.

Its concept started a quarter of a century ago, in 1986, when I came across a book entitled "Engines of Creation: The Coming

Era of Nanotechnology".[4] I read it in one night. I was mesmerized. The author, Eric Drexler, presented concepts that were nothing short of revolutionary. Drawing on ideas already talked about in the late 1950s, Drexler wrote about a world that was soon going to become our reality. A world in which microscopic machines could be built from individual atoms and then self-replicate from resources available in the ground, air and water. Once programmed, these machines, which he called "universal assemblers", could assemble into virtually everything one could think of. They could become shape-shifting clothing that would cocoon us at the bottom of the ocean or on other planets—or amplify our muscles to turn us into Supermen. They could turn into microbe-like tiny robots fighting viruses inside our bodies or morph into environmental scrubbers that would clear pollutants from the air and water; or flying micro-robots that would attack and destroy plant pests—or, perhaps, enemy planes. They could assemble themselves into robotized cities or spacecrafts. It was pure magic.

The world was going to be completely transformed by nanotechnology, and Eric Drexler has promptly set up an institute to prepare the world for its imminent arrival.

Eric Drexler's revolutionary book was not alone. Rather, it was the culmination of a series of books written in the 1970s and 1980s by many renowned futurists and forecasters. They were led by the most famous guru of all futurists, Alvin Toffler.

In his original 1970 book, "Future Shock"[5], printed in over 6 million copies and subject of a 1972 documentary movie narrated by no less than Orson Welles, Alvin Toffler argued that our society was undergoing an enormous structural change, a revolutionary leap from the old Industrial Society to what he called a 'Super-Industrial Society'. The speed of progress, wrote Toffler, was accelerating and this accelerating change was shocking and overwhelming ordinary people, leaving them disconnected and suffering from stress and disorientation, or "future-shocked". It was Toffler's belief that the majority of social problems—for example, people dropping out of the 'rat race' of high-stress careers and becoming homeless drifters—were mere symptoms of the "future-shock" and "information overload".

In his follow-up 1980 book, "Third Wave"[6], Toffler argued that since the late 1950s most developed countries were rapidly moving away from a 'Second Wave' (or industrial) society toward what he called a 'Third Wave' (or post-industrial) society. The 'Third Wave' world—the world Alvin Toffler saw taking place before his very eyes already in 1980—and for sure our world of early 21st century—was to be a wealthy, futuristic society with little hard work but with growing leisure time giving rise to a fantastic diversity of lifestyles, a Disneyland for grownups. It was going to be an 'Information Era'—a term coined by Toffler—in which processing matter was no longer going to be important. Instead, wealth was going to come simply from processing of information. The new type of workers—information workers, or 'cognitarians', working from home—would replace factory-bound proletarians.

The world of Alvin Toffler anticipated was the world of accelerating broad technological change, a world where problems that now seem to dominate our reality, both during discussions at the kitchen table and in the media—falling real incomes, sovereign bankruptcies, unemployment, rising prices of food, energy, real estate, worry about skyrocketing costs of education or medical care, or saving money for retirement—simply did not exist. In Toffler's world of the 'Third Wave', the affluent middle class people, living in electronic mansions, led the life of care-free leisure, short working hours and diversified lifestyles of their choice, telecommuting to school or to work, and producing at home whatever they desired. In this world, anticipated to be our world of the early 21st century, debt, unemployment, poverty, financial crisis, long working hours, jobs disappearing to India, China, or being taken away by low-wage immigrants—were unimaginable.

In theory, we are all living in Toffler's 'Third Wave' world, right now.

Like many young people I knew at that time, I was a great admirer of Toffler's ideas. I was also fascinated by the incredible possibilities presented by nanotechnology as described by Drexler. And so my book—this book—began as a part-time personal research project: I was trying to prove to myself that the brand new world, described by Toffler and Drexler was not only imminent, but already happening, that the great technological leap, resulting in full employment, short working hours, rising incomes and majority of us turning into affluent, leisurely 'information workers', was actually taking place. I pictured my future book proving we are already entering this brave new world of leisure, based on artificial intelligence, nanotechnology, robotization of the mundane tasks and even more—and that was going to be the new idea—rebuilding our bodies with implants that would offer our brains the memorization and processing capabilities of computers and supplant our failing organs or muscles with robotic inserts. I was fascinated by the idea of computers and robotic protheses or even largely artificial bodies becoming part of our everyday life, helping us to advance to the next stage of our evolution as a species. From there, physical immortality was just around the corner.

But as my research progressed over the last two decades, it began yielding mixed, not to say odd results. I discovered that, outside of improved information processing and transmission—delivered by what Intel began in 1971 calling the microprocessor—there actually was not that much broad technological improvement going on. In fact, Alvin Toffler seems to have hit the high point of change around 1980, when computers were already well entrenched in most offices and it was clear they were set to rapidly develop further. But outside of computers and IT, since around 1980, most areas have hardly showed any signs of technological progress or improvement—at least not anything with impact on our daily lives. Nanotechnology, artificial intelligence, omnipresent robots, and average people living life of leisure in their electronic mansions—all this was still talked about as imminent for a while, yet over the decades that followed it continued to be conspicuously and completely absent from our daily lives.

Against all expectations of accelerating progress, I discovered that research productivity—the ratio of patents to the number of research scientists and engineers—has declined sharply over the last forty years, in many different industries and countries. Between 1970 and 1990, it has dropped by 55 percent in the U.S. alone, with even steeper declines in Europe, raising the specter of 'technological exhaustion'—getting less and less innovation despite the ever-increasing levels of R&D investment.[7] Decline in research productivity was paralleled by decline in actual productivity—overall productivity growth of top industrial countries dropped by around half in the last three decades of the 20th century compared to the 50s and the 60s.[8]

I have discovered that—while lack of concern with financial issues maybe made sense for someone writing in the 1970s, as Alvin Toffler did, after decades of strong increases in average incomes, very low unemployment and declining inequality—since Toffler's visions the future has changed. And for most people in the developed countries, it has undergone a dramatic, unexpected change for worse.

I have found that the slowdown in innovation was paralleled by a steady, gradual economic slowdown taking place even as the futurists were penning down their rosy visions. In the 1960s real global growth averaged six percent. This figure dropped to 3.5 percent in the 1970s, below three percent in the 1980s, and barely two percent in the first half the 1990s. Since then it was only lifted by the phenomenal rise of the BRICs, barely offsetting the stagnation or even decline of the developed economies. Average American GDP growth—in the near-quarter century from 1973 to 1995—slowed down to only 1.64 percent.[9] Between 2005 and 2011, on a per capita basis, American economy did not grow at all. Not just America—Japan and Europe were stuck in a no-growth mode since the 1980s.

I have found that as less and less productive jobs were available to employ massively growing populations, and as real wages began to drop, governments had to pick up the slack by subsidizing the economy. But since many richest taxpayers were now tax-exempt and tax income could not match expenses, they were increasingly doing so on credit. By 2011, according to economist Gary Shilling, almost 60 percent of all Americans receiving any form of income depended on the U.S. government for most of their paycheck—salary, unemployment, welfare, medical benefits, whatever—double compared to 1950 percentages. By 2018, this was expected to increase to almost 70 percent.[10] Not only was public sector expenditure ballooning dramatically; worse—close to half of the public money being spent was borrowed. Among the hoopla of accelerating progress and supposedly growing wealth, real poverty was creeping in. Since the recession began in 2007, for the bottom fifth, family incomes in the U.S. have fallen by over 11 percent[11]. By late 2011, a new census revealed, nearly half of all Americans could be classified as poor or near-poor. In Europe, where official unemployment was over 11 percent, quarter of all people faced poverty. In the U.S., in a single decade between 2000 and 2011 the number of (means-tested) Medicaid recipients has increased from 34 million to 54 million people, and the number of people receiving food stamps shot up from 17 million to over 52 million. Spending on food stamps alone was projected to reach $800 billion over the next decade.

I have discovered that, far from massive affluence widely predicted by Toffler, Naisbitt and others as the result of the expected technological progress, poverty rates have risen since the 1980s in all almost developed countries, and especially in the USA.

In fact, in the four decades since Toffler published his work, I have never met any 'future-shocked' people, and 'information overload' was at the very bottom of people's concerns list. Instead, I have met a great deal well educated people living from paycheck to paycheck, insecure in their jobs and incomes, their existence a daily struggle with rising prices and declining real wages and benefits. They were not worried how to fill their leisure time or develop hobbies–they were worried about their and their children's future and working longer and harder to make ends meet. Shaky economy, constant, grinding, daily insecurity of jobs and incomes, disappearing welfare cocoon long taken for granted, grim prospects facing most people's children–items hardly ever mentioned by any futurist–were increasingly their first priority. The last two decades were especially hard on ordinary people, with the old mainstay of the society–the middle class–steadily losing ground. Finally, what some call the 'Great Recession' of 2008-2009 destroyed the western societies' illusions of affluence–until recently propped by massively growing debt–and brought the bleak reality to the surface. Since 2001, median middle-class income decreased by 5 percent; total wealth of American households dropped by 28 percent. The wealthiest 1 percent of the U.S. population now had 288 times the amount of wealth of the average middle-class American family.

By the end of 2012, a mere 400 richest Americans had more wealth than 150 million of the poorest, a stunning level of inequality, reminiscent of the centuries long past.

In the US, in the 1960s the richest country in the world, most people now lived a day-to-day existence, earning miserable incomes in permanently insecure jobs, squeezed between flat wages and ever-growing costs of living. The worst part was that there seemed no hope of things ever getting better.

The landscapes of the new, Hi-Tech Baroque that emerged over the last two decades would shock the dreamers of the 70s: slummy centers of once-booming cities, where the homeless searching for cans through the garbage bins and police on ruthless hunt for cash from parking or traffic offenses were increasingly the visible signs of economic activity; monumental city halls plastered inside with pictures of smiling taxpayers or admonishments to correctly recycle; outside, rough streets, peopled by beggars, hoods, muggers, drug addicts and skinheads in army boots, armed with knives; destitute families sleeping on the sidewalks; porn shops and hookers. In sleepy suburbia, illiterate kids on drugs, teachers with no time to teach between confiscating knives and filling government forms, a bleak reality of shrinking prospects and shaky employment, where hard work and moral values once advocated by parents no longer guaranteed success. Further away, discreetly hidden behind walls, guards, and electronic surveillance, there were luxury villas of the newly rich, at their apex the computerized palaces of the billionaires. Grandiose functions, new political dynasties steadily entrenching themselves in supposed democracies, incredible degree of corruption, cynicism and decay mirrored the reality of Baroques long past.

And increasingly, no long-term future visions were being offered. The entire futurology virtually disappeared as a discipline. Get-rich-while-you-can seemed to be the only motto of the day. Political programs lasted only until the next election.

The future was turning very unfuturistic indeed.

Instead of 'quantum leap' in productivity due to computers, such quantum leap expected ever since their arrival into U.S. offices in 1966–hailed at the time as the greatest invention ever–I have discovered that productivity in the services sector, strongly growing before, especially in the 1950s, has in many cases actually declined after services have seen massive computerization. I knew from my personal experience–and I soon also found from statistics–that working hours have not only not decreased, as firmly predicted by Toffler and most other futurists, but instead dramatically increased. 'Electronic cottages', where they existed, cost many millions of dollars and belonged only to the privileged few, at best top one percent of the population. I was shocked to discover that, in the midst of our 'Information Era', illiteracy was growing, and number of patents per scientist was steadily decreasing. I found that the same R&D investment that used to produce well over hundred new pharmaceuticals in the 1950s, now could not even produce one.

Instead of confirming the rosy visions of Toffler and Drexel, my research began to take me into a completely unexpected direction. The society was changing, even changing dramatically, but these trends had nothing to do with 'Third Wave' or 'information overload'. The society was polarizing between the growing numbers of 'underprivileged' people—the new working poor—and the elite-educated 'information professionals'—at best 10 percent of the population. This elite, led by the super-rich 1 percent—now establishing itself as a new-fangled investor class—was distinguished from the rest by soaring incomes and ostentatious displays of wealth. Skyrocketing prices of real estate, of elite private schooling, and obsessions with money and branded goods dominated these people's discussions, not diversification of lifestyles.

In this world the middle class was rapidly shrinking. By 2011 in the U.S. it shrank to only 44 percent of the population, from around 70 percent a generation ago. Its old role as the anchor of equality and democracy was increasingly meaningless. There was palpable financial stress and even fear, underpinned by unprecedented levels of debt at every level, government or private, seemingly the only way to support the old living standards and benefits. Wealth gap was increasing rapidly and by 2010 concentration of wealth in the U.S. was back to levels unseen since the Great Depression, or even in the last 100 years.

Against all predictions, the Holy Grail of futurists—Information Technology—was not making average people any richer and was failing to create significant employment. America, despite being a technology leader and a flag-bearer of Alvin Toffler's 'post-industrial society' by 2010 was near-bankrupt and deep in debt to 'factory of the world' China. It was also falling behind in GDP growth and its relative size on the world arena. By the summer of 2011, America teetered on the brink of default, its credit rating downgraded for the first time ever. It had federal government debt equivalent to almost seven years of revenues. Just like in Baroque Spain, close to half of all expenses had to come from borrowed money, accounting for the biggest debt in the country's history.

The central premise of all the forecasters of the last generation—that Information Technology would rescue us from all ills and make us richer—seemed to be turning into a complete delusion. IT sector was creating few jobs, and even fewer high-paid ones. Increasingly, more and more of the IT jobs that were being created were not in the U.S. but in places like India—places were companies could find both expanding markets and cheap yet educated labor.

On the global level, there was growing fear of how small the margin of error has become, and how suddenly vulnerable our world has become to catastrophic events, both man-made and natural. Commenting on a 2011 OECD report, an article in "The Times" so described the dire situation of the developed countries: "It is not hard to understand the sudden disquiet about how unprepared financial and political systems are for the ripple effects from random shocks . . . Consequences of events like sovereign defaults, natural disasters, commodity price surges, regional power failures and social upheavals have become the stuff of conjecture and policy discussions. But it is far less clear that anyone is actively modeling, planning and preparing for these risks. For many, increasingly myopic investment community is almost blind to long-tem horizons . . . 'Never before have global risks seemed so complex, the stakes so high and the need for international cooperation to deal with them so apparent'" said OECD in its recent report. [12]

Any long-term visions and programs disappeared from this reality struggling against daily debt, unemployment and financial problems unseen for generations.

By contrast to the malaise of the 'post-industrial' world, low-wage, fast-industrializing countries like China, Brazil and India—places hardly mentioned by Toffler or other futuristic gurus of the 70s and 80s—were booming, completely at odds with any futuristic theories. Today's China—already perhaps the world's biggest economy or likely to become so in a decade—was as unfuturistic as they come.

It was a pure 'Second Wave' reality, a smoke-stack Industrial Era country—a complete anti-thesis of Toffler's Third Wave utopia. It was full of sweatshops and back-breaking labor, corruption, bureaucracy and pollution. It was a country that grew into a superpower within a mere generation since Toffler's prediction not thanks to producing information or innovation—there was hardly any—but real industrial goods, at low cost, with tens of millions of peasants producing sneakers, toys, laptops, iPhones and all other imaginable material goods, often in sweatshop-like conditions, for rock-bottom wages. There was no leisure era in this new world leader, no short working hours, no 'third wave', no 'future shock', no 'information overload'. There was also no democracy, and the wealth gap was already terrifying and growing. Everything about China's rise was completely at odds with Toffler's forecasts on how our future was going to be.

Clearly, the way things were going, Third Wave visions of mass affluence and broad technological progress hailed by Toffler and other futurists were just a fantasy.

Instead, as I studied the rapidly changing reality of our last few decades, the new world taking shape in front on my eyes began to display a strangely familiar feel: a deja-vu. Instead of being futuristic, the trends shaping our world eerily resembled the trends of a Baroque reality we thought long past. Just as during the 17th century Baroque, the reality of 21st century America was that of workers 'on call', without job security or benefits, of speculation in grain prices, of swelling numbers of the working poor, of foreclosed family homes and farms, of growing numbers of homeless and illiterate underclass, of urban ghettoes and impoverished suburbia contrasting with fortified mansions of the wealthy—the elite-educated professionals, owners of financial assets, the new investor class. Slowly, imperceptibly, our world was turning into an overcrowded, Baroque-like world of educated nobles and illiterate paupers, of mercenary 'contractors' dying in distant wars, of soaring inequality and stagnant innovation. The only areas of progress, exactly the same ones that were the hallmark of the last Baroque, were processing of information and financial engineering.

Just like today, Baroque was the world of semi-literate poor in a world awash with abundant information.

Instead of trying to validate and follow Toffler's and Drexler's visions about the future, I decided to first understand where they went wrong and what drove the dramatic changes that altered our reality over the last few decades. I set out to discover what took us onto a very different path from the one that, in theory, we might have realized as per their predictions.

This book is the result of my research stretching over many years. In trying to understand the present and the future, it took me into the past, to periods of history marked by trouble and decline, falling incomes and skills, rising debt and de-industrialization, stagnant innovation, periods that experts often glide over trying to validate their comfortable, simplistic theories of steady, linear progress. It took me to conclusions very much at odds with the prevailing mantras.

The thesis of this book may be difficult for many to accept. It argues that all the signs of our present reality—virtually every element of the story of the past four decades—point to a structural decline, decline rooted, as in *all* other historical declines, in massively growing populations faced with declining innovation and lack of new energy converters or new cheap energy sources. What makes the situation worse in these circumstances is de-education and de-skilling of the rapidly pauperizing middle class and dramatic polarization of the society between rich and poor. Very high levels of inequality are proven by history to be absolutely destructive. As malaise sets in, they become a major contributor to decline.

I decided to call this deep-rooted, recurrent problem the 'Baroque Syndrome'.

Every Baroque Syndrome follows a predictable pattern. It invariably arises first in the leading economies, these with the highest operating costs and the least room to grow further given their stagnating energy and technology setup. These are the economies burdened with legacy costs—social and military liabilities, enormous bureaucracies and vigorous, expansive, voracious elites—societies like Obama's America, and also Western Europe and Japan, least able to implement any significant reform. In face of cheaper foreign competition, lack of broad technological advance and vested interests paralyzing their political machinery, they can only borrow and pass the burden onto the next administration and next generation. On the visible surface of events, Baroque Syndrome manifests itself as escalating energy costs and persistent inflation—especially inflation in energy, housing, food and other basic commodities. It invariably shows in flat or declining incomes of average people. The decline eras seem to be typically accompanied by soaring value of positional assets—assets that secure exceptional income streams. Such assets are top real estate, senior jobs in and contracts with the government or large corporations, elite private school diplomas, access to networks of decision makers or guild-like exclusive professions setting their own monopoly fees—the doctors, the lawyers, the top bureaucrats and chief executives.

In the decline stage, the society becomes increasingly polarized between rich and poor, and there is massive growth of personal debts and government deficits. The middle class shrinks and pauperizes at the same time. These trends are accompanied by growing neo-conservatism (and often obscurantism, religious or otherwise), outsourcing of manufacturing to low labor cost locales, increasing numbers of poor and homeless, decline of civil society and rise of street-level brutality and crime, all set against the escalating wealth of the rich: the investor class.

The only progress that takes place in such times is the rapid growth of information technology and financial engineering. These are attempts to introduce, at minimal expense, an injection of new efficiency into an otherwise stagnant system. Implementation of these efficiencies underpins the growth of, and brings outsize profits to the new, top-educated class—the investor elite. There is visible dearth of any other new life-improving technologies. Often, but not always, IT progress extends to warfare technologies; and wars, rebellions, riots and social revolts, driven by desperation and alienation of the impoverished masses, tend to mushroom on the back of the deepening decline.

Where did Toffler and other futurists go wrong? The future predicted by Toffler and other gurus was based on anticipated broad technological advance that simply failed to materialize. Even the innovation that took place in the thirty years preceding Toffler's visions—laser, plastics, nuclear power, microchips—was already living off the science created early in the 20th century, before WW2. Even in Toffler's time productivity of research and development was already on the decline, but he and other futurists chose to disregard this red flag. Instead of looking at what was actually happening, they chose to look at what was theoretically possible.

There is a big difference between forecasting what *may* happen—extrapolating latest cutting-edge technologies and inventions into imagined future breakthroughs, completely failing to take into account either economics or civilization's historical experience—and looking back at what actually *has* happened, looking for clues offered by real past events, events and trends that have consistently lead to specific historical outcomes. Unfortunately, technology and innovation do not develop in a vacuum. They heavily depend on underlying social and economic realities. Long-run historical events, typically spanning centuries, once you look below the surface—the stuff we learn in school, the kings, the dynasties, the dates, the battles—have a consistency that is almost chilling. In history, combinations of certain input factors *almost always* result in the same outcomes, time and time again. This is why people often say that history repeats itself.

Looking back at past trends provides a much surer footing to forecasting than extrapolating a few latest inventions and adding a lot of wishful thinking. Unlike futurology with its rose-tinted glasses, history is a hardened fellow that has seen many a civilization—in fact, most civilizations—destroyed and covered by sand or by jungle. You may say that it has also seen us rise from the caves to skyscrapers and space travel. Yes, we have made great progress over the last few thousand years, but this progress has been hardly linear. Instead, it's been in general slow and halting, sometimes rapidly accelerating—typically due to an invention of a new energy converter harnessing some new energy source—but subsequently *always* followed by prolonged periods of stagnation, even retreat from living standards and levels of technology already reached, often descending into a centuries-long plateau—a Baroque—at worst spiraling into complete collapse.

Historically, every wave of new growth, every blossoming of a new civilization was based on new energy coming into the system, every collapse due to this energy being eaten away by the combination of population growth and unbearable costs of supporting the elites. Spreading around pre-existing information—as opposed to true innovation leading to broad technological progress and increase of energy supply and improvement in living standards—never played a leading role.

Brilliant encyclopedias were written while people were starving in the streets, simply because food production and distribution technology was stagnant.

Until we understand how history—and progress—really works, futuristic forecasts will continue to be a sham. Despite the wishful thinking of many, history proves that we were only rescued from decline and propelled on a new path by invention of new energy sources and new energy converters—things like agriculture, sailships, windmills, iron ploughs, combustion engines, trains, cars and airplanes, or nuclear reactors—and *never by invention of new information processing technologies.*

IT advances, as we shall see in this book, usually come late in the historical cycle. Unfortunately, and due to reasons we shall also explore, IT advances—all the way from introduction of writing by the Sumerians—typically follow, rather than precede, other major technological inventions. They come at the peak. As such, rather than usher into a new era of plenty, they historically have signaled the incoming decline.

We should not delude ourselves that our era is somehow 'modern' and therefore exceptional, for some miraculous reason immune from the disasters that befell our predecessors. Unless technological progress effectively dispenses with human involvement in the economy by replacing our labor with robots and our minds and decisions with these of intelligent machines, as long as we are not immune from bias, error, greed, corruption and 'irrational exuberance', as long as human factors of self-interest and pursuit of power and wealth at all cost drive our economic reality, as long we have the very poor and the very rich, historical trends are unlikely to change.

Consequently, as of today, our reality is little different from that of our predecessors. Despite rosy hopes to the contrary, the very same problems that we once hoped were assigned to the past: hunger, unemployment, endemic war (even if so far only in poorer locales), poverty, massive inequality of income and wealth, corruption, job insecurity, eroding safety net—all are back with us. And now, we seem to be in a place in time where the inconvenient similarities with past eras of decline begin to be too close for comfort. They can no longer be ignored.

All leading civilizations of the past reached a moment when they began to suffer a debilitating decline. Other than perhaps pre-modern Japan, there wasn't a single exception. All these declines were signaled, before the collapse took hold, by the same factors as outlined above—overpopulation, lack of new energy sources or converters, dramatic social polarization, declining incomes of the majority and rise of small, educated elites of mandarin-like 'information professionals', invariably translating their educated status and access to information and peer networks into mushrooming wealth and ownership of income-producing assets. Such periods of decline would routinely witness de-industrialization and loss of basic skills by the 'post-industrial', once leading economies, and their swift eclipse by cheaper foreign competitors. Ancient Egypt suffered a decline similar to that of the Classical Maya; Classical Greece similar to that of Renaissance Italy. Stone-Age Chaco Indian culture collapsed in an oddly similar way—and basically for similar reasons—as dynastic China, the latter saved only by rebellions and civil wars at regular intervals officially known as the 'dynasty change'. Medieval Italy began, during the Renaissance and the Baroque, to de-industrialize in an undignified process of social unraveling and de-skilling strangely resembling the de-industrialization of early 20th century Britain and the one being experienced today by America.

The documented story of mankind has known, during its five thousand years run, dozens of unravelings affecting virtually all complex societies, all the way to the islands of Polynesia. But if there is a distant mirror reflecting the woes of our reality closest—the mirror of an age long past yet so eerily similar to ours—the glorious Renaissance and its ugly child, the disastrous Baroque seem to be just such a mirror.

Let us look into this mirror and see if we can learn from what happened and try to prevent it from happening again.

PART ONE

END OF THE AMERICAN DREAM

BAROQUE SYNDROME

"[In America] productivity rose by 83 percent between 1973 and 2007 but male median real wages rose just by 5 percent"

—The Economist, 2011[13]

"Our industrial base is vanishing, taking with it the kind of jobs that have formed the backbone of our economy for more than a century; our education system is in shambles . . . our infrastructure is crumbling. And American middle class, the driver of our creative and economic success—the foundation of our democracy—is rapidly disappearing."

—Arianna Huffington, Third World America[14]

AUGUST 2010, PORT of Piraeus, Greece. Heat and economic crisis hang over the city. Our cruise ship slips overnight activity programs for the following day under the passengers' doors. In the bundle, a note tells us to tightly close the balcony doors: in the morning an industrial robot will spray the windows with water under pressure. I make sure that the windows are closed, but hang around long enough to see what is really going on. No robots in sight. Instead, a couple of Asians with buckets and soapy dripping mops climb onto the balcony, clean the windows and then disappear with apologetic smiles.

We live today in an odd reality, very different from the one anticipated fifty or even thirty years ago by the futurists of the time. No robots. No automated colonies on the Moon. No short working hours. No full employment. No mass prosperity. No cold fusion or artificial intelligence. No flying cars or domed cities. No nanotechnology able to transform matter at will at the molecular level.

Oddly, of all the technological wonders predicted in the 1950s or 1960s only the computer flourished—and beat many expectations, even if the machines that emerged were quite different from what was once anticipated.

Yet few, if any of us, wonder why all these forecasts could have gone so wrong. Few notice—or maybe dare to articulate, in face of the prevailing mantra of accelerating progress—that our daily reality, with the single exception of computers and computerized IT gadgets—has hardly advanced since the 1960s. Few if any wonder why information technology developed but virtually all other forecasted techno-wonders failed to appear. Few look at historical events to learn from the past as to what the future might hold.

Are we destined for a bright future of rising incomes and prosperity—always just around the corner, as we have been persistently told for the last forty years—brought to us by the miraculous 'information explosion'—or are we destined to live in a world increasingly polarized between the rich and the poor, haunted by declining wages and unemployment, plagued by debt and disappearing safety nets, bankrupted, overpopulated and ravaged by climate change?

Very few people make a link between technology and our incomes and job prospects. Even fewer look at history of our race as the storehouse of information that allows us to predict the future or at least understand the present. Most people believe the prevailing mantra that we continue to make great strides in innovation and technology; that our 'Information Era' and shops full of computerized gadgets are somehow signs of technological progress and coming prosperity, somewhere just over the horizon. Most continue to believe the old mantra that we live in an era of accelerating progress.

Oddly, this well-worn paradigm is still being unquestioningly accepted even as most people increasingly believe that their personal future—and the future of their children—is likely to be a hard grind, with flat incomes, growing job and income insecurity, growing financial stress and disappearing social mobility—which now in America is among the lowest in the developed world. The 'accelerating progress' mantra is still being hailed even as a 2010 Wall Street Journal poll reveals that two thirds of Americans believe that the country is in irreversible decline and grinding financial problems daily fill the news.

How can this be reconciled?

The present is certainly disturbing, if not outright depressing. By summer 2012, Europe's debt problems and possible bankruptcy of eurozone countries were filling the news. The U.S. were growing slower than in any previous recovery, debt continued to escalate threatening future technical defaults, housing sector was weak, economy was not creating enough of the much needed jobs. The government seemed paralyzed. Official U.S. unemployment was over 8 percent, real one—the one that included people that gave up looking for jobs or were forced to accept jobs well below their skills—perhaps around 17 percent. "Not since records began has so deep a recession been followed by so shallow a recovery in employment" said 'The Economist' newspaper[15]. The country's economy was still far away from recovering the jobs it lost in 2008, and by end of 2011 real national per capita output was no higher than that of 2005.

Economists peddling stories that U.S. economy was on the brink of collapse were flourishing. Some were predicting doomsday scenarios where China, who owned almost a trillion dollars of U.S. government debt, might start selling it and send the U.S. dollar into a tailspin.

Gloom was pervasive. In stark contrast to how the futurists of the 1970s imagined the 21st century, in February 2010, UN head Ban Ki-moon told an international security conference in Germany that poverty, hunger and climate change were going to pose the major threat to mankind of 21st century. "[Thanks to dramatic food

price increases] there are now an unprecedented one billion hungry
people in our world" said the Secretary General. "In recent years
we have seen food riots in dozens of countries. Chronic poverty and
the worst downturn in generations, these two are emergencies [of
our times]."[16] Food prices hit a record in the spring of 2011, after
surging by more than a third in less than a year. Some, like maize,
went up by over 80 percent; sugar and wheat went up by around 60
percent. Unbearable increases in food costs were widely thought
to underpin the Arab Spring revolts in countries like Egypt, were
majority of people lived on less than two Euros a day. In 2012 in the
U.S., the worst drought in half a century has shown how vulnerable
we really are. In a single year, it drove up the prices of wheat by 26
percent, corn by 22 percent and soya beans by 38 percent. Food
production, said the experts, would have to go up by 70 percent by
2050 to feed exploding populations, rise of Asia's megacities and
changes in the diet caused by the migration to these cities from the
countryside. The 'Green Revolution' seemed exhausted: for the first
time since the 1960s yields of the world's key crops: wheat and
rice, did not keep up with the growth of population.[17] In July 2012
on CNN, an agriculture expert was predicting dramatic further food
price increases, in face of low investment in agriculture, stagnant
innovation in the sector and aging farmers.

If we contrast these dramatic stories with the rosy tales of
never-ending boom and Dow at 36,000—the stories of a relatively
recent 2006 vintage—we might be inclined to believe that our reality
somehow took a dramatic change for the worse in a mere three or four
years. This would be a wrong assumption. The reality of our world is
the product of a slow, consistent change that has been taking place
over the last 40 or even 50-60 years, until quite recently off the radar
screens of economists and the media, below the hooplas of New
Economy of the 90s and Globalized/Flat World hailed during the last
decade. Both the fake boom and the sudden downturn are its visible
signs, the flipsides of the same coin. The key sign of this reality in
the aptly named post-industrial economies is increasing population

pressure on resources—energy, food and raw materials—and stagnant innovation. As before, the underlying problems manifest themselves in steady polarization of societies, de-industrialization of the old leaders, growing inequality, lack of meaningful long-term visions, programs or R&D investments and dramatically rising debts. The declining societies experience stagnant or falling incomes, shrinking of middle class, inflation affecting daily necessities, steady increase in rates of poverty and inflow of low-wage immigrants brought in by businesses trying to cut down costs.

The flipside—and an integral part—of this malaise is the spectacular rise of a narrow, top-educated, transnational elite—the 'investor class'—controlling the vast majority of the wealth, income and consumption of our present reality. This reality—so different from the 1960s, the era of triumphant middle class—is now aptly described by Citibank analysts as a "plutonomy"—an economy totally controlled by and principally geared toward serving, the rich.

Whatever statistics one cares to look at, the story is the same, exposing a structural change that has been going for decades but which only the current crisis dramatically brought to light. In the middle of our 'Information Era', almost all of the once-leading economies seem on the path of decline. Productivity of American capital, yielding 30 percent on the average after the WWII, now stands at a paltry five percent. In the UK, millions of families are struggling to pay their bills, with about forty percent of households finding it tough to cope or falling behind on payments[18]. Any rise of interest rates over their record lows could tip many mortgage borrowers over the edge. Toffler might be surprised to learn that by 2011, British families would need to earn 20 percent more than a year earlier to remain out of poverty, as per report by Joseph Rowntree Foundation, since real increases in cost of living belied the understated official inflation statistics. Over the past decade in Britain, the cost of 'minimum' basket of goods and services rose by 43 percent, almost double official inflation figures. Another 2011 survey painted a dire picture of relentless squeeze on family budgets.

More than half of all households were spending all their income on basic bills and debt. In West Midlands, more than two thirds of all households have no money at all left after paying bills[19].

All the governments of the post-industrial world now carried extreme levels of debt. Economic reality of America in year 2011, the world's biggest debtor, was bordering on insane. Its government had to borrow forty percent of every dollar it was spending, relying on artificially low—significantly lower than inflation—interest rates to keep the interest burden low. It got itself into a situation where it was supporting one way or another close to 60 percent of all income-receiving Americans for most of their income. It also got itself into a situation where billionaires like Warren Buffett were taxed at lower rates than their personal assistants, yet—due to political paralysis—it was unable either to meaningfully raise taxes or slash spending. Analysts expected that by 2025 tax revenues would only be sufficient to finance debt interest payments and entitlement programs such as government pensions and Medicare—all expected to soar from $200 billion a year to $1000 billion a year. Anything else—for example, national defense, homeland security, energy and transport—would have to be eliminated or supported by additional borrowing. Japan financed half of its spending with debt, depending on near-zero interest rates. British government debt, now close to 100 percent of GDP, was by 2011 triple compared to where it was a decade ago[20]. The only way out seemed either politically unpopular austerity or devaluing the debt through inflation.

At the beginning of the second decade of the 21st century—the century that not long ago was anticipated to bring unprecedented progress, wealth and leisure—millions of Americans, Europeans and Japanese were experiencing instead unprecedented levels of financial stress and indebtedness, money problems on a scale they never had to cope with before in living memory, even as they were working longer and harder than ever. A 2010 poll revealed that half of Americans could not come up with $2000 in 30 days to meet an emergency. This meant that half of the population of this reportedly richest country on Earth was living a single paycheck away from potential disaster. In places like California, even before the crisis, official poverty levels were up to thirty five percent, up from just fifteen percent a generation ago[21].

The vaunted hi-tech economy and the prosperity and jobs it was supposed to bring seemed like cruel joke when one cared to look at the facts: seven out of ten jobs the U.S. economy was creating in 2010 were low-pay, low-skills and low-tech, many demanding only limited literacy. U.S. were increasingly importing high-tech goods from places like China or Brazil, while exporting commodities. Americans who lost their jobs found that their new jobs would pay, on the average, a fifth less than the old ones—if they could find jobs at all. Real incomes of the vast majority of Americans, Germans or Japanese have hardly moved in the last two or three decades. In many cases they have dropped. There were precious few mid-income jobs being created to replace the well-paying manufacturing jobs that the U.S.—and most other developed economies—was losing. Middle class, the traditional bastion of equality and democracy, was rapidly shrinking and losing economic clout in the new post-industrial reality.

"One in five Americans is unemployed, underemployed or just plain out of work" said Elizabeth Warren, chair of the Congressional Oversight Panel for TARP, "one in eight mortgages is in default or foreclosure. One in eight Americans is on food stamps. More than 120,000 families are filing for bankruptcy every month."[22]

The Great Recession of 2008-2009 brought about a decisive paradigm shift. Unprecedented wealth destruction, collapsing financial institutions, rising long-term unemployment—the partial unwinding of the debt mountain accumulated over decades has dealt a death blow to decades of self-delusion. The optimism generated by the debt-fuelled fake boom—reportedly generated by unstoppable technological progress, but proven to be essentially based on borrowing against inflated assets such as property—has collapsed. It has been replaced by skepticism and fear. The once near-religious belief that the "New Economy", based on new information technologies and college education, will bring growing, permanent prosperity to ordinary people, has been finally and completely shattered.

The American Dream, people tell you today, is over.

*

WHILE IT MAY seem today that the anticipated decoupling between the rich economies and the emerging markets has finally happened and is taking the two on radically differing course: the rich economies declining; the emerging ones growing, with accompanying reduction of poverty, expansion of the middle class and increasing real incomes, the driver of both trends is the same. The emerging economies of Asia, Middle East, Latin America, Africa and Eastern Europe are growing, yet—remarkably—all they are trying to do, and likely all that they can hope to ever achieve, is merely to catch up with the technology and living standards already reached, decades ago, in the West. Instead of using the now-popular acronym BRICs, it might be better to call them CUEs: Catch-Up Economies. But even there, even as this catch-up powers forward, wealth inequality is increasing: the average per capita income of the richest ten percent of Chinese is now 65 times higher than the bottom ten percent[23]. The Gini coefficient of income—the main measure of income inequality—worsened for most Asian countries over the last two decades.

In the post-industrial West, to get back to the low inequality levels, balanced budgets, and high overall living standards already achieved in the developed economies in the peak 1960s era, for some reason seems impossible to achieve.

Few of us realize that most of the changes we have been witnessing during the last forty years are all related. Almost everything we see around us: flat or declining real wages of most salary-earners;

persistent inflation, especially inflation in prices of assets and basics like energy, housing, education, medical care, transport and food; rising inequality and widening gap between the rich and the poor; waning power, size and wealth of the middle class; increasing job and income insecurity; evaporation of social rights and benefits taken for granted for over a century; globalization, or rather a global search to push down labor cost by outsourcing production of goods and services to the low-wage countries or to the domestic underground economy of 'illegal' paupers; frustrated attempts to develop new affordable energy sources; speedy progress of new information technologies set against odd slowdown of in almost all other areas of technology; and finally, the dawn of a transnational world of elite-educated, wealthy investor class, living in a world apart from the increasingly impoverished rest of the society—all these trends, without exception, are rooted in and are the reflections of the Baroque Syndrome.

Not only these, but virtually all, seemingly even more unrelated events we see and have seen around recently: from rise of the walled luxury estates to the collapse of the Soviet Union; from massive privatizations of government assets to longer working hours; from growing illiteracy, right in the middle of the "Information Era", to stratospheric increases in top executive compensations; from demise of the welfare state to rise of extremism, religious fundamentalism and other obscurantist trends; from skyrocketing number of people working temporary or contract jobs to stunning levels of personal and government debt; from massive rise in international trade to global obsession with elite private education and brand name luxury goods; from the return of Baroque-style homelessness and dramatic numbers of out-of-wedlock births to the biggest ever corporate bankruptcies and frauds going into billions; from asset inflation to the comeback of some long-forgotten diseases to odd phenomena of returning slavery and piracy right in the middle of our supposedly modern era—all these seemingly random phenomena are not only intimately related, but are in fact all surface signals of the Baroque Syndrome.

The first visible signs of this mega-trend, heralding our new reality, first surfaced almost exactly forty years ago, at the peak of America's prosperity and power in the late 1960s, when the first humans landed on the Moon, when the Internet was invented and only a few years before Apple unveiled its first personal computer, at the time when equality and rising incomes were taken for granted and homelessness and temp jobs did not exist. This peak era, like all the peak eras that came before—and possibly all these that are yet to come—was the time when the future seemed to hold every promise imaginable.

LES NEW *MISERABLES*

"We are moving towards a third-wave economy of full employment and short work hours."
—Alvin Toffler, Third Wave, 1980[6]

"Living standards will not get up again—ever. The reduction in Americans' living standards will be permanent"
—Howard Davidowitz, celebrity Wall Street analyst, Jan. 2009

THE FIRST VISIBLE signs of reversing trends surfaced in 1970s America. As always, they first showed among the poor. The '70s were the decade when the "new poor" suddenly and unexpectedly appeared—the homeless, the destitute, the underemployed part-timers or "contingent" workers. Nobody recognized their appearance as a reversal of the history's course, or the portent of a new Baroque reality yet to come. Instead, they were naively hailed by some futurists of the time as voluntary rat-race dropouts signaling the coming Leisure Era of 'diversified lifestyles'– Hollywood-style 'Easy Riders'. At first they were few. Typically, they did not own a home, did not have savings, and were either destitute or a paycheck away from it. Many were single, or single parents, who increasingly found it near impossible to support a household from a single income. The 70s were also a decade where U.S. annual productivity growth dropped from 1.4 percent to basically zero, and energy prices tripled or quadrupled in real terms. But no futurist paid attention to either of these phenomena.

This post-industrial social underclass of Baroque vagabonds—which today is omnipresent and seems near-permanent—did not exist in the

1950s or 1960s. But since the 1970s, its ranks have never stopped growing. Soon, poverty began rising not just among the drifters, the unemployed and the welfare recipients but also among the working class. By 1996, a third of American males 25 to 34 years old earned below the minimum required to support a family of four.[24] Crime and illegitimacy accompanied the unfuturistic rise of *les* new *miserables*.

The fall of the bottom earners into poverty was due to the falling wages. The American wages first began to drop in 1973, and since then have been dropping steadily[25]. "During the 1950s and 1960s, the halcyon era for America's middle class, productivity boomed and its benefits were broadly shared. The gap between the lowest and highest earners narrowed," said 'The Economist' newspaper in its 2006 study of rising inequality. But, "after the 1973 oil shocks, productivity growth suddenly slowed. A few years later, at the start of the 1980s, the gap between the rich and poor began to widen."[26] By 1995, real hourly wages of non-supervisory workers had declined fourteen percent, real weekly wages by nineteen percent compared to the 1970s. Real purchasing power was drifting back to 1950s levels[27]. Seemingly inconsistent with the futuristic Information Era forecasts, wealth and income inequality worldwide grew at spectacular speed, returning back to, and sometimes exceeding, pre-Industrial Era levels.

The decline was the worst at the bottom. Between 1973 and 1992, the real wages of the bottom fifth of male American workers fell 23 percent[28]. While elite wealth and power skyrocketed, the middle class visibly shrank. In the U.S. in the two decades between 1983 and 2004, a whopping 94 percent of all financial wealth created by the American economy went to top fifth of earners[29] In the 1980s, 90 percent of all income gains went to the top one percent of the earners; by the mid 1990s, the top 10 percent controlled nearly 90 percent of all financial assets in America.[30] Between 2002 and 2007, two-thirds of the nation's total income gains accrued to the top one percent of U.S. households; by 2007, this top one percent held a larger share of income that at any time since 1928[31]. By 2007, top fifth of the population owned a remarkable 85 percent of total wealth and 93 percent of financial wealth (i.e. wealth excluding family home) of America. The remaining 80 percent of the population (the middle class and the poor) owned only seven percent[32].

As the new millennium opened, millions of middle-class Americans joined the new, swelling underworld of the poor. Between 1975 and 2002 in California, the official number of people classified as poor grew from fifteen to 35 percent of the population, all at the expense of the shrinking middle class. Incredibly, with phenomenal increases in costs of virtually everything—from housing to transportation to food to schooling to medical care—not only real but even nominal wages of the vast majority of population have failed to significantly increase over the last three decades. By 2010, many fresh high school graduates were still making, in nominal dollars, not much more than $1200/month, roughly the same as in the early 1980s, in their first jobs; average middle-age, middle class wage earner would still make about $3000/month, comparable to nominal salaries thirty years ago, but now with less benefits and purchasing power. It was the same across all richer economies: KFC outlet in Singapore paid workers S$4.50 an hour in 2010, roughly the same as in 1985. These wages were all in nominal dollars, unadjusted for inflation—meaning that in fact they were lower perhaps by two thirds or more in real terms.

These numbers tell the story of low—and middle-income earners gradually drifting into poverty. While their wages for a generation stayed flat or dropped, most costs—from food to transport to schooling, but especially real estate, escalated dramatically. Some costs, like buying or renting housing in more desirable cities—cities that had jobs—rose by perhaps as much as 10 or 15 times in the meantime. Annual tuition cost of a public university—like Berkeley—rose from $650 in the 1970s to over $10,000 in 2010, an increase of 15 times.

By 2012, poverty has finally come to the American suburbia. It was here that during the last decade poverty increased the most, by over 50 percent. "If you take a drive through the suburbs and look at the strip mall vacancies, the 'For Sale' signs, and the growing lines at unemployment offices and social services providers, you'd have to be blind not to see the economic crisis is hitting home in a way these areas have never experienced," said Donna Cooper, a senior fellow at the Center for American Progress, a think tank.[33]

Faced with declining real incomes people began working harder and longer hours, moonlighting, saving less, borrowing more and retiring later. Increasingly, both spouses worked and sometimes even working children living with them supported one household budget. But nothing compared with the massive borrowing against the inflated values of real estate. The subprime phenomenon was not an isolated incident but a natural response to the typical Baroque trend of declining wages set against inflating property values.

Over the last thirty or forty years, we have witnessed a stunning impoverishment of the majority of not only American society, but most people in the developed economies. This was concealed only by massive and ostentatious increase in wealth of the small minority—at best top 10 percent of the population—and also by significant increase in wealth of many millions of people—no matter their income—who happened to own real estate (or some other positional assets) and lived one way or other of the inflating values of these assets. Casual evidence showed that most middle class people in developed economies that retained or increased their wealth during the last two or three decades did so by investing in real estate or stocks. Some lived of indexed government or corporate pensions or other similar inflation-proof 'legacy assets'. Very few got rich from truly productive—let alone innovative—activity and, apart from sports or media celebrities, those that did were mostly old-fashioned, Baroque-style professionals: doctors, lawyers, bankers, accountants.

The stellar rise of the rich elite was one of the most visible features of the Baroque Syndrome. By 2005 Citigroup memo argued that our world has largely become a 'plutonomy', a reality shaped by and principally serving the needs of the rich. "Our thesis is that the rich are the dominant drivers of demand in many economies around the world" said the memo. "These economies have seen the rich take an increasing share of income and wealth over the last 20 years, to the extent that the rich now dominate income, wealth and spending in these countries. Asset booms, a rising profit share and favorable treatment by market-friendly governments have allowed the rich to prosper and become a greater share of the economy in the plutonomy countries. Also, new media dissemination technologies like internet downloading, cable and satellite TV, have disproportionately increased the audiences, and hence gains to "superstars"—think golf, soccer, and baseball players, music/TV and movie icons, fashion models, designers, celebrity chefs etc. These "content" providers, the tech whizzes who own the pipes and distribution, the lawyers and bankers who intermediate globalization and productivity, the CEOs who lead the charge in converting globalization and technology to increase the profit share of the economy at the expense of labor, all contribute to plutonomy."[34]

This superb analysis was right on target. In the post-industrial 'plutonomy' world, the middle class was the clear loser. "Earnings [of the middle class] are flat, and likely to remain so in real terms, while cost inflation is steep especially for healthcare, energy and insurance. Globalisation, together with devaluation of western currencies and the apparently irresistible dominance of what Americans call the FIRE economy—finance, insurance and real estate—further pressures the salaried middle classes. At least part of what is happening reflects flagging competitiveness against Asia . . ." said *Financial Times* describing the situation in the UK in 2010. "[Lightly taxed] big spenders contribute to keeping our economy afloat . . . The political difficulties of persuading the middle class to pay more tax are compounded by knowledge that these big hitters escape relatively lightly. Statistics show that the gulf between top and median earners is wider than at any time since 1929. More and more companies are opting out of offering employees health or final salary pensions. Britain's average individual earnings are just over GBP22,000 [per year], a pathetically low figure . . ."[35]

The gradual slide of the middle class wage earners into poverty was a phenomenon witnessed by virtually all high-cost, developed economies. Between 1990 and 2010, Japan has experienced a continuous slide in wages; from 2009 to 2010 alone, winter bonuses to employees dropped a record nine percent, to the lowest figure in two decades[36]. Despite lower wages, working hours only grew longer.

Since early 1970s in America, real wages dropped for all income earners except the top fifth—the income elite—the only group where they increased[37]. Yet even in this category they increased by only ten percent. Within this group, the only people that made significant wage gains between 1979 and 2004 were the top five percent of earners, increasing their incomes by around half in real terms[38]. These modest gains were dwarfed by the soaring income growth of the very top earners: the top one percent of the population. Between 1985 and 2005, real starting salaries for lawyers joining big U.S. law firms went up 600 percent[39], with partners in top firms making maybe a million dollars a year; real pay of large-company chief executives increased by more than 1000 percent. By 2007, the income inequality in the U.S. was at its highest in almost a hundred years[40].

Same as in previous, pre-industrial civilizations experiencing their own Baroque Syndromes, one of the major visible surface signs of the mega-trend was a dramatic polarization of the society between the haves and the have-nots, and a gradual slide of what was once the middle class into poverty.

*

THE PRIMARY ORIGIN of the falling wages and the growing un—and underemployment was corporate America's drive to combat declines in profits as productivity gains declined and foreign competition increased. Despite increasing move of manufacturing offshore, the last four decades saw a steady decline in productivity of capital. While from the end of WWII until around 1980 it took an investment of only $2 to generate a $1 increase in the GDP, this increased—in the single decade of the 1980s—to $3 needed to generate the same GDP increase, and by 2010 it took $6 to generate such increase[41]. From the trough of 2002 recession to the trough of the recession of 2009, real U.S. gross domestic product grew only an average 1.7 percent annually, economy's worst performance for over half a century. During the previous six decades, growth averaged 3.9 percent a year[42]. Even during the 1991-2001 period growth has been almost twice as fast as in the decade just past[43].

Starting in the 1970s, as U.S. manufacturing began to face declining productivity at home and stiff competition abroad, it began to cut labor costs. Growing unemployment allowed to push wages down, not only in manufacturing but also in services. Millions of Americans got laid off from well-paying factory and office jobs as companies downsized, "outsourced" to Mexico and to China, automated production, modernized, or merged in order to boost profits. The new jobs paid less and had less—if any—benefits. By 1995, temporary, "contract," "on call," and part-time workers made up over 25 percent of all U.S. workers, and by 2000 the number was 35 percent[44]. Out of almost 1.25 million jobs created in the U.S. in the first half of 1993, 60 percent were part time; in February of that year, 90 percent of all jobs created were part time. These jobs all came with low wages and no benefits. According to a Senate Labor Committee 1991 report, 75 percent of U.S. workers were accepting wages lower than they would have 10 years earlier[45]. By 2010, the statistics showed that people who lost their jobs were on the average moving to jobs paying 20 percent less than their previous jobs, since many others could not find any jobs at all[46]. Sometimes they took jobs paying half or less of what they made before.

Few of the new substandard jobs carried any benefits, and they made a joke of unemployment statistics: In November 2009, if one added to the "officially unemployed" figure of ten percent those who were looking for work but did not meet the official tests, plus the involuntary part-timers, the U.S. unemployment rate would reach seventeen percent. If those who had completely dropped out of the workforce, involuntarily worked on call, or were involuntary "independent contractors" (mostly downsized professionals without much income), another fourteen percent would be accounted for[47]. The result would be America's effective unemployment/involuntary underemployment rate of 31 percent, nearly matching Europe's 33 percent effective unemployment/job market inactivity rate. In both post-industrial regions, only about two thirds of working-age adults were working regular jobs; in both between one-third to half of families have descended into poverty since Information Era set in.

In the very midst of this hyped Information Era, there was a stunning new trend: an alarming rise in illiteracy. By 1990, a third of American adults were functionally, marginally, or completely illiterate; in some U.S. cities, the school dropout rate reached nearly 50 percent[48]. A study of British middle-class teenagers found that their IQ, which was rising steadily during the past century, reversed this trend just as we entered the 'Information Era'; the 2008 IQ scores were 6 points lower than almost three decades earlier[49]. Dropping literacy and IQs seem to correlate with rising inequality and neo-conservative policies: A 2005 London School of Economics study found that Britain and the U.S.–the leaders of the neo-conservative creed–had the worst social inequality out of the eight richest countries studied, due to failing public education systems that precluded low-income students from moving up the wealth ladder.

At dawn of the new Baroque, in 1990s Arizona, almost one in every 3 households lived on less than $20,000 a year. Most of these new poor not only worked full-time, 40 hour weeks–many worked more than one job. Few of these jobs had benefits: pension, paid medical insurance, vacation, sick leave. These new *miserables* would eat cheapest fast food. They would put off seeing a doctor, even when they felt sick. One mistake, one illness, one accident, could push these people under: they lived on the very edge of the abyss. "A car breaks down and suddenly there's no money for mandatory insurance. No insurance means breaking the law just driving to work. Never mind that $50 for registration tags was already used for food[50]." There were stories of single parents who had part time jobs, yet lived with their children in a homeless shelter. Other new *miserables* might be fresh college graduates, sharing small flats in old buildings, always shopping for groceries with coupons and a list, and hardly ever going to movies, making long distance calls, or eating out[51].

With the advent of our new, Baroque-like reality of the last decades, the poorest of the new poor no longer had enough money to buy food. Even during the 'boom decade', in 2003, eleven percent of U.S. families reportedly experienced hunger. Increasing numbers of babies were showing signs of malnourishment, and pediatricians raised alarms that the problem was growing dire, especially for babies under one year old, for whom lack of food, or unsuitable food, could lead to problems with brain development[52]. In 2006 Britain, 4.1 million children—one third of all the children in the country—were classified as poor. Despite a much-publicized and costly program of tax transfers to families, Britain continued to have some of the highest child-poverty rates among developed countries, due to low incomes and high unemployment rates among families with many children[53].

The global economic crisis that set in 2007 only made things much worse. By February 2009, in a new suburban development Lehig Acres, Florida, after it was hit by dramatic drop in house prices and soaring unemployment, hunger became the chief topic of discussions in the community. Local food banks saw demand soar by three quarters in early 2009, with people of all ages, races and past income levels lining up for food[54]. These were not just the unemployed—more and more working people had to use the food banks because their wages dropped below the minimum necessary to cover rent and food.

Curiously, education did not seem to provide full protection from poverty—one fourth of the hungry in Toronto had college or university training. In the Philippines in 2008, half of the jobless had high school or college diploma[55]. By 2011, 360,000 Americans with master's degree had to rely on public assistance to survive, roughly triple 2007 numbers.

In our new 'Third Wave' reality, pauperism became global. In the winter of 2005, Russian authorities announced that in Moscow alone 17,500 unidentified bodies, the vast majority of them men, had been found over the previous five years, often lying under the snowdrifts all winter. These were the drunks, the poor, the unemployed, those who had failed to adapt to the new brutal winner-take-all reality[56]. By 1995, France already had an estimated 600,000 to 800,000 homeless, and the situation was getting worse[57]. Japan was not far behind.

The new poor of America's 21st century Baroque might work changing oil, flipping burgers, cleaning motel rooms, caring for the elderly, waiting tables, answering phones, delivering pizza, tossing boxes, or risking death by contracting themselves out to fight in distant wars. Many did not vote. Significantly, while some of these workers were hardly literate, many of the people stuck in such menial occupations were educated, some with a college degree. To this growing section of the society—the new servants of the new elites of our Neo-Baroque—the hyped New Economy and Information Society were at worst a cruel joke, at best a distant myth. Every year, their ranks were growing amid America's middle class.

"Low-wage bias is creeping into the economy" stated Bloomberg economist Joseph Brusuelas. MSN Money columnist Michael Brush pointed out that out the current minimum wage was "too meager to offer anyone the chance to climb out of poverty, let alone afford basic goods and services". He also highlighted an even more frightening trend: minimum-wage workers today were better-educated than they were three decades ago: in 2010, nearly 44 percent of them had either attended or graduated from college, up from 25 percent in 1979[58]. Why? Increasingly, minimum-wage jobs were all that was available to college-educated people.

Still, until quite recently, societies showed little alarm. Even as tens of millions of the unemployed, underemployed, and destitute emerged in post-industrial countries over the past few decades, most people still convinced themselves that the problems of the new poor were best solved by "the market," or by "college education." If people were poor or destitute, went the common thinking, it was their own fault.

*

"In the age which preceded the fall of the [Roman] republic, it was computed that only two thousand citizens were possessed of any independent substance"
—Gibbon, Decline & Fall of the Roman Empire[59]

THE SOCIAL IMPLICATIONS of the large-scale pauperization of citizens—reminiscent of the circumstances that preceded the downfall of the Roman Republic, or of the Baroque era of disasters and calamities—seemed to go unheeded. Few bothered to search for the hidden drivers that changed their world. Many denied the world was even changing. Until not long ago, throughout the 80s and the early 90s, media kept vehemently denying that the wealth gap between the rich and the poor was widening; even the use of the word 'poor' remained politically taboo.

Now, when we finally dare to admit that our world has dramatically changed and our 'Third Wave' has turned instead into a Baroque 'plutonomy', a world driven by, and serving the rich, what can we expect of the years to come?

WHEN FUTURE FAILS

N
OT A SINGLE forecaster in the rose-tinted 1960s or '70s predicted anything like the kind of future we are experiencing today. On the contrary, the 1970s and early 1980s, despite the clear signs of growing economic stress, gradually slowing innovation and increasing polarization of the society, witnessed the triumphant predictions of futurists like Alvin Toffler and John Naisbitt, both forecasting the imminent future of widespread affluence, full employment, short working hours and electronic cottages. Believers that the "information explosion" would somehow usher us into a wonderland of plenty and that part-time work is a lifestyle choice, still abounded. Even by 1989, visionaries like Frank Feather were still enthusiastic: "The use of artificial ears and eyes will be widespread by the late 1990s . . . The entire world is constantly moving towards the same kind of 5th wave leisure economy that is being created in the West. But it still will be a society of full employment . . . Balanced employment will be maintained because, thanks to technology, working hours in the West will continue to be reduced. Economic growth and higher incomes will come from increased productivity generated by the ongoing information explosion . . . we will see working hours reduced drastically—to 24-hours or fewer per week by the end of the 1990s—for most Western populations." Based on outside studies, he anticipated the cure for cancer to be found by the mid-1990s, robots to have supplemented 90 percent of U.S. factory workers by year 2000, and by 2025 robots to be handling virtually all manufacturing in America.[60]

Unfortunately, not a single of these predictions came true. Almost a quarter century later, despite the continuing 'information explosion' there was no trace of '5th wave leisure economy' (except perhaps for the top 1 percent), no widespread usage of artificial eyes or ears, no higher incomes, no full employment, and no shorter working hours, while full robotization of manufacturing still seemed a distant dream, in face of abundant supply of cheap human labor and exorbitant cost of the robotic machines. Instead, in the early 90s—two decades after the first *miserables* appeared, middle-class Americans suddenly woke up to a feeling that the world had changed. "[The] American mood seems dark and edgy," stated author Michael Elliott in his book *"The Day Before Yesterday"*. "There is a pervasive sense of slippage, a feeling that the country that carves colossal monuments to the ideals of freedom and democracy has somehow failed to live up to them . . . there [are] fears that the nation's economy may never again achieve its vaunted promise of prosperity—that the American Dream may be fading." The Americans felt rotten, argued Mr. Elliott, because they could not stop comparing their present to the nation's golden age, the 50s and the 60s, when the country seemed united, small towns and cities functioned, incomes were rising steadily, wives could afford not to work, families were stable and moral values secure. But, concluded Mr. Elliott, these conditions were freak and would never return: ordinary men would not find high-paying jobs again, small towns would stay dead, and cities might die as well. [61]

Increasingly, outside of the few iconic, splendid centers of conspicuous consumption—what began to be termed the 'global cities'—there was growing decay of physical infrastructure. By early 90s, reported one magazine, Chicago—still booming in the 60's—"seems more derelict than occupied. Nowhere along the route from New Orleans are as many buildings vacant, as many sidewalks cracked and weed-choked, or as many bridges visibly rusting and crumbling. The air of dilapidation contributes to a pervasive impression of physical danger. Chicago is well on its way to a record number of murders, with 29 on one recent weekend alone . . ."[62]

In was in the 90s that—for the first time since the Great Depression, and maybe even since the beginning of the Industrial

Era—a realization had dawned on most Americans that their future was not guaranteed and that it could yet fail them. In Canada in the early '90s, 54 percent of middle-class people said they expected their children to be worse off than they were—only 14 percent expected their kids to be better off—and more than 80 percent of those polled believed that it had become more difficult to get ahead on hard work and merit alone[63].

By the mid-1990s, as the middle class got fearful, forecasts increasingly turned from fantastic to bleak. Unlike the downfall of the destitute, the distress of the middle class could not be ignored. The first bleak forecasts appeared. In the future predicted in 1996 by economist Lester Thurow, middle-class motivation for working and being more productive would no longer be better incomes, but fear—fear of being fired into an economy of falling wages. "Fewer of them will be able to afford their own homes. They are going to live in a very different world, where inequality rises and real wages fall for most of them. They cannot expect rising standards of living over their lifetimes or for their children. The middle class is scared and should be scared."[64]

The main source of the distress of the middle class was job and income insecurity, and growing financial stress sparked by flat or falling real wages. Speaking at the National Press Club conference in December 1995, George David, President of United Technologies, summarized the new situation this way: "Since 1990 our company alone has eliminated 33,000 jobs in the United States, about one in three. During that same period, we have added 15,000 jobs outside the United States. We have no reason to believe that this trend for corporate America will change any time soon. If anything, it will accelerate." Going forward, Mr. David painted a bleak job forecast: "[Of the 120 million Americans working] as many as 30 million will be at risk: 18 million people in administrative support jobs prone to automation, 10 million in manufacturing jobs susceptible to foreign competition, and 2 million additional white-collar jobs that medium and large companies like ours, under the pressure of the competition, will learn to live without." Neither did he believe that market forces alone would be able to re-absorb the laid off workers into comparable jobs[65].

Just as during the original Renaissance, during our New Renaissance—the last four decades—income gap kept steadily getting wider. In 2005, the bottom 20 percent of U.S. households had an average income of only around $10,600 per year, 15 times less than the top 20 percent—the highest income inequality ever recorded.[66] The reason the bottom incomes were able to be continuously pushed down was very high unemployment among low-income people: in 2010, official unemployment rate among the lowest 10 percent was 31 percent, compared with only 3 percent among those making $150,000 a year. [67] This extremely high unemployment rate was principally related to the loss of manufacturing jobs through offshoring and automation, but perhaps also to the fact that it often made more financial sense to be on welfare than to work and earn poverty-level wages.

For the middle class, coping now meant both spouses working, and working harder and longer. Middle-class wage earners found tax cuts mostly smoke and mirrors: between 1971 and 1991, a median-income family saw its combined tax bill (Social Security and income tax) go up by 329 percent, while a family making more than $1 million a year saw its combined tax bill fall by 34 percent[68].

Even though, starting in the 1970s, many spouses began working to subsidize family incomes, the financial effect was mixed. Even with two incomes now generally supporting a family, real household incomes for 80 percent of American families either fell or, at best, stayed flat[69]. But the side-effect of both parents working created predictable strain, with escalating rates of divorce and children problems. Education standards were slipping as children were left to be raised by overcrowded municipal schools and by peers, fuelling the drug culture. "People have accommodated all they can accommodate," said Paula Rayman from the Public Policy Institute at Ratcliff College. "They have made trade-offs to get a better quality of life, and it's still insufficient[70]." Squeezed between family demands and employers requesting more and more, middle-class Americans felt they were failing. Working hours grew steadily longer, making a joke of futurists' predictions. From 1969 to 1989, the average American worked 158 hours more per year and had fewer paid vacations. Since then, the trend has only accelerated–by 1997 a married couple worked 256 hours a year more than in 1989[71]. By 2010, when U.S. companies were hiring almost exclusively temporary workers to cut costs, any productivity increase, argued private equity professional Byron Wien, was primarily the result of driving the labor force harder and harder, to the point of exhaustion, a situation that could not go on.

Juliet Schor, author of *Overworked American,* described a middle-class universe of over-stressed career parents, unattended kids in deteriorating public schools, part-time mothers who could only dream of old benefits such as sick days, health care, pensions or vacations, people working second jobs and moonlighting just to maintain their living standards[72].

The much-hyped college education did not guarantee job or income security. As employment became haphazard, jobs and incomes volatile and insecure, and the safety net faded, many top-paid middle class professionals began to fear unemployment which might bring instant destitution. A 2006 study shocked analysts by revealing that few professional women earning over $100,000 a year felt financially secure; as many as half feared they might one day become destitute "bag ladies."[73]

For the middle class, shrinking wages and unemployment spells had the effect of eliminating or draining savings, then cutting down people's spending to the basics. What these 'basics' were, was dictated by the legacy of the peak era lifestyles, now found increasingly unaffordable: it forced most middle class Americans into suburban living and lengthy commutes with related car, fuel and insurance costs. On top of this, artificially low interest rates combined with population pressure to result in soaring house prices. These in turn compelled many who could barely afford it to defensively buy real estate—the logic of saving, renting, or deferring purchase, just did not add up. Many bought with little down payment, or through 'interest only' schemes as the prospect of continuous property appreciation was the only potential source of the family's future financial security. The subsequent crash of the housing market destroyed family finances of tens if not hundreds of millions; the net wealth of many Americans dropped by 40 percent after the housing bubble blew in 2008.

At the dawn of our modern Baroque, financial squeeze on average working American, just like that on his early Baroque predecessor, was overwhelming. Combined burden of various taxes (federal, state, and Social Security) was around 30 percent, plus 20 percent for medical care (in Europe, where medicare was state-paid, taxes were around 50 percent), plus rent or mortgage costs (typically, at least another 25 percent of income), added up to combined cost of basics: tax, shelter, and medical care, to around 75 percent or more of income. With food costs adding another 15-20 percent of median income, it was clear that middle-class U.S. families had no room to save, provide for retirement or unexpected expenses like joblessness, major illness or accident, or fund private education for their children, to escape the public-education ghetto. If we add to it the growing cost of servicing consumer debt, sometimes running as high as 25 percent of income, we have the final picture: the middle class whose disposable income has largely been eaten away and which—just to maintain what the peak era established as an average living standard—is running itself into debt and financial ruin.

For prospective families, the ever-rising costs of housing, kids' education, medical care and commuting, against a backdrop of falling real incomes and both spouses having to work, resulted in people marrying late or never, having fewer or no children, dropping academic standards, and broken families. Typically, low-wage immigrants, often living in slums and working for rock-bottom wages, compensated for falling birth rates. As in previous such historical cycles of economic stress and disintegrating middle class, the number of illegitimate births soared. In 2004 America, the all-time record of 1.5 million births, nearly 40 percent of all births, were to unmarried women. Unlike in the 1970s, these mothers were no longer teenagers: women 20 and over accounted for 76 percent of the single mothers[74]. In many urban ghettoes, the institution of marriage seemed to be fading away, challenged by the reality of crude, insecure, and increasingly brutal day-to-day existence, depicted in Hollywood movies and in the rap music of ex-ghetto dwellers, in an eerie echo of the underworld culture of the last Baroque permeating the mainstream culture.

Just as in previous Baroques, vast elements of the new underclass morphed into the criminal underground of pimps, prostitutes, drug dealers, burglars and crooks. Away from cleaned-up city centers full of expensive condos, from London to New York, from Paris to Tokyo, desolate and decrepit suburban 'estates' in Europe and inner-city ghettoes in America, full of garbage, poverty and graffiti, were ruled by gangs of skinhead or immigrant youths dealing in drugs, girls and guns.

The steadily rising costs of real estate extracted a heavy toll. While families that already owned a house, resorted to borrowing against the home equity in order to keep or improve their old lifestyle in a reality of falling real wages, for new families it only got tougher: By 2005, 86 percent of families in San Francisco and Los Angeles could no longer afford to buy a new median-price family home[75]. With budgets already stretched almost to the breaking point, the expectations for the future became consistently bleak. Even among the retirees—one of the most affluent groups, those that still lived off the nation's past golden era of legacy entitlements, there was a chill. Confirming the fears of many American retirees, an *MSN Money* analyst in early 2006 stated matter-of-factly that now was as good as it would ever get.

America's future, for most of its citizens, seemed to be the future of decline.

*

THE LAST ERA of decline—the last Baroque—has seen almost exactly the same social and economic trends we are witnessing today. Following in the footsteps of the brilliant era of transition—the Renaissance—the Baroque saw government and private debts spiraling out of control and into bankruptcies, inflationary asset bubbles collapsing into deflations, pauperization of the middle class, the rich escaping taxation, urban slums ruled by gangs, rise of elite education, obsession with luxury goods, rise of what today's analysts would certainly recognize as 'plutonomies' or systems shaped by and serving, the rich. This was an era that saw massive population increases putting a strain on resources. It also saw technological stagnation, widening gap between the rich and the poor, outsourcing of manufacturing to cheap locales, financial wizardry replacing productive activity, luxury production increasingly dominating economic activity.

Same as today, the rise of new information technologies—mass printing with its tens of millions of cheap books, leaflets, adverts, maps and atlases, regular mail and newspapers—which all resulted in speedy, ubiquitous access to information—was taken as a miracle remedy for stagnation in every other area. Same as today, while coffee houses, newspapers and luxury shops proliferated, there was remarkable lack of progress in mechanics or new energy sources or new energy converters—almost, same as today, there was a technological stagnation bordering actual regression. Same as today, the remedy to this was outsourcing of manufacturing to cheap labor locales, globalized search for 'natural resources' (mostly cash commodities and slave labor) and above all, ruthless efficiency drive.

It affected all areas of economy and depressed wages of the swelling masses of paupers, among whom underemployment and on-call 'service' occupations became the norm. Same as today, the last Baroque saw rising class of information professionals, top-educated 'nobles', many of them bureaucrats or lawyers in government service, bankers, notaries, accountants, asset managers, tax collectors. Same as today, they were all using elite education, personal networking and access to new information technologies as tools to acquire assets and set up new dynasties of investors and asset owners.

Same as today, the Renaissance/Baroque era was the heyday of bankers and high finance. Same as today, the Renaissance/ Baroque period saw a rise of extremism, obscurantist 'religious wars' wrapped by propaganda experts into fundamentalist language we would certainly recognize, plus witch-hunts, all deftly manipulated by politicians. All this 'event theater' was growing on the back of steadily dropping living standards and economic decline. Just like today, Baroque saw rise of poverty-driven illiteracy, brutality and crime. Just like today, it saw obsession with money, luxury and ostentatious consumption by the educated elites—the Renaissance Men—mushrooming at the expense of virtually anything else.

And—same as its parent, the Renaissance—the Baroque saw remarkable dearth of mechanical inventions or harnessing of any new energy sources, a technological stagnation that lasted for generations, all the way to our Industrial Era.

For three centuries, progress almost stopped.

THE UGLY CHILD

T HE ORIGINAL BAROQUE began inconspicuously, somewhat like the present one is beginning today. It followed seamlessly on the heels of the era commonly hailed as one of the most glorious, ostensibly 'modern' and seemingly affluent in all of human history—the Renaissance. While the Baroque could be called the Renaissance's ugly child, it merely continued—with disastrous consequences—all the ideas, beliefs, social and economic concepts and legacies of its parent. In many respects, the Renaissance and the Baroque were the same.

A bizarre reality of fake luster, pomp and gilt; of expensive elite education coupled with narrow-mindedness, intellectual void, plagiarism and trivia; a world obsessed with money and status, luxury outfits, gadgets and accessories; a realm of snobbery and pretence, of corruption and fraud, the Baroque flourished in a reality of absolute extremes. It was a world driven almost entirely by the pursuit of money; by the desire to accumulate and display riches; and by eagerness to stamp down on the poor. In the Baroque world, absolute poverty contrasted with absolute wealth. This was the era of theatrically grandiose palaces, colonnades, and poses; of fantastic gilded churches; of swarming armies of semi-literate, disposable paupers covered in rags; of bejeweled, bewigged, and feathered top-educated investors and officials. This was the world ruled by real and wannabee urban barons derived from property investors, lawyers, *rentiers*, doctors, bankers, town councilors, estate managers, notaries, all elite university-educated, many with multiple degrees, most well-travelled, all savvy investors and asset owners, most of them already certified 'nobles'.

This was the time of splendid coaches, gilded tables, chairs made of solid silver, polished floors, theatrical décor, marble statues, gigantic domed libraries, fancy manicured parks the size of medieval towns. Just a few streets away, similar to many inner American cities today or suburban ghettoes of Europe, there were wretched hovels, creatures in rags, boarded up businesses, urban despair, and crime on an unprecedented scale. Entire societies of squatters and homeless vagabonds—often pauperized descendents of once prosperous middle class families—lived on the street or underground, in the shadows of the grandiose palaces of the new urban princes.

In this overcrowded and impoverished world, medieval urban democracy already became a distant memory. Just like the declining Roman Empire, Baroque Europe seemed to be reverting to a lower level of complexity: in a process we begin to witness today in the once-leading industrial countries, entire regions, even countries completely de-industrialized, to become poverty-stricken exporters of grain, cattle, wine, or olives, with accompanying loss of industrial skills and explosion of poverty, illiteracy and banditry. The heroes of the new criminal underworld were glamorized, same as the drug dealers and hoodlums in today's rap music, by the entire popular subculture depicting vagabonds, pirates and highwaymen. The entire continent of Europe de-urbanized and eventually depopulated, as economic collapse was accompanied by war, plague and starvation.

The absolute bottom of the Baroque era seems to have been plumbed during the horrible years 1647-1652. "Poverty was such in Florence in April 1650 that it was impossible to hear mass in peace, so much was one importuned during the service by the wretched people [begging], naked and covered with sores," reported historian Fernand Braudel. "Prices were terrifyingly high and the [silk] looms stood idle; on the Monday of Carnival week, to crown the misfortunes of the townsfolk, a storm destroyed the olive trees as well as mulberry and other fruit trees.[76]" Around that time a noble from Vincenza wrote: "Give alms to two hundred people and as many again will appear; you cannot walk down the street or stop in a square or church without multitudes surrounding you to beg for charity; you see hunger written on their faces, their eyes like gemless rings, the wretchedness of their bodies with the skins shaped only by the bones.[77]" In this world, at the nadir of the cycle, random brutality ruled. People in the street were arrested, judged and convicted based on their appearance alone. Old medieval ideals of social responsibility, and any notions of equality or community of any sort, seemed completely forgotten. Hard-fisted wealth and power were daily on display. Paintings from the Baroque decades uniformly depict the grim universe of absolute poverty, disease, quick and easy death, urban and rural abandonment, celeb-style glitzy and extravagant urban luxury co-existing with starvation and urban decay. Even among the privileged elites, there was a palpable feeling that the world had reached the bottom of some unfathomable abyss.

*

I WRITE THESE words sitting in front of Khazneh—also known as the Treasury—the key monument of Petra, an Arabian Desert city that flourished two millennia ago and produced fantastic, soaring classical-style monuments carved in living rock, only to be covered by sand and forgotten for almost two thousand years. The afternoon sun plays wonders with Khazneh's façade, bringing out the pink and the whole palette of colors, as I ponder on fragility on men's dreams.

Not long ago, a discussion of a 400-year-old blip in time would have been a topic of no interest. While it is impossible to deny that most—virtually all—civilizations that came before ours eventually failed miserably—sometimes to the point of being covered by sand just like Petra and completely forgotten for millennia—until recently we firmly believed that ours would be different. We declared ourselves immune from history; some gurus in the 1990s even triumphantly predicted history's end. Until quite recently, we believed we were crafting a brave new modern world, one that would eradicate all the problems of the past, eliminate want and poverty, and take us to the stars. From Adam Smith to Karl Marx to futurists like Alvin Toffler and John Naisbitt, we were all believers. Believers in steady, even accelerating, progress.

For almost two centuries now, continuous progress was taken for granted, as if it were a law of nature. Propelled by this mysterious force, if there was something on which various gurus all agreed, it was that ours was going to be the "Modern" era, the "Information" era, the era of "Globalization." Our era was going to be different from all the eras that came before.

But this fantastic future failed to arrive.

America of the early 21st century would be unrecognizable to the forecasters of a generation ago. The optimism of the '50s and '60s has been replaced by uncertainty and fear. "The conventional optimism that propelled generations of immigrants to work hard in the belief that they could better their lot in life and improve the prospects for their children has been shattered," writes author Jeremy Rifkin. "In its place is a growing cynicism about corporate power and increased suspicion of the men and women who wield near total control over the global marketplace.[78]" The improbable election of Barack Obama for president in 2008 was a desperate expression of hope, a cry for change coming from millions of ordinary people hoping that an outsider like him can upset the calcifying political establishment, turn the tide of decline, cronyism, lobbyism, nepotism and corruption, inequality and ineptitude and bring change, jobs, prosperity and hope back to America.

It is a measure of the incredible decline of expectations over the last few decades that even these simple hopes for the future had now to be considered audacious—and even these modest expectations have been generally disappointed. Nobody seemed to remember that we now live in a time when many forecasters of just a few decades ago expected mass prosperity as a given, plus domed cities, cold fusion, flying cars and colonies on Mars.

Outside of the computers, virtually none of the hopes and predictions of the forecasters from a generation ago have materialized.

As year 2011 opened, a 60-year old British journalist so summarized the incredible decline of expectations he had witnessed over the last four decades: "What particularly concerns me is not my own plight but that of the younger generations. My young friend Katherine is facing the new decade with the prospect of becoming 20. What strikes me about her, and her generation, is that when I was 20 I was looking at a world that had endless potential for a life that was well beyond the dreams of my parents. The economy was booming, working class children could go to university if they passed the exams, and we would all revel in a new-found wealth that was unimaginable to previous generations. There would be no return to recessions, no return to mass unemployment and no return to poverty. But now it is on our doorstep[79]."

*

WHY SHOULD THE future be failing us? And how could we compare our era to the dismal Baroque? Aren't we, here at the beginning of the new millennium, riding the greatest wave of inventions the world has ever seen—a churning wave of change that will surely counteract any decline? Haven't we invented more, as one InfoTech guru confidently stated not long ago, in the last 25 years than in the preceding 25,000?

To answer this, let us picture the daily life of the world's leading civilizations in 1820, 1910, and today.

In 1820, the leading civilization of the day, Europe, was living out the last days of the Baroque era. Outside of a few British industry towns like Manchester, where the new Industrial Era was being born in the midst of grinding poverty and cheap labor inherited from the Baroque, or a handful of glitzy, remodeled, tax-and-rent based, iconic capitals like London, Paris or Sankt Petersburg, Europeans of 1820 still lived off the old medieval substance of their crumbling towns, inside decaying centuries-old houses enclosed within medieval walls. Their daily life has hardly changed since the Middle Ages had waned. Horse-drawn carriages traveled on unpaved country roads, town streets were floating with raw sewage, laundry was washed by the river. Just like centuries earlier, ships were made of wood and powered by sails or even oars; swordsmen fought hand-to-hand; interiors were lit with candles and had no bathrooms, plumbing, toilets or running water. Chamber pots were emptied out the window. Cholera and typhoid were rampant, claiming tens of thousands of victims. Medicine, hygiene or food refrigeration did not exist.

Perhaps nothing can convey to us better the desperate existence of these last Baroque decades than the recent movie *"Les Miserables"* with its heartbreaking, haunting images of horrifying poverty, wasted lives, and hopeless dreams. Last decades of the Baroque were pure hell.

France of Victor Hugo, Germany of Goethe, was a stagnant, depressed landscape of sleepy towns, firmly in the grip of petty landowners, lawyers, notaries, and government prefects. Stendhal's Italy was a dilapidated world of smugglers, bandits and *carabinieri*, farcical government officials, and priests. Petty dukes were living in crumbling *palazzos*, in crumbling towns. In many, not a single new building has been added since the collapse of the medieval boom centuries before. Europe's landscapes were full of beggars and bandits, romantic revolutionaries and hopeless revolutions, intrigues spun in candle-lit interiors, fights fought with sabers and muskets, aboard sailships hardly changed for centuries. The continental elite could not even be described as the noble bureaucracy of old, in its yuppie, arrogant, "knowledge professional" Renaissance version. It was just too poor. It had eaten away all its surpluses, squeezed all value out of its peasants, disabled all productive sector. It was unable to find any new wealth on which to feed. Goethe's house in Weimar, so small and thriftily appointed, was not untypical for a princely minister.

In 1830s Berlin, Prussian princesses wore cheap percale dresses, saving expensive silk for state occasions. Cows still grazed within old medieval towns. Literacy and living standards were lower than in the 1400s.[80]

Outside of the grim cotton factories of Lancashire, where a brand new reality was being born, it was the world of stagnant technology. The fastest trip around the world, by horse and sailship, would take well over a year, same as centuries before. There was no concept of insurance for unemployment, health, or old age. Education was for the rich. Just talking about democracy was a sure ticket to prison. English prisons were full of poor people who could not pay back debts; in France, *les miserables* were really locked up for life as galley slaves—possibly just for the theft of a loaf of bread. It was an era of common poverty, slums in the cities, banditry in the countryside. Slavery and piracy were still very much a big business. In Goethe's Germany, a person that owned a house was considered rich. Wages were abysmal, in many places at their lowest ever, and complete destitution—vividly described in Dickens' novels—was commonplace.

One would be hard pressed to tell how average people's daily lives have improved during the preceding four hundred—or perhaps even two thousand—years, thus challenging the fanciful idea of the steady, gradual progress.

Even in England—the uncontested technology and wealth leader—poverty was horrible. It was in England, against the backdrop of ever deteriorating living standards, dropping wages, teeming masses and cholera-infested cities that Malthus conceived his famous theory and Marx came up with his vision of history as class warfare.

The beginning of the new reality seemed to prove both theorists right. As potato-fed populations grew unchecked and there were more and more laborers (especially women and children) ready for work, wages dropped steadily. There was an abysmal poverty in the growing industrial cities. Overcrowding, polluted water, raw sewage, all combined with the layer of coal soot that covered everything to produce the blighted landscapes of first-ever industrial pollution. British cities were breeding grounds for typhoid, cholera, tuberculosis, and smallpox. In some areas, London was worse than Calcutta today. Other cities were no better. In 1842 a Glasgow police superintendent stated: "I should be able to find a thousand children who have no name whatsoever, only nicknames, like dogs"[81]. These wretches inhabited areas where gentlemen never ventured, where tenements were filled with creatures dressed in rags, with gin alleys, drunks lying in the streets, places where crime, prostitution and whiskey shops were the key business, and wages never covered the food bill. Harsh winters, starvation, and typhoid, killed these creatures by the thousands. It was a Dickensian world of orphans, debtor prisons, pickpockets, and Scrooge-type tight-fisted businessmen. The growing masses of the urban poor were being preyed on by landlords and shopkeepers; the scale of adultering the food sold to the poor by "shopocracy" of the 1840s was infamous, only matched in some cities of China today.

Yet paupers fled to these cities because the life they left behind in the countryside was even worse. Late-Baroque English countryside of the 1790s was described as the only country in the world where free peasantry has been basically wiped out. Outside of the cities, England, like Egypt of the Ptolemies, was a gigantic landed estate, owned mostly by absentee asset owners and farmed by their agents. The physical degradation of people was brutal. The picturesque English villages we so admire today are usually leftovers of medieval textile towns, once vibrant with craft and manufacture. Later, battered by Renaissance and Baroque recessions, they reverted to village status, abandoned by industry, impoverished and depopulated. By early 1800s, in the countryside still suffering in the last stage of Baroque cycle, they all have turned into infamous "slum villages of the worst kind" where the new rural proletariat of farm laborers lived, eternally waiting for hire by estate managers, for steadily dropping wages. The poor who did not belong to a factory or slum village were arrested as vagabonds and made to work in the 'Poor Houses'. In Andover Poor House "paupers were employed in bone-crushing;

they were so ill-fed that they fought each other for the putrid gristle adhering to the horses' bone".[82]

*

BUT A DRAMATIC change was imminent. While in 1830, there was only one short railway line in the whole world (in England) and it was barely 5 years old, by 1860—within the following mere thirty years—railways, steamships, telegraph, electricity and mechanized factories—progress all based on fossil fuel-powered machines, plus new chemicals and medicines—completely transformed the world. This was accompanied by an explosion of wealth, escalating incomes, rebirth of the middle class and—against all expectations of the 1820s—rebirth of democracy.

Notably, little if any of this Industrial Era progress can claim to have been accomplished due to any advances in information technology. Energy injection provided by fuel-powered machines—for the first time ever machines that did not rely on human or animal muscle or wind or water power—was the principal, almost exclusive reason for this miraculous transformation. Critically, the chief driver of the arrival of the powered machines was the stunning profitability of such investments. Parallel—and absolutely amazing—progress in practical chemistry, physics, medicine, and basic sciences is due the rest of the credit. The century of the peak Industrial Era—let's call it the Industrial Century, roughly 1850-1950—brought an incredible quantum leap in our understanding of the world and ability to transform it.

This quantum leap has not been matched since in any shape or form. Truth be told, we still mostly live off its inventions.

The Industrial Century was a miracle. Changes from decade to decade, even year to year, were literally transforming every facet of daily life. In the amazing decade of the 1890s, inventions were coming like a waterfall, at a rate that was never seen before and never equaled again. Among these exceptional years, 1896 was probably the most amazing, mankind's 'annus mirabilis'. It saw, within a few short months, the advent of the first sewing machine, first electric light bulb, an improved telephone set, first typewriter, first flashlight, first radio, first production car, and first airplane.

The Industrial Revolution cannot be compared with our Information Revolution. Industrial Era has made the biggest strides in cheap energy sources, new energy converters, or daily-use powered machines such as cars, airplanes, trains, fridges, washing machines, telephone or radio. These were mostly things that amplified our physical power, substituted machines for our muscles, allowed people, goods and information to travel faster, or reduced our daily toil. These also happened to be areas where there has hardly been any significant innovation for centuries before, and—since Industrial Era has passed—for almost half a century since. On the other hand, Industrial Revolution has made little progress in terms of the medium of mass distribution of information. It remained, until the advent of the Internet and same as during the Baroque era, contained to books, magazines and newspapers. Radio and TV were broadcast media suitable only for news and entertainment, while telephone was one-on-one communication; neither could compare with the Internet as mass-access information technology tool.

Information Revolution, we will argue in this book, is not unique. Instead, it is a typical historical follow-up phenomenon, an 'efficiency event' with limited impact on the general technology or general living standards. It happened before, always at or past the peak of the relevant historical cycles, apparently as a tool to improve efficiency of the pre-existing system. It cannot replicate the breakthroughs in mechanical innovation and living standard achieved during the Industrial Revolution—the recent one or any that came before.

After getting a feel of what the world of the 1820s looked like, let's now picture the daily world of 1910, mere 90 years later. Only three generations have passed since the new fuel-powered machines began to be first introduced. We are now in America, the leading civilization of the day. While superficially there are still some similarities to the world of 90 years earlier—in clothing, manners, decorative styles—the underlying daily-use technology has changed beyond recognition. The world of the year 1910 has cars and airplanes, movie theaters and color movies, oil rigs, telegraph, telephone and radio, electric underground trains, air-conditioning, diesel engines, photo and video cameras, synthetic rubber, escalators, music records and music players, machine guns, chemical industry, oil industry, dynamite, skyscrapers serviced by elevators, electric stoves, electric power plants, municipal sewage and indoor plumbing. It has fridges, electric streetcars, vacuum cleaners, department stores, submarines, neon lights, advanced medicine and X-rays, typewriters, washing machines, sewing machines, canned food, all-steel refrigerator ships, Titanic-style luxury cruise ships, global multinational corporations catering to global consumers. It even has prototype television and a prototype moving sidewalk. Penicillin and other antibiotics are just a few years away.

In 1910, just like today, bright advertising neon lights already illuminate Piccadilly Square. British miners are months away from securing a 7-hour workday and benefits we now see rapidly disappearing. IBM is already around and is perfecting its numerical punchcards, precursors of computers. Magnetic levitation technology is already invented and Henry Rutherford has already presented his analysis of the structure of the atomic nucleus, the first step toward nuclear power. In Europe, cities have changed beyond recognition, for the first time in centuries outgrowing and demolishing their medieval walls. People listen to the radio, go to the movies. Within five years Americans will be able to call their friends across the continent; within a decade fly across the Atlantic. Many believe videophones will appear in a decade or two. In the leading countries of the world, there is now functioning democracy. It reappeared, as if by magic and without any revolutions, at the peak of the Industrial Century around 1900 and is likely more effective and less corrupt than today. Electric cars are staging races; first solar power plants are being designed; engineers are studying ways of sending a rocket to the Moon; Einstein has already written his relativity theory down. Nuclear power, first computers and the first space flights are just one generation away. Piracy and slavery have been wiped out. Aristocracy is now a relic.

This was the world of hundred years ago, at the very peak of its expectations. How they subsequently failed to be fulfilled by technology can be seen from newspaper headlines in the decades that followed:

- The New York Times declares that the electric car "has long been recognized as the ideal solution" because it "is cleaner and quieter" and "much more economical."–1911
- The Washington Post writes that "prices on electric cars will continue to drop until they are within reach of the average family."–1915
- The New York Times reports that the "old electric may be the car of tomorrow." The story said that electric cars were making a comeback because "gasoline is expensive today, principally because it is so heavily taxed, while electricity is far cheaper" than it was back in the 1920s.–1959
- The Los Angeles Times says that American Motors Corp. is on the verge of producing an electric car, the Amitron, to be powered by lithium batteries capable of holding 330 watt-hours per kilogram. (That's more than two times the energy density of modern lithium-ion batteries.) Backers of the Amitron said, "We don't see a major obstacle in technology. It's just a matter of time."–1967
- The Washington Post reports that General Motors has found "a breakthrough in batteries" that "now makes electric cars commercially practical." The new zinc-nickel oxide batteries will provide the "100-mile range that General Motors executives believe is necessary to successfully sell electric vehicles to the public."–1979[83]

CAPITALS OF FINANCE: LIVING HIGH ON OLD INVENTIONS, OIL AND DEBT

SEEN FROM AN AIRCRAFT landing in Dubai, Burj Khalifa–currently the tallest building in the world–seems unreal: standing incredibly tall and ghostly thin in a flat desert landscape. It fits perfectly with Dubai's cultivated image of a spectacular desert mirage, a Disneyland for grownups. Driving on the city's main thoroughfare, Shaikh Zayed Road, I still find it sometimes hard to believe that this desert Manhattan was wished out of the sand by the will of one man, Dubai's ruler Shaikh Mohammad Al-Makhtoum, and that most of it is barely 10 years old. But will alone is not enough and in order to build this city, Shaikh Mohammad needed money: tens of billions of dollars. Some of it was directly invested, much was borrowed. But why would anybody invest in a place that was hardly on the map not long ago and still has a tiny resident population? Both investors and lenders ultimately expected the return on their investment from Dubai's future income as the financial capital of an oil-rich region, with oil now priced at over $100 a barrel.

Dubai's rise is based on debt, oil and need for international financial capitals. It may look spectacular, but other than computers, just like in the rest of the world, it hardly has any technology that is less than half a century old.

Similar in many ways to Dubai, the reality of high Industrial Era–the world of skyscrapers, metropolitan cities, subways and suspension bridges, railways, ports, giant factories–was built quickly, with grand visions, panache and lots of money. The money that fuelled this explosive expansion initially came from huge profits of spectacular productivity increases in manufacturing and agriculture. But ultimately, like Dubai, the whole reality of the Industrial Era was built on energy from new fossil fuels: it was built on oil and coal.

By 1910, the stagnant Napoleonic world of creaky wooden sailships, pirates and slavers, saber-wielding hussars, candle-lit houses, laundry washed by the river, leisurely *rentiers* reading books in their stately manors, notaries controlling dilapidated towns: all this decayed late-Baroque 'Information Era' reality was absorbed by the new industrial world. Gradually, it dissolved in it, as if it never existed.

What replaced the old Renaissance/Baroque system of tax-and-rent squeeze was the idea of making money from innovation and growth. Suddenly, there were solid financial reasons to be innovative and inventive. Why? Inventions of the early Industrial Era were relatively simple to make. Many, like first car, electric light bulb, telephone or airplane, took few people working in a barn and did not require huge budgets. Yet these inventions brought phenomenal profits. Unlike today, many got to the market within mere months. Most of Industrial Century's practical inventions were introduced into mass-use very quickly and—just like Googles and Facebooks of our InfoEra today, make their creators rich.

The combination of low initial investment, relative ease of inventing, lightning speed to market and phenomenal financial return gave tremendous impetus to mechanical innovation. How things have advanced in one sector only—transport—in little more than a century can be seen by comparing a horse-drawn coach—the fastest mode of transport in 1820—to a prototype Nazi-designed 'Amerika Bomber' spaceplane a mere century or so later. This 1936 hypersonic, orbital prototype was supposed to reach a top speed of over 22,000km per hour, flying up to 280 km in space above the Earth.

It is hardly credible how little time this kind of leap took. It is equally incredible to realize that—unlike today—*virtually none of the practical inventions already operating in 1910 (or especially in 1930) existed in 1820*; most of the 1910-1930 technology described above did not exist even as remote ideas or concepts in 1820. Even more amazing, *even the basic science leading to the practical inventions of 1910 was mostly not invented yet in 1820.* Within mere ninety years humanity has made an incredible leap. Nothing like this has ever happened before—or since. By contrast, *by 1940 all the basic science on which our current reality is based was already in place,* including science leading to DNA splicing, nuclear energy, magnetic levitation, solar power generation, space travel, spacetime theory, quantum physics, computers and all.

Here is something that may be difficult for some of us to swallow: over the last seventy years, since around 1940, there has been very little progress in basic science, despite astronomical amount of money invested in all types of research and in technology development. If anything, the pace of progress kept steadily decelerating, with a virtual void in discoveries in the last two or three decades.

The reason for this seems fairly simple, even though you won't find it splashed all over the news. One needs to first accept that innovation is ultimately driven by money, one way or another. Very few innovations are or have ever been done without initial financial investment and reasonable expectation of a financial return. The simplicity of the early inventions—things like power spinning, electricity or railways—combined with the massive productivity increases they brought about to ring in prompt and spectacular profits to the cash register. Only these kinds of profits enabled the brisk and massive adoption of these inventions. This profit-driven adoption then allowed all the tremendous changes of the Industrial Century to take place and alter the entire psychological makeup of our civilization. These profits, fortunes, fame, careers were what sparked interest in mechanics, engineering and science.

As reality changed, it ended up promoting almost a new type of human and a new culture. It sobered up the outlook, created a virtual cult of hard work, responsibility and strict morals, quickly replacing the Baroque ideal of noble idleness, living off financial income, endless partying, gambling and sexual license.

Eventually, after the pivotal year 1850, industrial abundance was released overland via development of railways. It pushed up wages and living standards as food, fuel and industrial goods became cheaper and cheaper, finally transforming the destitute servants of the Baroque into the new middle class.

Amazingly, in this ascending cycle, with rising incomes and declining inequality, industrial abundance also created democracy.

The stunning productivity jumps were the critical base on which the lower prices, higher wages and resulting rise in living standards—these cornerstones of every era of real progress and something we can hardly find around today—were based. We are not talking about improvements of 10 or 20 percent. In areas where there can even be comparisons—such as speed of transport, or speed of transmission of communication, or volume of food or goods produced, the productivity increases typically went into thousands, sometimes tens of thousands of percent.

The initial invention that launched the Industrial Revolution was the power spinning machine. It produced 200 times more fabrics than a manual spinning wheel, a 20,000 percent productivity increase. The next key invention provided a similar, spectacular increase in productivity and profits: a single locomotive could pull a load that before required hundreds of horse wagons, at ten to twenty times the speed, a productivity increase of perhaps 50,000 percent. Telegraph, radio and telephone improved the speed of communication—previously reliant on horse-mounted messengers or sail ships—by such an extent, any percentages would be meaningless. Almost any machine one would look at could boast phenomenal productivity jump. Shown in 1851 London Exhibition, a single printing machine could print 6,000 newspapers a day. In 1855, at the Paris Exhibition, where a newly-invented American threshing machine was displayed—displacing the labor of 16 men—salesmen took pride demonstrating to onlookers the 2,055 percent productivity increase the machine could deliver. By 1885, thirty cigarette-rolling machines—a design patented just four years earlier—could fulfill the entire U.S. demand for cigarettes, using only a handful of workers.

With most new so-called 'continuous-process' machines productivity improvements typically went into thousands of percent.[84] An airplane cut the time of crossing the Atlantic from a week or two to mere hours; invention of a washer and dryer machine cut the time dedicated to doing laundry from hours to few minutes; antibiotics, vaccines and other medical advances reduced child mortality rates by maybe 60 percent, almost doubling the average age at death within less than a century.

The key indicator of Industrial Era's success was the wage trend. Again, same as during the ascending cycle of the medieval era, production of goods and food began to run ahead of population growth—even if both grew much faster than ever before. Massive increases in productivity made prices drop and wages go up. Average real wages in the USA likely tripled between 1830 and 1910. In the 45 year period between 1914 and 1960, despite intervening Depression, they more than tripled again.[85] In England, by some measures, real wages of building craftsmen quadrupled during the 19th century.[86] At the very peak of the cycle, in a trend exactly opposite to the one we experience today, the highest gains were at the bottom: between 1950 and 1980, the real wages of the bottom fifth of American families shot up by 150 percent[87]. Not only wages: all the ascending cycle trends were pointing in the same direction—opposite to the trends of today. The run-up to the peak 1960s era was the time of declining income and wealth gaps, declining inequality, low unemployment, low inflation, high societal cohesion, low crime and illegitimacy rates, and broadly distributed prosperity. Between 1900 and 1968, wealth and income inequality decreased steadily. Income share of the top 20 percent of U.S. population dropped from around 60 percent in 1920s to mere 45 percent in 1960. Wealth share of the richest 1 percent of U.S. families dropped from around 40 percent in 1929 to around 20 percent in 1969.

All these trends were the exact opposite of what we have been observing in the last few decades.

There cannot be a more dramatic difference in terms of quality of life and practical changes brought by technology than that between the world of 1820 and 1910—all result of an Industrial Revolution and its breakthroughs in new energy sources and new machines, all having happened in just 90 years. We have nothing remotely comparable to show for practical benefits of our "Information Era" revolution over the last four or five decades. Even worse, as of today, unless current trends change dramatically, the next forty years will bring more of the same. If so, we are looking at an entire century of decline in incomes and living standards: a true Baroque era.

It was the massive improvement in productivity, generated principally by labor-saving and productivity-boosting mechanical technology (and not, like today, by deregulation, privatization, globalization, delayering management levels, longer working hours and lower wages) that drove the economic miracle of the high Industrial Era. As the new system delivered goods in abundance, in the period between 1870 and 1896, wholesale prices in Britain fell by 50 percent, while economy kept on growing, on the average, by an impressive 4 percent a year, with minimal debt. In other words, the economy of the Industrial Century was also exactly opposite of the one we experience today with our "Information Era", the time of persistent inflation, stagnant or declining wages, weak or non-existent growth, and massive, rapidly growing debts.

Virtually every other aspect of the ascending cycle was opposite to what we experience today. With growing prosperity, there was a dramatic decline in crime rates, and not because more police on the streets and millions of people in prison. In London, violent crimes convictions dropped from 12 per 100,000 people in 1850 to 4 in 1900; Chicago arrest rate dropped by more than half between 1870 and 1900; alcohol consumption, out-of-wedlock births, all declined dramatically between 1850 and 1900.[88]

Within a couple of generations of the late 19th century, the high Industrial Era, the whole outlook of humanity changed. The world of 1910 was a self-assured, liberal, optimistic world of affluence, a time of high wages for the growing middle class, which began to include skilled factory workers. Virtually all the leading industrial countries either had or were considering the full social security package—holiday with pay, maternity leave, unemployment, old age and medical insurance, free and compulsory education, a security blanket which fully materialized within a generation and which we now increasingly consider too expensive for our debt-ridden post-industrial society to provide.

Unlike today, when socialist politicians advocate conservative policies, in the ascending cycle, conservative politicians advocated socialist policies. Aristocrat Otto von Bismarck invented public old age pensions and public health care in the 1880s. Aristocrat Winston Churchill pushed for introduction of the first large-scale public unemployment insurance in 1911. Patrician Franklin D. Roosevelt was the chief designer of the welfare state.[89] Concepts like fairness, social justice, and economic planning were discussed and relevant programs implemented in all seriousness, with long-term programs constantly on the agenda.

The mantra of the Industrial Century was progress, which increasingly meant widely understood social progress. A commonly held idea—not much mentioned today anymore—was that the individual was responsible not just for his own actions, but for the improvement of the society at large, under the principle that everyone should strive to fight injustice where they saw it. It was subscribed by many top politicians and industrialists in America—from Abraham Lincoln to Andrew Carnegie—and other countries. Unlike today, over-the-top consumption wasn't glamorized. Instead, visible inequality in general, and slavery in particular, became targets of popular outrage. Despite its huge profitability, under extreme popular pressure slavery was abolished in virtually all countries and actively prosecuted by governments worldwide. Serfdom–still present in Russia–was abolished by tsar's decree, gambling and alcoholism increasingly curtailed. Amazingly, many of these actions were taken under little or no pressure, by the most conservative of leaders. Today, there is hardly any country in the world guided by such lofty principles, with gambling being re-introduced more and more to generate profits; taxes on gambling, tobacco and alcohol continue to be one of the main public revenue earners.

Why did this happen? Just like during the early medieval boom, the steadily growing productivity of the industrial system based on newly found, cheap fuels, enabled the governments and corporations to afford their largesse. It was the industrial abundance that drove the social change.

During the Industrial Era, there was a thirst for knowledge we would be hard pressed to see around today. Technical and scientific books were printed in millions of copies and avidly read. There was a cult of work and machine bordering almost on religious. Some 19th century industrialists promoted salvation through 'self-employment in co-operative workshops'. Most notably, even as fantastic profits were being made, Adam Smith and his market-driven ideas were ignored. Instead, everyone–from Robert Owen to Otto von Bismarck–had an idea on how to improve the world. Radical–by our standards–ideas were commonplace. Paradoxically, the reason Communism could be born in such a world was that the reality of the time could financially afford it.

It was a strange time indeed.

According to social historian Howard Newby, Britain's zenith of prosperity–coinciding with its industrial peak–was reached in 1911. Since then the real income per capita has steadily fallen, depressed by the usual combination of rising costs and taxes, especially consumption taxes that hit poor the most. The working hours have also increased steadily since 1919 when–as we mentioned before–British miners managed to achieve a seven hour week.[90]

THE GREAT SLOWDOWN

"You might wonder why aren't there any robots that you can send in to fix the Japanese reactors. The answer is that there was a lot of progress in the 1960s and 1970s. Then something went wrong. [Today] you'll find students excited over robots that play basketball or soccer or dance or make funny faces at you. [But] they're not making them smarter. [Marvin Minsky]

Many people would protest the view that there's been no progress, but I don't think anyone would protest that there could have been more progress in the past 20 years. What went wrong went wrong in the '80s. [Patrick Winston]"

—Marvin Minsky and Patrick Winston,
MIT conference 2011[91]

FLYING ABOARD THE 'Concorde' is an incredible experience. The aircraft takes barely 3 hours to get from Paris to New York; the cabin is small and narrow, but the flight is absolutely smooth. Part of the flight is at such a high altitude, I can see the curvature of the Earth and darkness of space above.

Now that the era of supersonic passenger travel is over, the memory is even more special; I am unsure if I can ever repeat it. We have glimpsed the future, but now it's gone.

*

WHEN WE CONSIDER the failed forecasts of the 1970s futurists like Alvin Toffler, we may want to simply dismiss all such forecasts as fantasy. 'Well', one might say, 'such forecasts either never materialize or take much longer than any futurist expects!'

Sounds plausible; except it is not true. Take Jules Verne who, when writing in the 1860s about electric submarines, rockets to the Moon or 20th century Paris full of cars and pollution—well before the relevant machines were invented—was considered a daring visionary. Verne's own characters talk about such inventions not ever materializing, at least not for another hundred years. Yet Jules Verne seriously underestimated the pace of progress of his own era: first cars and submarines materialized within less than 30 years or so; within less than a century not only cities were chocked with cars and pollution but nuclear submarines traveled under the polar cap and humans stood on the Moon.

By the 1960s, reality of the Industrial Era delivered more than the forecasts of the most daring of its visionaries a century earlier.

Exactly the opposite has been the lot of our Post-Industrial Era futurists. Even though, as the "Information Era" was progressing, many forecasts of the last few decades got increasingly tentative and more and more timid (and recent ones hardly base future forecasts on any new breakthrough technologies), despite this unappealing timidity their accuracy rate has been abysmal. Virtually none of their visions of future progress and leisure eras came true, and—see Alvin Toffler's, Drexler's or Frank Feather's forecasts—*most seem more fantastic today than when they were written a generation ago.*

Something clearly went wrong.

If you still need proof that progress if failing us where it counts—in visibly improving our daily reality—why not look around your home, your town, and your workplace and try to identify new things invented during your lifetime, things that are now part of your daily life. At home, the only new thing invented in the last forty or fifty years would be your personal computer and its various derivatives like smartphones. All the other electric devices and machines, from the fridge to the TV to the dishwasher to the vacuum cleaner, from electric heaters to double-glazed windows to air-conditioner to telephone or microwave oven are generations-old inventions.

If you went out, the only thing different from how many a street looked half a century—or perhaps even a century—ago would be the large plasma screen on a corner building, a 1970s invention but which took forever to implement. Everything else, from steel-and-concrete skyscrapers to buses to streetcars, from TV screens to neons, from airplanes flying overhead to electric subway trains below, from streetlights to telephone wires hanging from the poles, was introduced before 1930 and has not changed much since the 1960s. And by the way, none of it—not a single item—was there in 1830. Some of these things may look different than generations ago, but that does not change the fact that they are all century-old inventions and their modern equivalents are based on the same basic science. One decade the shapes of our cars are square; the next they are rounded; but—incredibly—under the hoods, they still conceal polluting engines invented in the 1880s. And if there are some new buildings that catch your eye, remember that construction technologies and materials have not really changed in the last forty or fifty years. All that has changed is fashion.

In your workplace, again the only things that are really different from a 1960s office are the computers—only they have significantly evolved from their large mainframe models, when they made in 1966 their debut in American workplaces. Everything else: from plastic-cum-stainless steel furniture to fluorescent lighting; from all-steel building structures to panoramic glass windows, from central air-conditioning to fast elevators, was there when we were children—or even before many of us were born. Incredibly, the passenger cabins of the airplanes we fly in today look like exact replicas of the cabins of the 1960s aircrafts, with tiny windows and cramped seats. And the

aircrafts themselves, again except for computerized controls, have
hardly changed for over a generation. Even the physical airplanes we
sometimes fly in can be 30 years old, something unheard of before,
when technology was evolving much faster.

These comparisons could go on and they would be equally
revealing. *Outside of the computers in their different guises, there
hardly has been any material technological change in our reality,
over the lifetime of most of us.*

*

IT IS ACTUALLY quite odd that we should be so caught up in the
mantra of accelerating progress as not even to notice these rather
obvious facts. Yet there are first signs that this outdated mantra
is finally starting to be questioned. Participants of MIT-sponsored
conference "Brains, Minds and Machines" on robotics and artificial
intelligence held in May 2011 agreed that since the 1980s there
has been basically little or no progress in these two critical areas,
once widely held as the key to humanity's future. They also agreed
that the 60s and the 70s were the decades when most of the
innovation in robotics and artificial intelligence took place, followed
by disconcerting stagnation. The leading specialists stated that
excessive specialization in various sub-fields of study and increasing
superficiality of approach ('how to make robots play football' or
similar theatrics) were the key causes of failure.

In August 2011, Michael Greenstone, MIT economics professor,
admitted in a TV interview that innovation in America has slowed
down since the 1970s.

Even bolder statements, completely at odds with the ruling
paradigm, began to recently appear. Tyler Cowen, in his 2011 short
e-book "The Great Stagnation" argued that technological stagnation
was the reason for flat wages, anemic job growth and rising wealth
inequality. The author argued that the world experiences "periodic
technological plateaus, and right now we are sitting on top of one."

Today's America is ageing, stagnant, overgoverned and waiting for a new burst of technology to get its engine going again, states the author[92].

Economist Robert Gordon of Northwestern University seems to agree. He argues that U.S. productivity increases have peaked. Most economists, he writes, believe "economic growth is a continuous process that will persist forever." It may not, he argues. Gordon is not impressed with the current "Information Revolution". He argues that productivity gains stemming from it "had faded away by 2004" and that at present the Internet, smartphones and tablets increasingly focus on entertainment, not labor-saving.

"Technological innovation, though faltering, will continue" writes journalist Robert J. Samuelson reporting Mr. Gordon's vision of the future. "Think more driverless cars and new cancer drugs. But [Mr. Gordon] argues that the effects on average American living standards will be muted. Less-skilled workers from lackluster schools will cut productivity and wage growth further. Greater inequality will steer some gains to the wealthy. Higher taxes to cover budget deficits and transfers to the elderly will squeeze take-home pay. . . . Though not preordained, Gordon's prophecies suggest a long era of stunted economic growth." [93]

Writing as early as 1975, technology historian Jean Gimpel stated simply: "We are witnessing a sharp arrest in technological impetus. No more fundamental innovations are likely to be introduced to change the structure of our society. Only improvements in the field of preexisting innovations are to be expected. Like every previous civilization, we have reached a technological plateau."[94]

A simple survey of our existing reality, accounting for what is and not for what could be, shows that our world is stagnant, and getting increasingly so. True breakthroughs, despite massive and accelerating R&D investment in the decades since WWII, are hard to come by, one might frankly say, are almost non-existent.

This slowdown in innovation translates not only into our daily life basics—the suburbia, the commutes, the cars, the downtown skyscraper offices—resembling the world we or our parents grew up in the 1960s, but also in dramatic slowdown in productivity improvements coming from technology—and ultimately in the economic stagnation we increasingly witness in the once-leading economies. The "energy crisis" that first surfaced in the 1970s—or rather technological inability to devise new, cheaper or more efficient energy sources in face of massively growing human populations and demand—was just one visible, critical facet of this technological slowdown.

If we take a hard look at one industry after another, we see a persistent, accelerating pattern of decline in the pace of innovation. Technological progress is steadily slowing down. In pharmaceutical industry, for example, "The [R&D] statistics are horrendous" says Sir Richard Sykes, ex-chairman of GlaxoSmithKline, one of the biggest British pharmaceutical companies. Innovation in the industry seems to have suffered a stunning, exponential decline since the 1950s. Statistics are truly sobering. In early 1950s a billion dollars (inflation adjusted, in 2008 dollars) invested in R&D would result in almost a hundred new drugs coming to market. In 2008, it took two billion dollars to develop just one drug—something even twenty years earlier cost just $150 million. "To some observers, that reflects the end of the mid to late 20th century golden era for drug discovery"[95]

Why? "Regulatory demands to prove safety and efficiency have grown firmer. The result is larger and more costly clinical trials, and high failure rates for experimental drugs.[96]" Fear of astronomical legal settlements—in case there is any problem—acts as additional brake on the speed of commercialization of the drugs. The result is that you see dramatically less new drugs coming to market, something that may be then casually linked to few medicinal breakthroughs and then maybe linked to life expectancy, dramatically rising before, hardly increasing in the last four decades.

Great hopes for wealth generation and productivity improvements were pinned for decades on computers. Yet, even as computers were being introduced on a massive scale over the last four decades, productivity improvements during this era—especially in services, the area best endowed with IT—have been remarkably modest. Some areas actually experienced productivity drops. Since the service sector accounts for about 80 percent of the post-industrial economies, snail-pace productivity improvements in services became a huge drag on any economic growth—exactly the opposite of the late 19th century situation where rapid mechanization of the dominant (meaning, employing the most workers) sectors of the economy: agriculture and manufacturing, with massive productivity growth in these sectors, drove the economies at a brisk pace.

We could venture here that this inefficiency of services may be the only saving grace for jobseekers—the efficient, relatively automated industries like agriculture and manufacturing need dramatically less workers today than they did a century ago, yet they still produce in relative abundance. Yet even there, pace of innovation has been slowing down.

How about our daily life? Instead of tangible material progress and rising real incomes, we have better communication and data processing devices, iPhones and other communication gadgets, plus big flat-screen TVs—the only things differentiating us from the reality of the 1960s. Yet having access to data-crunching computers and the Internet does not seem to have made us richer, more intelligent, or even truly better informed than having access to books, newspapers, telephone, radio or TV. Life-improving change—the proven, tangible improvements in incomes, living standards, lifespans, and daily comforts that Industrial Era has brought in—somehow has slowed down to a crawl once the Post-Industrial Era has set in. The critical comfort—the one that comes from knowing that the lives of our children will be better than ours thanks to technological change—that type of technological change that *really* makes a difference—has evaporated, replaced by fear of the future.

Technology improvements—even relatively small improvements, far from technological breakthroughs—increasingly seem to be taking longer and longer to reach the market. Flat-tube plasma TVs, announced in the 1970s, only really made it to mass market an incredible 30 years later. Solar power plants, first designed in 1905, are still a rarity; the technology is still costly and inefficient, despite many decades of improvements. Videophones, widely predicted around 1915, have only now become relatively common. Electric cars, staging races more than 100 years ago, are still talked about as novelty. Hybrid car technology has existed for decades, yet hybrids, being expensive, are still used by a relative few. For some strange reason, any significant switch away from the century-old internal-combustion engine seems to take us forever.

The inconvenient truth is that we have not yet invented a cheap, practical replacement for the fossil fuel engine, this basic driver of our reality—or any new cheap and abundant fuel to replace petroleum. To illustrate the problem: a fuel-cell bus you may have seen cruising the streets of your city likely cost your city fathers around US$3 million, more than 10 times the price of a regular bus, and worse, the hydrogen to operate it was likely manufactured and transported to your city using traditional methods (meaning by burning fossil fuels both to produce it and to transport it) at a huge cost both to the pocket books and to the environment. Solar panels require high-quality polysilicon, a material that consumes tons of fossil fuels to produce, and both high capital cost and low efficiency of the generation-old solar technology makes it impractical without massive subsidies. Bottom line? Other than the centuries-old wind and water power generation methods, the more recently invented renewable technologies—solar, fuel cells—are expensive, inefficient and actually not yet fully environmentally friendly when all is taken into account. No real breakthroughs are yet on the horizon, despite decades of research and investment.

It seems that the key problem of our reality is that we are yet to invent or discover truly revolutionary, cheap and non-polluting energy sources or an alternative: something like Drexler's universal assemblers, able to manipulate and transform matter easily and at minimal cost.

The record of practical inventions of the last 50 years, a very long time in Industrial-Era terms, is really quite modest: the transistor, the laser, fiber optics, the quartz watch, and the computer chip, plus steady improvements in artificial organs (the process started in 1951 with the first successful artificial heart implant). I wanted to add microwave oven, holography and maglev train to that modest list, as they all seemed so recent and modern, but then I discovered that the first was invented in 1945, the second in 1947 and the third in 1902! Hydrogen fuel cells, seemingly so recent, were invented in 1839 and commercialized in the 1950s.

Of the inventions of the last 50 years, only the computer chip (invented in 1958, so really more than half a century ago) has had the biggest practical impact so far, enabling the mass production of small, affordable computers and computerized devices (including things like ATMs and digital cameras) and allowing the mass use of Internet communication and computerized data processing. Paste-ups of some older inventions resulted in photocopy machines, faxes and mobile phones (combination of radio and telephone already in use in the 60s but only made practical for mass use with the invention of computerized switching). What is significant is that *all* of these inventions arrived before 1980, some, like laser—invented in 1960—long time before that date, leaving the last 30 years with even less to show. Personal computers were unveiled in the mid-1970s. Internet, while it only began getting popular in the early 80s, when World Wide Web was introduced, was actually invented in 1969. Other than 3D printing, invented in mid-1980s, very little was invented after 1980.

If we look at the record of the last quarter century, since 1990, the result is even more remarkable. In technology—other than Segway, the personal transport device—it shows essentially nothing. While steady improvements have been made to some old machines, especially TVs, cellphones and computers and various combinations of these, *no new popular-use machines or technologies were invented in the last quarter century*, an incredible blank in the records of human invention and a direct contradiction of the naïve "accelerating change" hype.

Biology shows only two breakthroughs, both still questionable: human genome mapping with related promise for genetic engineering (with creation in early 2010 of the first artificially-rearranged DNA), and cloning. In other areas, scramjet tests and continued nano-research, especially on nano-tubes, may result in some interesting breakthroughs in the future; graphene, a carbon-based nano-conductor just one atom thick, invented in 2006, may replace silicon in future computers; 3D 'printing' of objects layer by layer—something similar to sophisticated injection moulding—is likely to revolutionize many manufacturing processes and enable people to 'print' objects at home; a new generation of cheaper industrial 'robots' may finally prove economically cheaper than Western-wage factory labor. However, even if ultimately successful, these improvements, likely resulting in lower costs and higher efficiency of manufacturing, but contributing little to improve the dismal inefficiency of the biggest sector—services—won't change the already dismal innovation record of the past two or three decades.

Remarkably—and completely at odds with the accelerating progress myth—the scarcity of new inventions is increasingly matched by the growing number of abandoned or under-deployed inventions already achieved. Supercavitation technology, invented by the Soviets in the 60s, a technology that allows torpedoes and possibly submarines to travel underwater at speeds of over 400 km/hr by creating an air bubble around the object, has not been widely followed. Instead, today's sea and subsea vessels—like nuclear subs—use propulsion technologies invented generations ago, with slow speeds to match. Our popular techno-showcases are getting very long in the tooth: the high-speed trains in France and Japan, still admired by school kids as state-of-the-art, date from the 1960s; the space shuttle, still in use by 2010, is the relic of the early 1980s, and was scrapped by mid-2012. Yet was replaces it—picture American astronauts hitching a ride on an old-fashioned Russian rocket in October 2010—is a technological throwback to the 1960s or even earlier.

The Space Era, as declared 'The Economist' on its cover in the summer of 2011, is over.

Incredibly, we travel today slower than our parents (or maybe grandparents!) did in the 1960s, not only because of congestions, interminable airport security checks and flight speeds designed to save fuel, but—most importantly—because supersonic passenger travel, implemented in the 1960s, no longer exists. In the U.S., passenger trains take almost twice as long to get from Chicago to Minneapolis than in the 1950s. Similar examples abound.[97]

Reversal in the speed of travel is the first such step back in centuries; maybe ever.

*

NOT ONLY SUPERSONIC passenger jets disappeared. There have been no landings on the Moon since 1973; every subsequent plan to send humans back there has failed, with President Obama's cancellation in April 2010 of the Constellation Program topping this dismal list and effectively marking the end of America's meaningful involvement in space. As daily worries about our future bite, the ISS (International Space Station) seems to many people to be a pointless, costly exercise. Science coming of its experiments has been very weak, no revolutionary results to report. The biggest success seems to have been a new kind of air purifier. If no new funding can be found to support the station into the 2020s, it will be broken up and destroyed, a sad witness to the failure of mankind's dream about venture into space[98].

In a true hallmark of a new Baroque, the era of engineering and exploration seems to have ended with the bells marking the end of the 20th century, to be replaced by a déjà vu 21st century Baroque-like world of luxury shoppers, near-destitute middle class masses, domestic servants, and super-connected global investors. The rise of *plutonomy*–this brand new world of financial wizardry coupled with technological slowdown, spiced with fraudsters, drug-pushers and even return of piracy and slavery, seems to be the fitting symbol of the retreat from the technological highs achieved at the peak of the Industrial Era around 1969 and the visible sign of the onset of the era of decline.

*

THE KEY ISSUE with the technological advance of the recent decades is that, despite the soaring numbers of scientists and research dollars available, this advance–once very broad–has gradually narrowed to basically two fields: computerized information-processing and genetics. Unlike the broad creative achievements of the peak Industrial era–a time that gave us electricity, medicine, cars, telephones, jet airplanes, TV, atomic energy, x-rays, lasers and space travel–the expected inventions of the new tomorrow are either info-gadgets, like foldable and wearable computers, or anti-ageing cures, computerized prosthetics, or perhaps cloned bodies, for those able to pay the price. New power generating turbines, arguably a more important element of our reality than laptops or iPhones, are basically the same as the machines used quarter century ago, with basic technologies themselves more than half a century old. Power generation experts anticipate that another quarter century into the future, the same machines, maybe slightly more efficient, still will be employed.

After half a century of reported accelerating progress, our 3-D movies still use 1950s-style 3-D glasses in the theaters. When the "Back to the Future" movie was showing in the mid-1980s, we still could believe that the world of 2012 might have cold-fusion powered flying cars and other dramatic technological breakthroughs. Since then, we forgot we ever had such dreams, focusing on our struggle for daily survival.

Contrary to all the futurists' predictions—even where labor-saving devices (such as in the automotive industry, the one that uses most of the simplistic industrial 'robots', or rather, pre-programmed multi-movement arms for spot-welding) have replaced workers, wages have not gone up. Instead, generally, they have come down, while the numbers of unemployed went up. The once implicit linkage between technological advance and the growth of mass prosperity has completely broken down.

This breakdown was global. "Even in countries experiencing rapid economic growth," said UN assistant secretary general Jomo K.S. in 2006, "an array of factors, aggravated by tremendous demographic changes, has conspired to transmit inequality of knowledge, social responsibility and life chances from one generation to the next . . . few countries, rich or poor, have proved immune to the global trend of rising inequality, or to its consequences for education, health and social welfare." Noting that "growth in much of the world during the past quarter century has been slower than in the previous 25 years," Mr. Jomo K.S. concluded that "the economic liberalization carried out in much of the world in the last 25 years was a flawed policy from the start, and its consequences have become glaringly obvious."[99]

IN SEARCH OF LOWER COSTS

"The [Communist] Elders sowed the seeds of one of the biggest challenges to the party's authority. They entrusted some of the state's key assets to their children, many of whom became wealthy. It was the beginning of a new elite class, known as princelings . . . Twenty-six of the heirs ran or held top positions in state companies that dominate the economy. Three children alone headed or still run state-owned companies with combined assets of some $1.6 trillion, equivalent to more than a fifth of China's annual economic output."

—Heirs of Mao's comrades rise as new capitalist nobility, Bloomberg News editorial, 2012[100]

THE VIEW FROM my breakfast restaurant in the Grand Hyatt Shanghai, as of 2009 still the tallest hotel in the world, is truly breathtaking. This is despite the drizzling rain and smog that reaches all the way to the 87th floor of the Jin Mao Tower, the top floor of the hotel. From the restaurant, I can see over the spires of the lower skyscrapers to the renovated buildings of the famous Bund Street across the river and the vast panorama of the giant city beyond.

It changed beyond all recognition since I first came here in the mid-1990s, to later settle and live for a decade in Hong Kong. Then, Shanghai's streets were still full of bicycles navigating the narrow streets between old shops and brick houses. Now, other than the neoclassical buildings of the Bund, most of these areas are gone, demolished in the modernization drive. The area where my hotel stands, the new quasi-city of Pudong, did not exist, or rather, was a vast construction site in the mid-1990s. Around that time, I've seen similar landscapes of giant construction sites in the new factory towns growing around Shenzhen, across the border from Hong Kong. These scenes were repeated across much of China, as the country was becoming the world's giant factory.

The reason the landscape of China changed so dramatically within little more than a decade is simple: just like Western Europe during its decades of supercharged growth in the 1950s and 1960s, China opened up to the market system and the efficiency of the US-style production, management and credit-cum-advertising driven consumption models. As it provided its cheap and hard-working labor for the benefit of inflation-wracked global consumer, industrialization of China created immense riches for upstart entrepreneurs, corrupt bureaucrats and the new wealthy insider dynasties of 'princelings' sired by Communist elders. It lifted from poverty tens of millions of people and created a new, affluent and growing middle class. This process of rapid industrialization involved the wholesale modernization of infrastructure.

We might say that what I saw, maybe the most dramatic change of physical reality one could witness in such a short time, was the visible sign of the global paradigm shift. This shift took us all from the idealistic social ideologies of the 50s and 60s, through the collapse and bankruptcy of these ideologies in the 70s, the time of the Gang of Four, Khmer Rouge, Idi Amin and Red Brigades, to not merely the global adoption of the market system in the 90s, but most importantly, to the desperate search for efficiency and lower labor costs that this lightly-regulated market system brought with it.

Move of China and Russia to market economy in the late 80s was part of the same search for improved efficiency that drove Thatcher and Reagan reforms in the UK and the USA earlier that decade. Reacting to the deep economic malaise that set in during the 70s, they waged a war on the unions and their weekly strikes, on layers upon layers of government and corporate bureaucracies, on customs barriers and red tape, punitive taxes and disincentives to excel—that war was a process that was driven by the same reasons that propelled China to reform. And the reason was basically the same: bankruptcy of the welfare state.

Was this global move to unregulated, raw market economy a 'flawed policy'? From purely economic point of view, it might be argued otherwise: many ex-socialist countries, from the UK to Chile, from China to Poland, have embarked on a new growth path after introduction of such policies, functioning much more efficiently than before—albeit with dramatic increase in social polarization and wealth gap. Similar to the onset of the Renaissance economic system, the 1980s and 1990s privatizations have generally introduced efficiency and been largely successful, with few notable exceptions. Lowering of tariffs and taxes and allocation of various tasks of the global economy to various locales specializing in their relative strengths was one of the key drivers of growth in the last few decades. It contributed greatly to the increased efficiency—read cost saving—of the global economy, in face of declining productivity growth, rising fuel and commodities costs and dearth of new inventions. We may only speculate that without this global triumph of the market economy, the economic crisis we are witnessing now might have arrived much earlier. The 1970s were an early sign of what the increasing inefficiency of the system could bring, as the late Industrial Era was beginning to malfunction, falling victim to a combination of high costs, especially energy costs and declining innovation.

The fact that Communism and welfare state began to collapse in the 1980s—the decade when old illusions and ideologies were shattered across the globe and the reality went back to its eternal rut, governed by money, not dreams of social change—was not an accident. It was a sign that we could no longer *afford* welfare systems run by inefficient bureaucracies. As growth rates declined, the social benefits of the late Industrial Era—universal welfare programs, never-ending pensions, guaranteed employment and ample salaries for factory workers and the middle class, bloated bureaucracies, padded unions—suddenly began to appear as costs that hardly any countries in the world could any longer afford, without the risk of going bankrupt like 2010 Greece, where we started this tale. Even the heavily-reduced social welfare systems—like the U.S.—now face the stark risk of going bankrupt unless growth dramatically accelerates. Part of the problem is that many more high income earners today—same as in the Baroque decline era—pay either no or very low tax, thus forcing governments to borrow. Part of it is that post-industrial governments now act as paymasters one way or the other to over half of the population as private jobs get scarce and low-paid. Part of it—especially in the U.S.—is continued heavy military spending.

However, the key part of it is that productivity growth and GDP growth in the developed countries have slowed down to a crawl, combination of many factors but no doubt due to rising energy, commodities and food costs and stagnant innovation. Unlike before, vanishing economic growth can no longer solve the public debt problem. Consequently, it's either austerity or bankruptcy.

We can no longer afford what our grandfathers could still afford, since the wealth-generating broad growth and rapidly increasing productivity is no longer there to underpin our spending.

The slowing pace of progress exposed the economic weaknesses of the welfare states, as the ever-growing government spending and massive population growth overwhelmed generation-old productive technologies. Crumbling economic foundations deflated ideologies built on abundance. They dealt a death blow to the ideologies of people-power, to the redistributive systems of social justice—the 'people's republics', ideologies that were with us since the French Revolution, deflated the entire secular church around which all the social revolutions of the recent past were built. This collapse of populist ideologies underlies the feeling of inertia at best—and silent despair at worst—permeating our reality. We now have—collectively—very little idea what to do about fixing our problems. Worse, we seem to invest very little time in analyzing where these problems really came from.

The consensus, as always, is to deal with the visible signs of the malaise: tax the rich, cut the bankers down to size, clean the corrupt political system, get the government to create jobs by spending money on infrastructure, get the unemployed to engage in community work. But even these simple ideas seem impossible to implement, in face of vested interests controlling the legislative process and political deadlock. As the result, there is a curious feeling of quiet hopelessness that underlies our reality. There is also a strange intellectual void where little meaningful discussion on any key issues—other than maybe climate change—is taking place anymore. Few people, even if they are not happy with the prevailing neo-conservative political and economic system, can offer any workable, meaningful alternatives. Some of the 'religious' terrorism seems to be clearly related to this economic frustration, hopelessness and creeping poverty. People resort to terrorism or similar radical solutions as they have no confidence in venting their frustrations or solving their problems any other way. Taxing the rich would likely go a long way to pay off some of the public debt and perhaps rescue the public pension programs from bankruptcy, but the money is unlikely to be simply distributed to the poor to boost consumption and so would not contribute much to the revival of the economy. Considering how much spending in the present 'plutonomy' system is generated by the rich, some argue that reintroducing high taxes on the better off would significantly dampen consumption. Short of reigniting high rates of growth there does not seem to be an easy solution in sight.

*

IN MANY WAYS, the Thatcher/Reagan revolution met with spectacular success, taming inflation, reducing inefficiencies, facilitating doing business, promoting competition and creating incentives to run efficient systems. The rise of international finance and private equity enabled the new globalized economy to function much more efficiently than before. This process of eliminating various legacy costs and inefficiencies—through management, financial, and regulatory solutions—was one of the drivers of growth and improving corporate profitability we have seen over the last few decades. Wave of corporate mergers and acquisitions; push down on wages; removal of welfare nets, entrenched unions, tariffs, taxes, subsidies and trade barriers; currency unions; opening up of the new 'emerging' markets, both as suppliers of cheap labor and as consumers of industrial goods; rise of derivatives and various financial tools—all contributed to the rise and efficiency of a neo-conservative system that gave primacy to the market and profits. Together with growing availability of cross-border debt, just like during the last Renaissance, these efficiency trends drove and shaped our reality. And just like during the last Renaissance, the new global educated investor elites largely—in fact, almost exclusively—reaped the rewards of this process.

However, even as it improved the efficiency of the late industrial system and enriched the new elites, the 'neo-conservative revolution' generally exacted a heavy price on societies. It was a process strangely similar to the one that took place during the Renaissance. Absent broad technological advance, new energy sources or new energy converters, or lowering the heavy 'professional services' costs of the elites, globalization of business and creation of the global labor market—were bound to have a negative social impact. Sometimes, as in Chile or Iraq, deregulation was imposed from the barrel of a gun. Often, for example in places like Yeltsin's Russia or in the UK in the early 1980s, it caused widespread increase in poverty, as government industries privatized and shed hundreds of thousands of jobs. In the developed economies, as labor costs were cut, jobs moved to places like Mexico or China. In USA and Europe, as management levels were delayered, inefficient companies restructured, broken up, merged, or bankrupted, many middle class salarymen ended up seeing their careers destroyed, incomes and benefits cut. Against all futurist forecasts, working hours got longer, benefits evaporated and job security vanished.

The neo-conservative revolution pushed millions of middle class people into the ranks of the poor. It forced millions of others to finance their lifestyles from home-equity debt. Lightly-regulated, international finance gave rise to outsized profits of the financial industry and effective abolishment of taxes for the wealthy—the users of the new phenomenon, the offshore banking. Growing unemployment and especially underemployment in the developed countries kept wage increases down to inflation (or for many, below inflation) level: the result was growing financial stress, impoverishment, and steadily growing underclass phenomena such as illiteracy and breakdown of traditional family—all related to job and income insecurity, and to massive social polarization. When deregulation and hyped "self-regulation" combined with the mantra that 'greed is good', fraud, corruption and ostentatious wealth display came back with a vengeance. The efficiency drive, fresh from removing old evils: inefficiency and entitlement, rapidly bred new ones: neo-conservatism, inequality, hopelessness and dramatic wealth gap.

*

THE DARKER VISIONS of the present and of the future found in recent Hollywood movies and other mass media closely mirror the dark vision that the last Baroque left with us. Transition from the Renaissance into the Baroque was marked not only by economic distress but also by a deep cultural change, transition to a world dominated by dark and irrational visions of reality. With economic distress, when search for secret codes and wizarding formulas leading to imagined riches all became obsessive, Prague became the global center of the occult. This was where Emperor Rudolph II was working daily, locked in a secret laboratory inside a black-walled castle. With his astrologers and alchemists, he would search until the end of his days for the Grail of the Baroque—the Philosopher's Stone, able to transform base metals into gold. Rudolph had as teachers the famous astronomers Tycho-Brahé and Kepler, but he lavished his honors and his money on the Irish alchemist, magician, and visionary medium "Kelly," who was reputedly able to transmute metals, and on Kelly's friend John Dee, the English alchemist, astrologer, and magician. Responsible for the Enochian system of magical intercourse with a hierarchy of angelic beings, Dee was the court astrologer to both Queen Mary I and Queen Elizabeth I. According to legend, he conjured a windstorm that defeated the invading Spanish Armada.

Baroque, this era of contradictions, was the world of information wizards worthy of our dotcom billionaires; of magic and superstition; of financial barons no different from Wall Street sharks or Russian oligarchs; of inequality not seen in centuries; of torture chambers matching Abu Ghraib; of mountains of sovereign debt no worse than those of today's Greece or U.S. Treasury; of continuous financial problems facing not only governments, but most average people, especially the vanishing middle class; of cryptography and anagrams straight from *The Da Vinci Code*. But at the heart of this era of dark fears, wealth gaps, debts and plagues lay a generations-long societal, technological, and economic decline.

And this decline had its source in the brilliant era that preceded it: the Renaissance.

Let us take that as our cue. As we embark on a search for the answers about what kind of future is in store for us, and what we can do about it, let's begin by examining the patterns of the past. Let us see how Renaissance came to be and how it became the Baroque. For in the past lies inevitable prologue.

PART TWO

THEN

MEDIEVAL FIRE

"Machines of navigation can be constructed, without rowers, as great ships for river or ocean, which are borne under the guidance of one man at a greater speed than if they were full of men. Also a chariot can be constructed, that will move with incalculable speed without any draught animal . . . Also flying machines can be constructed so that a man sit in the midst of the machine . . .

Machines can also be made for going in sea or river down to the bed without bodily danger."

—Roger Bacon, Opus Maius, 1267[101]

F YOU CLIMBED the spire of your parish church in a European village in the year of the Lord 1300, you would not see much forest, orchard, fishpond or pasture. All you would likely see would be uniform fields of wheat. And not far in the distance, you would see three or four other spires of nearby village churches, so close were the villages to each other. You would be in a world of wheat, a world with exploding population, similar maybe to India or Brazil today.

Around the year 1300, at the peak of its cycle, medieval Europe had the fastest-growing population and the fastest-growing economy in the world. One of the main reasons Europe—non-existent as an entity in the Antique era and marginal during the Dark Ages, suddenly became a world power during the Middle Ages was demographics. Hard to imagine today, by 1340 Europe's population—estimated by some at around 120 million, a record only matched in the 18[102]ᵗʰ century–exceeded the population of India or China.

This was the time when Paris, from a tiny river town, within just a few generations grew into a city of 200,000, one of the world's largest. Genoa was just as big, and Florence even bigger. First-ever universities on the planet were already famous at Bologna, Oxford, and Paris. Rivers, empty today, were full of barges and ships. Cities were growing so fast that they had to employ armies of masons to constantly enlarge the walls and build new public buildings. In France, with 20 million people the most populous country in Europe, more than 80 cathedrals, 500 abbeys, and 10,000 parish churches were constructed within two or three generations, an immense building program that consumed more stone than the great pyramids of Egypt.

Everything was spanking new. Europe of 1250 was just like today's China, covered with construction sites and gleaming new buildings. Everywhere, there were new cathedrals with spires as tall as skyscrapers, new castles, new brick townhouses, new factories and new machines. Centuries later, during the interminable Baroque downturn, most cities still used the same medieval physical substance, same (by then decaying) houses, city halls, watermills and ports–all well into the industrial era. Medieval substance of most European cities did not get significantly enlarged until the 1860s, at the onset of the Industrial Century.

This was a very different medieval world from the one portrayed in Hollywood movies, full of poverty, plague and starvation. On the contrary, at the peak of the medieval cycle famine virtually disappeared from Europe. Only two were recorded in the entire 12ᵗʰ century; in the 13ᵗʰ, only a single region, Aquitaine, saw a single year of famine[103]. Warm weather supported bountiful crops. People grew taller and lived longer. In England, the average age at death rose from 32 in the Roman era to 48 in year 1276, only to drop back again to 38 after the medieval peak had passed.

Letters and reports from medieval Europe at its late 13th century peak all resemble those from other societies at their respective peaks: Classical Greece, 1870s Britain, 1960s America. They were snapshots of societies at the very zenith of their economic success. The Italian chronicler Bonvesin della Riva hailed the "abundance of all goods," and noted the "innumerable merchants with their variety of wares, ample employment opportunities." Artist Ricobaldo da Ferrara painted dramatic improvements in living standards between 1250 and 1320, echoed by historian Galvano Flamma of Milan, who ridiculed the frugality and simplicity of past generations. "Today, instead, everything is sumptuous," asserted Galvano. "Dress has become precious and rich with superfluity. Men and women bedeck themselves with gold, silver, and pearls. Foreign wines . . . are drunk, luxurious dinners are eaten, and cooks are highly valued.[104]" The 13th century, this century of prosperity, "raised the level of material life and transformed the whole psychology" of the civilization, summed it up the great historian Braudel.

"Abundance of wealth," we are assured by Giovanni de Mussis, describing the latest-model houses, complete with fireplaces, arches, courtyards, gardens and sun-parlors, "applies not only to the nobles and merchants, but also to those who practice manual trades, who make reckless purchases, especially on clothes for themselves and their wives . . . ." Giovanni Villani, gloating about his 1330s Florence, described it as an industrial city, where 30,000 people lived from wool manufacturing, there were 80 banks, 600 notaries and where 40 percent of children went to school. And to top it all, "during the month of July 4000 loads of melons came through Porta San Friano" said Villani.[105]

Around 1300, medieval society displayed the typical signs of a peak economy—high wages, massive liquidity, increasing inflation of assets, a large and affluent middle class, low unemployment and crime, overconfidence, complacency, liberal attitudes prevailing over the conservative ones, and wealth gaps just beginning to grow. It even had the first welfare programs, free schools, public hospitals for the poor, and doctors and teachers for those who could not afford them—all paid from the public purse. The banking system was flush with money.

And why was this? The answer is simple. Medieval Europe was where the first Industrial Revolution happened. This was the time of machines, of records, and of inventions. For the first time ever on such scale, machines multiplied the energy of this society beyond what humanity has achieved before. Based on new power sources and new machines, the medieval technological revolution resulted, just like the later 19th-century Industrial Revolution, in massive productivity increases and massive growth of prosperity. Mechanical inventions were coming in a cascade, decade after decade—energy converters like sophisticated watermills; rotating windmills, tidal mills; portable firearms; fulling mills; complex mechanical clocks; pontoon bridges; spinning wheel (first ever example of belt-driven transmission); interchangeable, prefabricated machine parts; knitting machines; cannons, timber-sawing machines, paper-making machines, cranes for loading ships, fully mechanized factories; gunpowder, musical organs, eyeglasses, magnets and compasses. Widespread use of waterpower and camshaft enabled millwrights to mechanize a whole series of industries previously operated manually. Dramatic productivity increases resulted in massive prosperity growth. While innovation and investment in it were generally driven by profit—a new windmill of Glastonbury Abbey, leased in 1342 to an enterprising farmer, would yield 26 percent annually to the Abbey[106]—medieval era had an obsession with mechanics and records which went beyond mere profit. The highest building of the medieval era, the spire of the Strasburg cathedral, reached 466 feet, height of a 40-story skyscraper. No higher stone buildings were ever built again, and Europe had to wait until the 19th century, building of the all-steel Eiffel Tower, to surpass this record. Dozens of engineers were trying to build a magnetic perpetual-motion device.

Of all the medieval mechanized industries, no other transformed more or had more social impact than fulling. Mechanizing all cloth-making operations in a fulling mill—a breakthrough, according to experts, as decisive as mechanization of spinning and weaving in late 18th century—transformed the face of the medieval civilization. Production of woolen clothing completely altered—one might almost say created—the destiny of both Flanders and England. Without their sheep and wool both would be poor, marginal countries, as they were in antiquity.

In Venice, naval manufacturing reached an assembly-line level. The top-secret Arsenal, Europe's biggest single industrial complex, had several assembly lines on which technicians could put together an entire war galley—a ship—from prefabricated interchangeable parts, in a single day. China, while richer overall—thanks to unmatched productivity of its rice fields—could not compare with medieval Europe in mechanics.

Just as in the 19th century—or even still in 1950s America—people of the peak medieval era were obsessed with mechanics. Soon they were looking for sources of power beyond hydraulic, wind, or tidal energy. Bold inventions and concepts abounded. In 1328 a doctor, Guido da Vigevano, wrote a military treatise for the king of France that included drawings of a prototype tank driven by wind power, and with windmill-type wings moving its gears. In the same book one can also find a sketch of a boat powered by propellers, siege towers with mobile platforms acting as elevators. Other books of the time depict submarines, pontoon bridges, sophisticated diving gear, portable firearms, and multiple tube cannons rotating like machine guns[107]—all this generations before Leonardo da Vinci's famous drawings. In fact, some of Leonardo's drawings seem to be simplified copies of earlier medieval inventions, now long forgotten[108]. In his treatise, 13th century philosopher Francis Bacon—in this chapter's quote—was describing a flying machine controlled by pilots, and with a passenger cabin. In terms of mechanics, no more advanced concepts appeared until the Industrial Revolution, which put a powerful and mobile energy source into these medieval concepts and devices.

A medieval Cistercian monastery like the one in Clairveaux, France, was in fact a fully mechanized factory. All operations—crushing wheat, sieving flour, sawing timber, fulling cloth, and tanning hides—were mechanized by water power from a channeled river. There was mechanical watering of the vegetable garden and also mechanical drain flushing. Water operated bellows for the beer-making vats, along with dozens of other mechanical gadgets. Hundreds of such factories were operating across Europe. Watermills hardly existed in the Roman world, but the medieval countryside was saturated with them, using them to the point of obsession. In 1066, England already boasted some 5,600 watermills. Around 1320 in Paris there were 68 watermills in a short upstream section of the river Seine, between rue des Barres to the tip of Ile de la Cite, a distance less than a mile long. Only under the Grand Pont (located where present Pont-aux-Changes now stands), some 13 watermills were moored; the restricted water moved the paddles faster.[109]

Machines powered everything imaginable, from water pumps, bellows, and hammers for making steel to mechanical saws for cutting logs, to presses for producing paper. Tanning mills, beer-making mills, paper-making mills were everywhere. With advances in mining, machines moved the complex gears of cranes lifting ore. Other machines ventilated the shafts. There were mechanical cranes to unload ships. The average town had one water-powered machine for every 30 inhabitants.

Water power enabled massive advances in metallurgy, essential element of Europe's newfound technology. Unknown before, mechanical hammers were now used in iron forges. The biggest ones could weigh as much as 1600kg, dramatically improving the quality of steel products. On the other end of the spectrum, light hammers weighing only about 80kg and used for finishing work, could deliver as many as 200 strokes per minute[110]. Water-powered bellows could heat up the furnaces up to 1500^C, for the first time ever producing molten iron. The first ever blast furnace on the planet was built in 1380.

At the late 13ᵗʰ–century peak, some castles began to be equipped with sophisticated central heating systems, later forgotten. By 1450 in Germany, gigantic machines were employed to pump water to the mines, lift loads onto ships, separate lead from silver. At the same time, the great ships of Venice reached 1,000 tons, and great Portuguese carracks 2,000 tons. Ships of the later Renaissance and Baroque eras were much smaller.

The idea that the peak of pre-Industrial European civilization was reached around year 1300, with subsequent Renaissance and Baroque being a time of overall economic decline or at least stagnation, may sound astounding. Yet it is true. This applies not just to everyday technology, but to the general commercial activity and overall wealth level of the civilization. Every recent study tells the same story. In 1310, not a particularly good year, at least a thousand ships sailed out of Bordeaux carrying wine. That was more than double, in number of vessels and tonnage, of what was going through Boston harbor in the 1760s. Studies show that equipment, books, accounting methods of a typical Boston trader in that decade were a virtual copy of those of a Genoese merchant in 1300—only the American's profits were much lower. Machines of 1760, just before the Industrial Revolution, were virtually identical to those of 1400; in terms of general technological advance, European civilization stagnated for four centuries.

Year 1293 is the one when many figures reach a record. In that year, volume of cargo going through Genoa harbor was worth an incredible figure of 4 million Genoese pounds; an increase of more than 400 percent in mere nineteen years. Never again, including the brief Renaissance boom, did the city's turnover come even close to such figures. In the same year, Venice reached a peak of yearly production at 160,000 pieces of cotton clothing. Virtually any other numbers we look at, whether values of yearly export of Florence's cloth, or even minor once like, say, trade between Barcelona and North Africa, all confirm that the peak of wealth and prosperity was reached somewhere in the 1290s[111]. In England, wool exports to

Flanders, a business that developed in the 1190s and grew steadily throughout 13th century, was reaching record figures after the key year 1300; records say that already by 1230 every year, 6 million sheep were sheared in England to export their wool to Flanders. Turnover of the Flemish wool production was nothing short of phenomenal. Between 1306 and 1313, production of wool rose in Ypres by 900 percent.

As with most other civilizations in their dynamic growth cycles, medieval Europeans were wonderfully efficient at applying and improving foreign products and inventions. Paper, which had been manufactured manually for a thousand years or so, first in China and then in Islamic countries, began to be manufactured mechanically as soon as it reached medieval Europe in the 13th century. Things like gunpowder, or printing, were invented in China, but fully applied, and on a massive scale—to the extent that they became game-changers of the entire Renaissance reality—only in medieval Europe[112]. With enormous success, Syrian sugar cane plantations were imitated in Cyprus and Italy, sheep from the Middle East were introduced into the Spanish Meseta and into England, new yield-enhancing scientific agriculture was introduced into Poland and Prussia. Toledo produced watered steel swords better than Damascus, Italy silks better than China. Trade records show that by 1330, people in Egypt, Syria, and Byzantium wore imported western textiles, used imported western soap, and wrote on imported western paper. Even lamps in a Cairo mosque, complete with their Koranic inscriptions, were imported from Italy. Those western products, while sometimes of lower quality than the local ones, were—thanks to being mass-produced—so much cheaper and plentiful that they soon dominated the markets the same way cheap Dutch (and later English) products dominated Europe during the Baroque, and the way cheap imports from China now flood the world.

It was not just its global search for gold and commodities, or its superiority in armaments, but also its ability to mass-manufacture and export—perhaps not yet to China but to Africa, Middle East and later the Americas—what first gave European civilization its leading edge and its global outlook. This process started in the Middle Ages and continued during the Renaissance and during the Baroque.

Same as today, not the economies best endowed with information technology, but those with a competitive edge in manufacturing and exporting manufactures—plus ability to practically apply others' inventions for a profit and produce trade surpluses and economic growth—who were the ultimate winners.

Hundreds of practical innovations originated in medieval Europe, innovations that neither the Roman 'benefactors' nor their servants-clients ever had any reason to invent before. Where Rome hardly used wood—even in forested regions like France or England—now an entire civilization was built of it. Hundreds of labor-saving machines and implements—even clocks—were completely made of wood. This wonderful flexibility in usage of resources was accompanied by an extremely rapid growth of a novel commercial infrastructure. Things completely unknown during the Antique era or outside of Europe: modern banking (being creation of new money as multiple of deposits), letters of credit, double-entry bookkeeping, joint-stock companies—appearing out of nowhere—all were in place by the end of the 13th century.

*

HANGING FOR DEAR life onto your church spire and looking at the wheat fields stretching to the horizon, you may have already guessed how all this originated! The abundant fields of wheat—a storehouse of energy—were what created Europe. Or, rather, the creator of the new civilization was a new converter that enabled Europe to produce abundant surplus energy.

Around the year 950 AD, Europe was still one of the most backward and under-populated peninsulas of Eurasia, submerged in barter economy and primitive 'Dark Ages'. The region has been declining for centuries—in terms of population, wealth, and by most other yardsticks. The nadir has been reached around the year 900AD, when Europe was savaged by Viking, Arab and Hungarian raids. This was the time when there were hardly any towns, money, manufactures or any tradable surplus, a miserable era of feudal manors in the woods, poverty and little surplus, time when impoverished papal Rome was ruled by "pornocracy".

Yet after the pivotal year 1000, Europe—even though still inhabited by only about 30-40 million people—emerged transformed. Its population and wealth began to rapidly grow. It was transformed into the global leader through a single technological invention, an invention unlocking a new source of energy. This invention was a brand new energy converter—a heavy, wheeled, iron-edged plow. It enabled people to cultivate the thick damp soils of Northern European Plain, soils that had for centuries resisted the light Roman wooden plow. Combined with the parallel invention of a field rotation system, the iron plow literally created what later became known as the Western civilization. It completely shifted the population centers. Before, people concentrated in the South-Eastern Mediterranean, essentially lands south and east of Rome. After year 1000, this completely reversed. Now, lands north and west of Rome, lands that were the most marginal, backward and underpopulated under the Roman Empire—France, England, North Italy, Low Countries, Germany—came to be the most populous and prosperous. By 1200, they already became the very center of the new civilization. By 1300, population density in these new regions was much higher than in Eastern Mediterranean. A new civilization—what later came to be called Europe, or the West, was born.

The newfound soil productivity, due to the iron plow and invention of field rotation, resulted in population increases that were nothing short of dramatic. Already by the year 1000 England had three times as much population as under Roman Empire; by 1340 France, before a sparsely populated rural backwater, became the most populous country in Europe. At 20 million, it had half as much population as in the early 20th century.

With the iron plow, the well-watered soils supported a new, more productive three-field system of agriculture. The new system doubled the average disposable grain harvest. In some areas, yields tripled or quadrupled. The new system also resulted—for complex ecological reasons—in better human diet and could support a massive population of domesticated animals, including horses.

Animals, especially horses, soon came to provide a key energy booster to the new civilization. A horse could deliver 10 to 20 times more mechanical power than a human and was much faster than the ox, previously used for plowing. As long as Europe had sufficient pasture lands, the proverbial horsepower enormously leveraged medieval man's energy supply. Where Roman horses could not pull more than 500kg loads, medieval horses, with completely redesigned harnesses, could pull loads of up to 6,400kg per wagon and for the first time ever, were massively employed in agriculture. Dozens of medieval inventions—starting with nailed iron horseshoes—continued to add to the effectiveness of the horse, turning the animal into a multifunctional "engine," one of the many medieval machines. Soon, medieval Europe became a world of wagons and carts, horse-pulled plows and horse-pulled coaches. All this was due to combining animal energy with a machine—a vast energy subsidy not available elsewhere and an incentive for further experimentation with later powered machines. Massive deployment of wind—and water-powered machines completed the transformation of the continent into the global technology and efficiency leader. By 1300 Europe was well ahead of any other civilization—including China—in mechanics and technology.

What is important is that the medieval explosion of ingenuity—the first such period since Greek times—happened not only because of the heavy plow, just as the Industrial Revolution was not merely a follow-up to the invention of the steam engine. What could have been a simple 'grain boom'—similar to the later 18th century 'potato boom' that was exhausted in a couple of generations—became instead an explosion of a new technological civilization. This was because, for the first time in centuries, peculiar conditions favored the rise of individual free enterprise and democracy.

Conditions in early medieval Europe were in many respects similar to those in 19th-century America—a largely empty continent with weak political control, open for pioneers, colonists and enterpreneurs. Both medieval Europe and 19th century America were new, expansive, barnyard technology-based civilizations, with exploding populations keen on cutting forests, on settling virgin lands, and on advancing individuals' fortunes through free enterprise. They did not rely much on any information technologies—late stage inventions such as the later printed books or Internet—inventions that marked the late stages of societal evolution during the stagnation and decline stage.

Both high medieval Europe and pioneer-era America were unusual places, places where ordinary people could become affluent or even rich not through special "wizard" talents, contacts, or years of elite schooling, but merely through hard work, business initiative and adherence to society's basic rules. Theirs were the circumstances very different from those we experience today. Both civilizations were based on mostly self-governing, bulk-trade and bulk-industry towns, with low or no bureaucratic overhead and self-administered taxation. In both civilizations, such towns were initially egalitarian—free from lawyers, urban barons, politicians and bureaucrats, information professionals of whatever sort, or passive asset owners.

In both Industrial Revolutions—the one that took place during the Middle Ages and the 19th century one—simple machines were invented and massively deployed in order to multiply the profits of business. In both, small and medium businesses found unobstructed room to grow. There was an incentive to invent labor-saving devices because—unlike in the slave-based Greek and Roman world—in these free societies settling virgin lands and clearing forests, manual labor was in short supply. It carried value. Its reality was based on high participation of individuals in production, ownership and exchange of basic, bulk goods—whether grain or timber, fish or wine, wool or cloth. Few people worked for wages before the medieval peak; initially both peasants and artisans controlled their own tools of production—if we use Marxist terms—to produce food, cloth or manufactures.

This was not a society focused on luxury manufacture. Unlike in later times, during the medieval peak era 95 percent of all cargoes and 75 percent of all profits came from bulk trade, and not trade in luxury goods or 'intellectual property'. Just like in 19th-century America, medieval Europe was powered by a large, affluent, enterprising urban class. In both cases, successful people weren't cocooned—like today or during the last Baroque—in a few 'financial capitals', acting as the civilization's top-educated, mandarin-style elite. Instead they were spread across the continent in hundreds of cities and towns. Significantly, none of the peak medieval businesspeople were yet landowners or rentiers. There were no passive investors, and there were no homeless.

But outside the city walls the democracy ended. While European civilization—and, by extension, our own western civilization—was born out of the invention of a single, simple energy converter, it inherited from Rome one key, essential feature of the collapsed Antique system: the land ownership. The Roman senatorial latifundia, turned feudal manors with the collapse of the Empire, still existed through the Dark Ages, supporting the barbarized descendants of the ancient officials, lawyers, and clerks, intermarried with dynasties of tribal strongmen. During the Dark Ages, these people became feudal warlords. Some of these latifundia, like those in the South of Spain, were controlled by the same families from Roman times, on through Gothic and Arabic rulers, all the way until late Baroque: an incredible span of some 1300 years. Religions, languages, empires, kingdoms and caliphates, all came and went, but the asset ownership arrangements survived them all, testifying to the incredible tenacity of asset-owning system and ancient elites that benefited from it.

*

SIENA IS DIFFERENT from any city I have ever seen. It has a strange feel I cannot identify, even though I myself was born in such an old medieval European town, Cracow in Poland. As I walk Siena's narrow streets, they all look pretty much the same to me: built of red brick, uniform, solid and undecorated. I peek up at tall, narrow windows that speak of readiness for assault and preparation for warfare. Even the town's central square, the Campo, and the city's seat of government, the City Hall, all look the same. Everything is built of somber, red brick.

Yet there is something strangely appealing in this city, even though it is so different from Venice or Florence, with all their frills, fancy outdoor art, marbles, statues, columns, palaces and luxuries. Here, there are almost none.

And then, suddenly, it hits me. That's it! This is why Siena feels so different from most other cities. Siena has no palaces and no slums, no fancy artistic wonders contrasting with hovels not far away, no visible inequality enshrined in stone. Siena speaks of republican equality. The reason it does is simple. It used to be a medieval peak-era republic and flash-froze in this stage of evolution. Once the High Middle Ages—and the city's independence—have past, Siena never became a royal or ducal capital. It never even turned into a fancy rentier-town, a place where the nobles of the Renaissance and the Baroque would spend their rent and tax money. Consequently, it never went through Renaissance 'model-city' beautifications and palace-building frenzies of the financial aristocracy of the decline era. Once Siena was conquered by Florence in the 14th century, you'd swear that life stopped, and the city froze in its medieval, republican shape. Walking through its streets we see it as it was around year 1300. It has never changed since.

At their medieval peak, most of Europe's cities were just like Siena. Hard for most of us to imagine, medieval cities were very different from what we are used to. They were communes—societies composed of citizens, all equals. Some analysts have compared life in a medieval city to being enrolled in a boarding school, or to being in the army. It was all about team discipline, hard work, and the complete power of the community. It was a place of family-based business where the impersonal, behind-closed-doors bureaucracy of today's institutions was totally unknown. Instead, everything was laid out in the open. Everybody watched everybody else, because the very survival of the community relied on the utmost contribution of every living soul within the city walls. The basis of existence was a family; there was no place for singles living by themselves. Every citizen belonged to some community within the larger community—a family, a craft, a guild; everyone had a communal responsibility to fulfill. Everybody had a business and everybody worked. The expensive and often corrupt complexity of the modern society was unheard of. Citizens did everything themselves—guarded the walls, prescribed in every detail the rules of the community, acted as night watchmen, militiamen, judges and councilors, chased and prosecuted crime[113]. In a unique reality of utmost personal responsibility, each one felt responsible for the whole. In these cities, there were countless documented examples of heroic civic spirit, ingenuity, and selflessness, because each individual life directly depended on the success of the community within the city walls, and the community shared its success with every individual[114]. During these strange times, there were countless instances where citizens would and did sacrifice their own life for the life of the city. The city was run like a competitive corporation in which every citizen had a vital share—his only real store of wealth. In such a commune, it was unthinkable to have lords and subjects, palaces, unemployed mobs, or corrupt bureaucrats.

While its time lasted, a medieval city was, even more than its Greek predecessor, a unique organism animated by a single spirit, set up, owned and controlled by a body of free and equal people: the citizens. People of medieval cities believed in progress and achievement, both personal and communal. The Christian hells and purgatories were to them stages of individual responsibility, on a personal way to perfection. For all its cruel and brutal side, the medieval time had a unique vision, one that appeared perhaps for the first time in history of mankind: a vision of a hopeful future, of salvation, of progress brought by dedication of men to their self-improvement, hope for change for the better, of equality of rich and poor before God, of love and charity due to all. There was a marked absence of cynicism, and frequent, strong, sometimes childish belief in all-transcending spiritual standards to which all, kings and beggars, were to be held. In this medieval morality play, in people's minds, there was a role assigned by God to everyone, king or priest, merchant or baron, a societal role and societal responsibility, a job that each one was expected to perform, and no one could ever dismiss. These beliefs, of responsibility of even the most powerful before God, that even the poorest had dignity and rights, and that all were held to some common standard of behavior, were uniquely medieval concepts, rarely articulated before and infrequently heard after.

Uniquely among all ages of man, the medieval world believed that we all have a soul and that we all have a purpose. Unlike previous civilizations, from Greece to Rome to China to our new Baroque, it did not divide humanity into superior people—elite-educated, rich, handsome, well-mannered, sharp, cool, well-born, articulate, predestined to greatness—and inferior people, low-born, dim, crude, homely, poorly educated, ill-mannered, ordinary, inarticulate —predestined for miserable servitude. Despite countless attempts to suppress them and to rationalize them away during the cynical ages that followed, medieval Christian ideals of self-improvement, charity, personal freedom, and equality before God never fully died. Wherever commercial and religious freedoms survived, in Holland and in England, they solidified into a simple set of personal principles and beliefs, finally finding their highest expression among those believers who drafted, ages later, the American Constitution.

THE TEMPLAR CURSE

"At a certain point the dynamism of the Middle Ages began to fail and the symptoms of decline became evident. The populations ceased to grow, difference between the classes hardened, and there was less social mobility. Restrictive practices were introduced in many industries, and there was growth in violent unrest in the big industrial centers. There were increasing indications that the level of efficiency was dropping and at the same time there was resistance to change. Energy production and mechanization has reached a peak and the standard of living began to decline. Inflation began to get out of hand; currencies were devalued and banks crashed."

—Gimpel, Medieval Machine[115]

The Great Master of the Templars Jacques de Molay was burnt at stake on March 11, 1314. It was ordered by the king of France and approved by his puppet, the Pope. The order of the Temple was disbanded, its officers arrested and tortured to reveal the locations of the hidden treasures: it was the money that the king was after. For a century the Templars acted mostly as bankers, the king owed them a lot of money, and their riches were reported to be fabulous. This way, the king resolved many problems at once: he cancelled his debts, confiscated new treasure, and also found a convenient scapegoat, somebody he could blame for increasingly shaky economy and rapidly increasing poverty of the masses. Some say that the Grand Master, before he died in flames, has put a terrible curse on the royal house, and called the Pope and the king to the judgment of God. Both died within a year.

Somewhere between 1293, arguably its peak year, and the first decades of the following century, when disasters began to multiply, the dynamism of the medieval civilization began to fail. Everywhere, the usual signs of decline suddenly all began to show up—growing income and wealth gaps, growing numbers of poor and unemployed, the first homeless, accelerating inflation (especially asset inflation), declining productivity and innovation, creeping neo-conservatism. Same as today, large fortunes were being built rapidly, accompanied by ostentatious display, just as the general living standards stagnated and began to drop. There was growing conservatism and resort to privilege, along with restrictive practices and parasitism in industry and trade. Same as today, there were alarming signs that returns on investment and productivity were dropping. Energy production and mechanization have both reached a peak. There was hardening class divide. Beginning around 1300, overland trade went into dramatic slowdown, damaging badly the once-busy Champagne markets, and Genoa began its slow decline as a commercial center. Textile manufacturing in both Flanders and Italy began declining; mining industry went into a slump; colonization and land development virtually ceased.

Even for a casual reader, this list of signs of decline must ring with an eerie familiarity.

By the first decades of the 14th century, even as the poor began to be pushed into starvation, the elites were growing richer than ever before. The opulence of Papal Court in Avignon was reported to be unbelievable, with banquets served on gold plates and (according to Petrarch) even the horses were "dressed in gold, fed on gold, and soon to be shod on gold"; one cardinal required 51 houses for his servants alone[116]. Similar displays were repeated in every royal court.

The century opened, just like our century, with a financial crisis. During the booming 13th century, national governments that fed on the boom grew in size and wealth at fantastic rates. Even before they began to get real muscle with mercenaries and artillery during the Renaissance, already in the 13th century they started to throw away the trappings of the layered feudal system. They began to hire lawyers to re-dust old Roman laws, engage public servants, remote-control provinces bypassing the feudal system—through sheriffs armed with writs—and set up treasury departments. They began borrowing money, not only from banks but also by issuing first-ever bonds. As the liquidity returned to the system, power began slowly to be associated with money, rather than with the feudal system based on personal system of dependencies associated with the pre-cash Dark Ages era. Beginning in the 12th century, new royal fortresses, aimed at keeping both own barons and neighbors in check, were mass-constructed everywhere by their hundreds. They controlled trade routes, coasts, and borders, and even some cities in the midst of which they managed to be built. They exercised control and extracted taxes.

Just like today, exercising power and displaying and enforcing authority needed more and more money. Royal taxes were tentatively introduced, even if still not enforced in a regular way, convoluted by noble, Church, and city tax exemptions and rights, and lack of real arguments in form of cannons. In Siena, municipal tax revenues rose from 12,000 lire around year 1200 to twenty times that amount half a century later and fifty times that amount by the century's end, a measure not only of prosperity but also of increasing tax rates and enforcement.[117]

But whatever the revenue, government expenses were always growing faster. To meet them, Venice issued first ever government bonds in the world in the 1260s. And since peaks of government spending came only well after 1300, a few decades after medieval Europe's economy has already peaked, this usual time lag between the peak productivity of the system and growing tax squeeze on it, could only accelerate the collapse.

The growing tax and rent squeeze, wealth inequality, and legalized oppression broke the long-lasting social peace and centuries of relative calm. The decades around year 1300 saw soaring waves of rebellion: from England to Sweden to Denmark to France, kings were overthrown. Townsmen of Flanders rose against the French oppressors, slaughtering them in Bruges, and then winning a battle against the French nobles in the Battle of the Spurs. The 14th century, the century of crisis, was also just like the Baroque, a century of continuous war.

Emergence of government debt resulted in appearance of world's first ever centers of international banking. The world's very first financial capital was Siena, seat of Gran Tavola of the Buonsignori. It was the first ever world bank, with agents across the known world. All Europe borrowed from the Buonsignori: great merchants, nobles, kings, even the Pope. Yet, increasingly, these loans were going bad. In 1298, Siena experienced its first great banking panic. While Buonsignori still survived, they were brought down in 1307. Together with Buonsignori, many other smaller Siena banks collapsed alongside[118]. Yet, as demand for credit was growing stronger than ever, Siena's place as Europe's key banking center was instantly taken over by Florence. By 1300, Florence already had 3 giant banks: Peruzzi, Bardi, and Acciaiuoli, accompanied by a host of smaller banks. Peruzzi bank quickly grew to dwarf even the Buonsignori. By 1315, it had branches across the known world, and was the biggest bank of the era, bigger than the later Medici Bank was ever going to be. Peruzzi's principal borrowers were kings of England and Naples[119]. Yet, same as for lenders buying Greek or Spanish debt today, lending was a dangerous business: if you stopped lending, there was a risk that previous loans would go sour—and size of loans was getting bigger all the time.

Same as Siena's banks before, Florence's banks soon began to succumb one after another. In an eerie preview of Lehman Brothers, the weakest failed first. The bank failures reflected growing insolvency of borrowers: as the 14th century opened, same as in today's Europe, governments of many European nations were virtually bankrupt. In France the government, desperate for cash, began outright extortion: by the royal decree, money of Jewish bankers was confiscated in 1306, the same happening to crown's Italian bankers in 1311. Torturing and killing the Templars was the last and most desperate step, but it managed for a while to enrich the growing class of government officials and hold off the national bankruptcy. Runaway government spending was accompanied by the usual expedient, coin spoiling, which brought inflation. When coin spoiling reached an unsustainable level, governments often resorted to re-coinage: issuing new currency. This brought prices down again, resulting in growing instability and increasingly erratic economic see-saw cycles between inflation and deflation. The increasing insolvencies continued to bring down the banks: the Scali Bank collapsed in 1326 and six other houses failed in 1342. Then, in 1343 and 1346, the three great houses of Peruzzi, Acciaiuoli and Bardi all collapsed with a great crash. Banking business disappeared in Florence for more than a generation[120].

*

THE KEY DRIVER of the 14th century economic collapse—as virtually all other historical collapses—was overpopulation and overexploitation of resources, all in face of a stagnant energy regime. Unlike when the heavy iron plow and field rotation system almost single-handedly created medieval Europe starting around year 950, by year 1300 the continent was completely covered with fields and people—forests almost disappeared. As mentioned earlier, if you climbed a spire of your village church, you would see four or five other church spires not far away, so close were the villages to each other. There were hundreds of towns in Europe that do not exist anymore. And, as incredible as it may sound, some of the existing ones have fewer people today, 700 years later, than they did then. This was a continent of small towns. Europe's population reached perhaps as many as 120 million, a record that held for the following 400 years, almost until the Industrial Revolution. In some places in France, the population was as dense as in China or ancient Sumer. But the agricultural productivity of Europe could not compare with either Sumer or China.

By the early 14th century, Europe's population had exceeded its energy and technology limits. As forests and pastures were turned into fields, there was hardly any space left to graze cattle. The shortage of pasture and forest drove up the prices of meat and the main energy sources, firewood and charcoal. More workers competed for fewer jobs, more farmers for less good land. The first caused a drop in real wages, the second asset inflation. Productivity of assets fell as marginal lands were brought under cultivation. Yields dropped as fertilizer began to be in short supply—all at the very same time that population numbers were reaching their peaks.

Economic see-saw cycles, inflation, erratic price movements of commodities, and the increased demand for hard assets such as land—all facilitated, same as today—speculative gains and steep increases of returns to capital. While inflation destroyed the wage-earners and people on fixed incomes, rising value of commodities and hard assets, combined with speculative swings favored the building of large fortunes faster. The 1330s saw a Wool Bubble: as pasture shortages restricted the output of English wool, a wool bubble began building, with prices and profits skyrocketing, up to the peak year 1340—when the bubble burst and the Flemish wool industry, one of the key manufacturing industries of the continent, collapsed.

The asset bubbles and financial crises were, same as today, symptoms of a systemic problem of the civilization as a whole, caught between overpopulation and stagnating energy regime.

As populations kept increasing, and as underlying technology and energy supply had reached their limits, real wages began to drop. By 1320 they were 25 or even 40 percent lower than they had been a century before[121]. At the same time, rents, land values, and interest rates rose sharply, well ahead of general inflation. Rents reached their highest recorded medieval levels in the late 13th century, after having inflated for decades at double the rate of grain prices. So did real estate—land values in Picardy more than tripled between 1200 and 1300; in Germany, land rents more than quadrupled[122].

In hindsight, we can see these were all pre-collapse trends, similar to the ones later witnessed during the late Renaissance, and also the ones we've seen drastically alter our reality over the last four or five decades: rising population, dropping wages, dramatic increase in prices of basics like food, fuel and shelter.

With power shifting from producers to asset owners, the latter began to aggressively enforce their old privileges and create new monopolies. In England, the Abbey of St. Albans, after constructing its own grist and fulling mills, forbade the local people to take their grain and cloth elsewhere—while charging them monopoly prices. In Italy, the richest of the merchants, seeking to enforce their power in the communities, began manipulating the economic instability to their advantage. Some arranged for the city councils to give them the privilege of always being paid in gold ducats (which held their value), while they—the merchants—paid wages and taxes in often spoilt silver coin[123]. With the rise of competition and communal complexity, and with basic production and trade uncertain or even producing declining returns, men of wealth and influence began to discover thousands of ways through which they could create a parasitic claim on reality and drape it in the cloak of the resurgent legal system.

Previous urban equality began to rapidly unravel. Studies show that in 1307 in the community of Santa Maria Impruneta, a town six miles south of Florence, the richest one-tenth of families still controlled only about 33 percent of the community wealth. But by 1427, closer to the onset of the Renaissance, the share of the total assets owned by the richest one-tenth had grown to 50 percent. Correspondingly, the wealth of the bottom half of the population had dropped from 21 percent to six percent. While urban inequality was not yet as dramatic as during the later eras or today, the late medieval statistics began to mirror the later Baroque and our own era. In addition to the growing evidence of the rich getting richer and the poor getting poorer, there was also rapid growth of the disturbing new phenomena—destitution and homelessness in the rural countryside. Both, unknown before, first began to show up in the records starting in the late 13th century, at the onset of this medieval Baroque, as reality began to collapse.

As the Middle Ages began to wane, the centuries of boom and general prosperity were followed, like in the biblical Pharaoh's dream, by generations of plague, stagnation, and decline. Ominously, in 1284 the first limits to engineering were met, as the vault of the choir of Beauvais cathedral in France collapsed. It had been intended to be the highest ceiling in the world, suspended at the height of a 14-story building.

Just as in our last few decades, there were plenty of other signs that the tide was turning. In addition to usual slowdown in broad technological innovation, the other standard and ominous decline trends were all in place—rising neo-conservative trends, political correctness and repetition replacing creativity, plus a growing net of restrictions imposed on freedom of expression and even thought. After the amazing spiritual revelations of Saint Francis in the 1250s, the following decades brought a steady narrowing of intellectual horizons. In 1277 the professors of the University of Paris condemned what they termed "Two hundred nineteen execrable errors" of faith. Some of these were ideas cherished by Saint Thomas of Aquinas—now judged too bold for the emerging neo-conservative reality. The medieval world, getting set in its ruts, was no longer open to the revolutionary experiments of the earlier generations. The year 1277 effectively marked an end to the era of enlightenment, that exciting time when all ideas about the nature of the world (some definitely un-Christian) were still openly discussed[124]. Now came a darker era of bias and rigid paradigms and soon—arrival of the Inquisition, this hallmark of the Renaissance and the Baroque.

*

IN 2010, RAJEEV Devendrappa , farmer's son from a small village near Bangalore began his new job processing foreign insurance claims for a London-listed business process outsourcer. The job was based in a small Indian town of Shimoga, 22 kilometers from his native village. Mr. Devendrappa, who has a master's degree in commerce, was once was planning to move to Bangalore, but after his father died suddenly and he was left in charge of the family, he abandoned the idea. The job in Shimoga opened up as Bangalore-based outsourcers began to face rising salaries, increasing attrition costs and general manpower crunch. Just like their 14th century and Renaissance predecessors, they began to look to smaller towns and villages to cut costs and stay competitive.

Another Indian process outsourcer, RuralShores, has moved even further: in the small town of Thirthahalli, 60 kms from Shimoga, around sixty percent of its workers are now women, typically married and with children, and thus with low geographic mobility. Wages are low, lower than in Bangalore and maybe even lower than in Shimoga: "The income is not much, but I was getting bored at home. I wanted to use my education, mingle with other people" says Jyoti Kishore Seth, a 35-year old mother with a commerce degree working in Thirthahalli[125].

RuralShores business model strikes us with an eerie feeling of a déjà vu. In the first decades of the 14th century, as technological limits were reached and soaring costs in the leading cities—whether of labor, regulation, property or overhead—could no longer be absorbed, there was a drive to cut expenses by outsourcing manufacturing to low-wage, rural countryside. This trend, this outsourcing, became pervasive in the 14th century and continued growing through into the Renaissance. Now, undercut by low-cost competition, old industrial cities—the old medieval communes—found themselves squeezed between growing unemployment, rising inequality, falling real wages for the average worker, and new methods of manipulation by the elites.

The result was growing social unrest. The biggest and richest of the cities–Bruges, Ghent, Florence, and Paris–all saw a sudden surge of riots, social rebellions, and assaults on calcifying privilege, just as parasitism and abuse of authority emerged in each of them on a massive scale, and began to grow by leaps and bounds.

THE RENAISSANCE MEN

"The fourteenth century opened with a flag of optimism flying high. In the course of the thirteenth century, Siena had erected a magnificent Duomo, a most refined and elegant demonstration of greatly increased wealth. At the beginning of the fourteenth century, the Sienese were convinced that wealth and population would continue to increase, and, in 1339, L. Maitani was charged with the preparation of plans for an enormous church, of which the existing cathedral would only be a transept. The plan was made and the work begun. But it was never finished. The empty arches, the unfinished walls which break away from the old cathedral bear sad witness to the fragility of men's dreams."

—Carlo Cipolla, Before Industrial Revolution[126]

By the mid-1340s, Europe's cities were overcrowded beyond all imagination. Tens of thousands of urban poor now lived in urban slums, crowded a dozen to a room. The stench of open sewers filled the air. Domestic garbage piled up in the streets and in the yards, or was just thrown outside city walls. This world was just waiting for the plague. When it arrived, in 1348, the Black Death killed between one-third to one-half of Europe's population within two or three years it ran rampant. After this, it returned frequently over several decades, keeping population numbers down. Devastated by war, plague, and economic collapse, Europe became a chaotic, depopulated world, an eerie landscape of half-empty cities. In 1420, during a horribly cold winter, roving packs of wolves attacked people inside the walls of Paris; three years later, 24,000 houses reportedly still stood empty in this once-bustling metropolis[127].

What happened in Europe during the late 14th century, during the decades of the Black Death, can only be compared to the sudden depopulations that seemed to occur in dynastic China every 200 or 300 years—the times when the raging civil wars marked the transition from one dynasty to another. Such wars were typically sparked by peasant uprisings against increasing taxes and oppression by the educated landowning Mandarin elite. These bureaucrats, often low-born, always managed to parlay their education, cunning and position of power into land investment, which quickly led to inheritable, dynastic wealth. When their oppression became insufferable, and poverty of the peasants unbearable, the massive peasant uprising would spark a civil war that would routinely kill off many millions of people and put to sword most of the Mandarin investor class. This was accompanied with routine deliberate destruction of land titles and debt records. Such destruction of both people and their parasitic claims on assets would thus clear the key productive asset—land—for a new cycle of growth, enabling the Chinese civilization to regenerate, albeit at a tragic cost.

The same happened in Europe after the devastation brought by the Black Death. The plague did not differentiate between the rich and the poor, and the survivors found themselves in a new universe, where land and food were plentiful, but labor was in short supply—with weak demand for industrial goods, as populations shrunk. In this new, super-competitive world, efficiency and cost-cutting became the key.

In a process we have been observing in our own reality, in the transition period of the late medieval and early Renaissance period, regions and cities began to specialize in their relative strengths. Since the cash-squeezed economy of Europe could no longer support the high prices of goods carried over long distances, local production became favored. Cheaper English cloth, produced by countryside labor, squeezed out luxury Flemish and Italian woolens—in fact, the wealth of Tudor England was to be based on its cheap woolens. Flemish cities and Florence managed to hang on in the business of "luxury detailing"—the dyeing and finishing of English cloth. Italy, formerly a merchant middleman with the Orient, almost overnight re-invented itself as the manufacturer of many "Oriental" luxuries, especially silks, which were now prohibitively expensive to bring from the Orient itself.

Yet the late medieval world did not come up with a steam engine. Instead—just like today—rather than create new technologies enabling increasing productivity, wages and rising living standards, businesses increasingly trawled the rural countryside seeking to explore all available human resources at the lowest possible cost.

Just like today, the search for lowest possible labor cost was matched by searches for monopoly, for rent, and for the ability to derive tax revenue. Some cities bought from cash-strapped governments the right to either tax passing merchant caravans on the roads, or to detain them, seize their goods, and liquidate them at prices set by the cities themselves. Extra profits from such "sales" went into the pockets of those in control of city councils. In some cases, collusion between the government and private business resembled the one between city government and property developers in today's Hong Kong . In late-medieval cities, councilor positions increasingly came to be treated as sources of rent. These positions were coveted, limited to a circle of insiders, and eventually were bought, sold, and inherited.

Gradually, the late medieval city became an unrecognizable, distorted version of itself a mere few generations earlier. During the glitzy Renaissance, medieval urban democracy became a meaningless show, a parody that we begin to observe in our own reality, with power increasingly rotating within insider cliques and a few wealthy families.

There was almost constant social turmoil reported in all major urban centers. Its source was the growing struggle of ordinary citizens—factory workers, small merchants, shopkeepers, apprentices—against the rising wave of extortion and abuse by those who, merely rich merchants before, now began to assume the profitable cloak of civic power. Hundreds of restrictive regulations now entered the picture: fixed tariffs, regulated wages, guild monopolies, and royal edicts regulating prices. Tax records of the depressed manufacturing cities show soaring inequality—as one Renaissance historian put it, the patron-funded artistic flourish of the Renaissance rose on the back of commercial decline[128]. Urban risings multiplied. In Florence in 1378, the so-called "Ciompi uprising" pitched the new poor—those without assets ("popolo minuto" or "little people")—against the wealthiest families of the city.

As in every other era of decline, conservatism and authority entrenched itself. Trade associations, called guilds, gradually became instruments for rich master craftsmen to keep their students in apprenticeship forever and pocket the profits of their labor. Mastership, which before merely reflected individual excellence of a learned skill, became regulated so that it could be inherited within families, leading to quasi-officialdom much like city councilor positions, enabling investors to extract value from yet another positional asset. They resembled the restricted-membership 'professional associations' of today—medical, legal, academic and many others—who set their own fees, restrict outsider access and ensure that any outside competition is illegal, and so maximizing the benefits of the insiders.

Increasingly, predation replaced business. The territorial expansion of late-medieval city states such as Florence was largely driven by the search for tax revenue. These taxes and other sources of cash extraction then came to be concentrated in the hands of the new elite—hereditary councilors, wealthy bankers, now styling themselves as (a new, Renaissance phenomenon) the wealthy "urban princes." The progress of the Medici family to political power was a good example of how some of the equals of the medieval commune became more equal, and eventually evolved into hereditary princes. During the medieval commune era, the Medicis were simple moneychangers, operating from a bench ('banca', hence 'banks') in the street. From there, as their fortune grew, they gradually turned into money lenders, bankers, city councilors and then, once their wealth allowed them to manipulate city councils, to self-styled 'princes'. As Florence expanded to squeeze tax income from subjugated cities—cities like Siena—these cities in turn began squeezing wealth from the surrounding countryside through escalating tax, rent, and food demands. In that way, the affluent rural areas of the peak medieval era gradually became a thing of the past[129]—in a process of slow decay of the small towns not very different from what we witness in America today.

*

LONDON'S GLOBE THEATER is a faithful replica of the Renaissance original, the one that Shakespeare used to write plays for. Sitting on a narrow, hard bench high above the stage, I enjoy one of these rare sunny London summer afternoons while watching the "Merchant of Venice". As the actors perform onstage, I ponder what this play is really about. A love story? An anti-Jewish pamphlet? As the familiar narrative unfolds, I feel that this play, more than most other plays by Shakespeare, conveys what Renaissance was all about: money. Antonio almost loses his life because of money losses from his trading activities, his freefall into debt and misery mirroring the Baroque financial collapse of that once-merchant metropolis that was Venice. Shylock is the model for the new up-and-coming breed: a cunning, ruthless banker. Bassanio, who uses Antonio's debts to dress well and make a show in order to marry into some major cash, is the model of a new Renaissance wannabee noble. All key characters are symbols of the new, deeply indebted, completely money-driven reality. Finally, the outcome of the story hinges on the sophistry of a sharp lawyer; and in Shakespeare's play, same as in real life of his era, it is the lawyer who has the last laugh.

Shakespeare's vision was right on target. Renaissance was all about money, debt, status show off through fancy material goods, money-driven marriages, and sophistry of the newfangled 'information professionals'–bankers and lawyers–bent on squeezing every penny out of the decaying reality. Just like in Shakespeare's play, as profits from productive activity–commerce or manufacturing–decline, the time comes for the well-informed, the rent-seeking, the well-dressed, and the unscrupulous to take over. Renaissance is the theater of bankers and lawyers, and of *nouveau-riche* investors–who make money just like many do today, from passive investments into property or shares, then buy noble titles to escape taxes and to show off their elite social status.

As the Renaissance dawned, it seemed to many contemporaries–dazzled by its opulence and artistic polish–that a new golden era had begun. Many of its direct beneficiaries–as well as its victims–hailed it as the dawn of a more brilliant, polished, aggressive, resilient and pragmatic civilization. And for the first time since Antiquity, it was a civilization led by a new kind of nobles–nobles who were highly educated, rich, and cultured: the Renaissance Men.

The Renaissance Men all were, to use Toffler's term, 'cognitarians', or information professionals. Indeed, it was typically their elite education, extensive network of contacts and access to insider information that allowed them to make money in the first place, so that they could eventually 'turn noble'. It was the golden time, the time of getting rich for upstart lawyers, army suppliers, royal advisors, court clerks, property managers, notaries, bankers, and all kinds of cunning speculators–the well-informed insiders and 'cognitarians' morphing quickly into the noble investor class. And this investor class routinely would try to buy land as investment, then soon after buy–or marry into–noble titles. Many factors facilitated their rise.

First, land became a commodity. In England, by 1422, say the analysts, the feudal system that still persisted in the countryside since the Dark Ages, effectively collapsed. Land ceased to be linked to the old warlord structure of power, the web of allegiance and societal responsibility. It simply became a rent-yielding commodity. It could be bought, sold, or rented, by anybody who had the cash.

And with this, the entire medieval political concept of multiple power sources, rapidly unravelled. Now anybody with cash could buy land and then aspire to noble titles. As investment in land opened up, it created a new and enormous business opportunity, incorporating land–before jealously inherited–into the urban cash economy.

Second, a highly educated investor would extract from land much better returns than those that the old warlord aristocracy–or illiterate peasants–could ever hope to extract. Third, as post-Plague populations rose rapidly and demand for food–both simple grain and new fancy cash crops–grew dramatically and so did the prices, land became an excellent investment. Fourth, as artillery finally allowed central governments to assert authority and collect taxes, the massive increases in state revenues needed to be collected and administered by large, complex, highly-educated bureaucracies, thus opening a myriad career and cash-squeeze opportunities for the educated and the ruthless. As taxes needed to be collected–and then collected cash spent, as assets and future income needed to be borrowed against, careers as tax collectors, lawyers, notaries, clerks, bankers, accountants, councilors, judges, surveyors, mercenary captains, asset managers–many of these occupations largely unknown in the simpler medieval times–now appeared, offering advancement and wealth opportunities to the educated, the ruthless and the insiders.

And the educated mushroomed in numbers and wealth, riding on the back of the Renaissance information revolution–the invention of printing, so similar to our own information revolution. Printing, this key invention–just like the computerized gadgets and the Internet today–offered incomparably cheaper, wider and easier access to information than ever before–without necessarily improving much the quality of the content.

Renaissance truly opened a floodgate of information. During the long Middle Age centuries, all books produced in Europe might be counted in mere thousands. They were rare and expensive collectors' items, often true works of art. But by 1500, mere fifty years or so after printing has been introduced, books were already printed in tens of millions, at cheap prices, enormously increasing access to information for the newly educated. Hundreds of various investment guides and land management manuals and other sources of investment information were printed in the 16th century alone, in hundreds of thousands if not millions of copies. Just like email and Internet today, printing, newspapers and regular, ever faster mail services became the new normal, an information highway that turned the unsophisticated medieval world into a wonderland for the well informed.

The Renaissance Information Revolution was the critical medium in creating the new investor class, even more so than email and Internet is contributing to the creation of our educated transnational elite today. In the previous medieval era, information was either passed verbally, or through letters, or (very rarely) through extremely expensive hand-written books, treasures cherished and inherited for generations. Few people, even among the nobility, knew how to read or write. Most had priests read them the lives of saints or similar religious works.

Now information was flooding the Renaissance reality, in form of tens, soon hundreds of millions of cheap printed books, pamphlets, leaflets, atlases, posters, wall maps, advertisings, and soon daily newspapers. Whatever could be printed, was printed. Regular mail services appeared and opened up ever cheaper and faster ways of transferring information over distance. There was a marked increase in the speed of mail across the continent, as demand for information—same as today—was driving the new reality.

The nobles of the Renaissance were not only "new people," the phrase usually applied to prosperous second—or third-generation merchants or peasants turned noble. More importantly, they were also a new *kind* of people. Unlike the old medieval warlords—typically illiterate, focused on honor and loot, and operating through face-to-face personal interaction with their lieges, peers, subjects, and enemies—the Renaissance investors no longer operated with a fist. They operated in a completely modern fashion—behind closed doors, through an appointment letter, a bank account transfer, a lease, a notarized loan contract, through a personal information network maintained by email-like daily letter writing, and through a writ of foreclosure. They were more than merely literate—virtually all had degrees from elite universities. Many had more than one. Most had traveled widely to gain education, learn languages, establish personal networks of elite contacts, copy ideas and manners, and acquire both information and cosmopolitan polish. Just like we see again today, many would travel abroad to study at top international 'brand name' universities—whether Oxford, Sorbonne in Paris, Bologna, Cambridge, Padua, or Salamanca. They maintained contacts across international borders, interacting mostly with the similarly educated, cosmopolitan, wealthy investors, with common interests in politics and luxury, in art and travel, in 'branded' goods produced by celebrity artists and craftsmen, and in elite sports.

But the driving interest was the common goal of making money.

It was an era eerily similar to ours.

The educated tastes of the newfangled nobles turned the Renaissance into an era of luxury. The new information professionals built glitzy marble palaces inside the old medieval communes, and these homes were full of books, statues, pictures, gardens, tapestries, art galleries, and luxury objects and furnishings. They competed with other wealthy investors, patronizing brand-name artists, collecting expensive objects, outdoing each other in luxury spending, with the resulting flourish of lavishly-funded art. Entire centers of a few key cities—the new *rentier* capitals—were redesigned to suit the new elite-educated tastes. We see their fantasies of the 'ideal cities' depicted in early Renaissance paintings.

Just like the wealthy of today, they were no longer citizens, comparable to the increasingly impoverished ordinary urban folks: When their pocketbooks could afford it, they fancied themselves urban barons, even princes. The top earners were spending lavishly and conspicuously, and—to the relief of many—the old no-fun religious inhibitions finally gave way to cynical attitudes of self-enrichment, expediency, and unabashed displays of wealth. This was the original time of 'greed is good'. The high Renaissance was marked by triumphant pragmatism and selfishness, spun by contemporaries as the 'humanist' triumph of modernity and reason over the old backwardness.

Just as today, for a long time the Renaissance seemed to be a glorious transformation toward efficiency, rather than an early sign of decline. While huge wealth gaps opened and many old trading cities declined, new areas of economic boom emerged. The key one was South Germany, which by early Renaissance became a hub of manufacturing and silver mining. While the progress of bulk technology had already stagnated and—as in other eras of decline—only information and war technologies were advancing, few noticed these early signs of trouble. Gigantic machines, based on old medieval models, were still being built, especially for mining and metal working—huge blast furnaces for making iron for cannon, machines to separate lead from silver, pumps to clear the mines of water. Few might have guessed that by the year 1500, machines had already reached their limits; none bigger or more advanced would be built for the next 300 years, until the advent of the Industrial Era.

During the Renaissance, instead of mechanical progress, the money supply and the speed and sophistication of financial transactions reached unprecedented levels. At the peak of the Renaissance, reminiscent of our recent management-cum-globalization revolution, the efficiency of asset—and invention-utilization reached a zenith, even as the once-broad technological innovation and advance of previous centuries stalled and narrowed to a few select fields, and declining wages combined with soaring inflation to impoverish everybody but the select few.

Yet nobody during the Renaissance decades suspected a Baroque future. How could they? The rapid flow and massive amount of available information, fancy artistic polish, financial wizardry, trips around the world, new information technologies, growth of luxury manufacturing and global trade, general economic expansion based on population increase, efficient outsourcing, massive liquidity available, sophistication, wealth and polish of the new top-educated elites–this Renaissance New Economy seemed as impregnable as ours seemed not so long ago. Growing efficiency and productivity of assets seemed to support the claims of economic miracle. As in the 1990s 'New Economy' hype, the world seemed renewed.

As the new class of investors acquired the best assets–typically prime land for cash crops and urban real estate–they turned the monotonous grain fields of medieval times into a more varied and more profitable landscape of vineyards, pastures, gardens, fishponds, and orchards. By 1600, these scientifically managed, investor-owned "agricultural assets" reached average yields of six to one, twice as high as during the medieval peaks[130]. Scientifically drained and canalized, entire regions, like Lombardy, reached amazing levels of productivity. Just like today, massive circulation of information, such as asset management books, helped to achieve this, as it quickly disseminated information, new ideas, concepts and 'lessons learnt' experiences among the educated, literate elite. Growing sophistication of the new investor class did the rest. It was a sort of 'globalization' of management styles, techniques and solutions across the continent that produced a wave of efficiency. Again, the similarities with the recent rollout of Chicago School style of capitalism around the world seem uncanny.

Just like today, in our current commodities boom, with growing populations putting pressure on resources, speculative and rental returns from real estate, mines, vineyards and food-producing land grew. Strikingly, after around 1550, in once-commercial cities like Venice, property investment became the key economic activity. "In olden times we all lived by trading and not on fixed incomes" commented Renaissance writer Girolamo Priuli describing this new post-industrial reality of living from either dividends from investment or government pay. "Now few of us live by trade. Most subsist on their [rent] incomes or on their [government] official pay[131]". Everywhere, as populations and food prices steadily rose, this 'noble' investment in land and urban real estate brought to the new *rentier* class increasing returns compared to the yields from the declining and risky commerce[132].

As the Renaissance wore on, simple medieval cloth turned into large, heavy, imposing robes of velvet, silk, fur and brocade, adorned with lace and jewels. And the new urban nobles no longer walked: by 1550, splendid urban coaches became common, to transport them around town. A full-blown costume of a new city baron would cost perhaps the same as today's Mercedes. His gilded coach would cost much more.

Yet, just like during our lifetimes, in the midst of this apparent economic boom, only those affected noticed that living standards in the countryside began to slip, and, after 200 years, the homeless began to reappear.

*

JUST AS IN THE 1970s, the early sign of the incoming decline was the reversal of real-wage trends. Prior to around 1465, the year that happens to roughly correspond to the beginning of the Renaissance, real wages were going up, returns to capital were declining or flat, and so were asset prices. Now, as populations were growing strongly and were putting pressure on land and resources, this began to reverse. In the Renaissance century, real wages began to fall and returns to capital began rising sharply. Between 1480 and 1530, while the overall economy was strongly expanding, real wages dropped 30 percent. Women's wages dropped most, their status noticeably deteriorated[133]. Farm laborers saw their real wages–previously inflated by a post-plague shortage of labor–drop by 75 percent between 1470 and 1570. By the end of the Renaissance, from France to Poland, real wages dropped by over 60 percent from their medieval peaks[134].

During the 16th century, the overall purchasing power of the average person declined at least 50 percent, and in some areas, like

Normandy, it was as much as 70 percent. Measured in kilograms of rye, monthly workmen's wages dropped from 15kg in 1460 to a mere 4kg in 1570. Even by 1750, the peak of the late Baroque mini-boom—a boom mostly based on new energy staples: potatoes and maize, supplemented with imported sugar—they only reached a mere 7kg equivalent[135]. It might not have been by coincidence that Marie Antoinette, told about bread riots, reportedly suggested that people eat cake instead: by early 19th century, sugar—from near zero a few generations earlier—came to account for well over twenty percent of the dietary energy supply: sugar and potatoes replaced bread.

During the Renaissance and the Baroque, expensive meat gradually disappeared from peasants' tables, and this drop in demand caused butchers shops to close. In Germany, per-capita meat consumption dropped from 100kg a year in 1400 to 20 kg a year in 1800, reflecting the steady pauperization of the average consumer that began during the Renaissance[136]. The number of people without jobs or property—the destitute—rose from around eight percent in the 15th century to around 20 percent in the 16th, even as rising prices and dropping wages pushed those that still had a job into poverty. It was a process not very different from the one we have been witnessing in the last few decades.

Just as during our last three or four decades, it was during the Renaissance that a whole array of ominous signs of impoverishment appeared, heralding the incoming Baroque reality. There was creeping poverty in the small towns and their surrounding regions. Just like today, inflation kept advancing, kept at bay only by the outsourcing of industrial production to cheap countryside labor—exactly the same solution that today lowers rich countries' manufacturing costs by producing in China and—for now—subsidizes American consumers' illusions of affluence.

During the Renaissance, as populations and demand grew, so did the prices, eroding the high wages of the late Middle Ages. Prices first began to rise around 1472 in North Italy and Southern

Germany, then the leading regions of the civilization. By 1500, inflation had spread to all of Europe, and it continued for more than 150 years—well into the 1650s[137]. Same as today, the fastest rise was in life's necessities, such as food, fuel, and housing—things most in demand when the population was accelerating, but least elastic in supply. Same as today, the relentless squeeze of taxes and rents pushed millions of people into financial problems, eventually into Baroque destitution.

Just like our own Renaissance, the original Renaissance had its own energy crisis, attested in countless documents, as firewood and charcoal began to be in short supply and their prices skyrocketed. English firewood costs increased sevenfold between 1500 and 1630, forcing England to intensify its use of coal for domestic heating. As populations grew unchecked, forests began to be cut again: Denmark lost 80 percent of its forest cover during the Renaissance and the Baroque.[138]

During the Renaissance, prices of food and fuel inflated twice as fast as wages, and land rents inflated more than four times as fast[139]. As real wages kept falling, stagnation and then a decline in general living standards began to be noticed by some educated observers—those who bothered to notice things that were happening outside their own charmed circles. But, same as today, few bothered about the growing inequality and widening wealth gaps. Just as today, the wealthy assumed that the growing divide between them and the rest was good for the society and inequality was part of the divine order. These beliefs echoed the beliefs of today's preachers of infallibility of the markets.

As wealth kept polarizing, overpopulation caused food supply instabilities and hunger, making people vulnerable to environmental disasters—just as in the last few years, where massive food price increases pushed the number of starving people on this planet to over a billion. As darker era approached, after 1560, a series of hunger-related epidemics caused some villages in the prosperous Bureba valley in Spain, to lose up to half of their populations. Food riots would break out in Antwerp, as people were literally starving in the streets.

The incoming decline was accompanied by soaring asset inflation. While (in nominal money, unadjusted for inflation) wages during the Renaissance merely doubled, land rents increased by about 800 percent, and landed property prices increased by a factor of nine in England, eleven in Belgium, and fourteen in parts of Germany[140]. While poverty was creeping in, escalating prices of positional assets and rising investment incomes fed the opulence of the elites and accounted—together with growing reliance on debt—for the false impression of economic boom.

This was exactly the same as in our present reality.

As before and as ever since, the growing inequality between rich and poor was reflected in a decline of human rights and freedoms and a rise in crime statistics. In Poland in the 1520s, soaring prices of cash crops encouraged landowners to turn cash rents back into labor obligations, essentially re-introducing serfdom. In most backward places, resurgent serfdom was turning into effective slavery; by the 1700s, in some Swedish provinces, peasants could be bought and sold in town markets, just like cattle. In an echo of our present reality, slavery, during the medieval era of no economic significance, now became a big business, underpinning huge sugar and cotton plantations and other businesses like mining or domestic service. Slavery dramatically grew during the Renaissance, with millions of slaves working not only in the Americas, but also in Europe, especially in places like Spain or Italy.

The decline signs were consistent everywhere: As the elites became richer and the poor poorer, the number of beggars and vagabonds, out-of-wedlock births, and amount of general crime increased rapidly[141].

RISE OF THE GLITTERATI

MANY IF NOT most of the nobles we call the Renaissance Men were of humble origin: Second–or third-generation peasants, lawyers, bankers, moneychangers, accountants, doctors, merchants, notaries, property managers, tax collectors, slavers, upstart legal clerks, or army suppliers. Dreams of becoming a noble drove all the desperate actions of Columbus–this one time sugar trader, married with a petty noble's daughter from Madeira, venturing into the ocean to become an admiral. Starting around 1480, virtually all of the English nobles were such new people[142]–as the original warlord aristocracy slaughtered itself on the battlefields of the War of the Roses. Similar, even if less dramatic social transformations were happening elsewhere in Europe, where money bought landed estates and then nobility. The keys to the financial success of this investor class were education, information, and investment cunning. In what strikes us as strangely 'modern' approach, some of Italy's 'new nobles' claimed that not aristocratic lineage, but 'merit' and education gave them the right to the noble titles. A Renaissance saying in Poland used to say: 'learn Latin, boy, so that you [too] can become a noble!'

In the same process we are witnessing today, the combination of elite education and informed asset investment drove the Renaissance reality, securing the new nobles' grips on all the possible income streams–top government positions, access to insider information and other people's money, land rents, government bonds, siphoned-off taxes, loan-sharking, and foreclosures. Loan-sharking was commonly practiced even by top-level aristocracy. A lawyer in the family was increasingly a must, someone to draft a debt contract to his family's advantage, control a town as a judge, squeeze money from the uneducated as a notary or—the ultimate glory—join the glitzy "*noblesse de robe*", or the "noble bureaucracy", in the distant tax capital.

In this new information era, a top-degree education from a brand-name university became an absolute must. Like today, it became a mandarin hallmark, an exclusive ticket to top positions, contacts, and titles. Like today, it not only secured the right contacts and access to best information networks, but, ultimately, it provided real skills. As the prospective and actual new nobles remodeled the castles they bought into palaces and replaced wall-mounted displays of loot with more subtle libraries and Greek statues, they proved themselves to be avid readers. They read not just the romance books of Amadis, but also land management manuals, legal treatises, atlases, accounting principles, newspapers and investment tips. The top players owned libraries of hundreds—often thousands—of books. Every day, they wrote dozens of letters—in some cases over 50 a day—to leverage for profit their personal information networks. Even for busy professionals of today, to write 50 emails a day might be a record! These peer networks, constantly maintained by daily letters—as good as today's Blackberries, iPhones and Facebooks—kept them abreast of global affairs, financial trends, commodities' prices, results of faraway battles affecting markets and all key events and resulting opportunities for profitable speculation. Then, as now, social networking and speculation was the *rentier*/investor's tool for making money without dirtying one's hands.

These upstart nobles held the old, rustic, illiterate and indebted aristocracy in contempt, yet aspired to their titles and past glory. The new people often hid their humble ancestry behind elaborate and rigid manners, invented family trees, fabricated coats-of-arms, and sumptuous, pretentious clothing. The nearest cultural precedent of this new class, closely related to government service, was the old imperial bureaucracy of Rome, and exactly by this association they chose to advertise their arrival. They invented the senatorial décor for the era they themselves named the Renaissance, unearthed and dusted off the old classical statues, temples, designed parks and fountains, geometric city plans, libraries and theatres—the whole frigid landscape of the "urban benefactors" of antiquity, into which they now slipped with ease. They lavishly funded artists to re-create this antique world for their private pleasure, to portray their features in imperial poses, to immortalize their faces inside quasi-religious paintings, to create beautiful objects for a life of daily pleasure. And while commerce and technology languished, this re-dusted culture flourished. Children were taught once again to recite Greek hexameters.

It was not a coincidence that the revival of the antique called "Renaissance" coincided perfectly with the birth of the *rentier* economic system. Renaissance was the artistic expression of the new *rentier* reality—a luxurious show. The gracious villas set in manicured gardens, the senatorial landowners, the triumphal arches, the statues of the noble bureaucrats again adorning the city plazas, stripped of the crass medieval commercialism and beautified with marble—that was the ideal world they wanted to re-create and be associated with, at least in art or in their own immediate surroundings. The display of wealth, jewels, statues, marble columns, brand-name paintings, gilding, costly fabrics, tapestries, palaces, artistic objects became near-obsessive after 1460, with hundreds of glitzy new "designer" objects appearing almost daily, and urban fashions changing almost every year. Among the new glitterati, there were fads for antique gems, for cameos, for nudes and pornography, for crystals and bronzes, for portraits by famous "brand-name" artists, or for imported Chinese porcelains or lacquer screens. And instead of the crude battlefield chopping of medieval times, the self-invented Renaissance princes spiced their lives with intrigue, poison, and murder.

The fellow citizens of the new investor-barons, now pushed into the service economy and pauperism, had only one outlet—theatre. In theaters like London's 'Globe' that began to appear everywhere, the favorite theme of early Baroque comedies was the merchant-turned-noble. In Shakespeare's England, where one could buy a baron's title for 10,000 pounds sterling, theatergoers were "laughing at knights who could not ride, in Spain at hidalgos who could not shoot, and in Italy at counts whose hands still smelled of the fish trade".[143]

But the new nobles—and the lawyers—had the last laugh.

*

EVEN AT THE time, people sensed that something major had changed with the arrival of the Renaissance, that a dramatic transformation of reality had taken place. But, just as today, they found it hard to pinpoint the key to change. Just like today people point to computers, Internet, or globalization, they pointed to printed books, to marble palaces, or discovery of America as the major elements of change. The truth was more dramatic.

With the arrival of the Renaissance, urban democracy died. Where before there had been communes composed of free businesspeople, now there were city mobs ruled by bankers like the Medicis or by royal bureaucrats. Where before the only civic businesses had been trade and manufacturing, now there were tax and rent collectors, lawyers, bankers and notaries, all displaying their new wealth. Where before medieval factories and watermills stood, and citizens walked to their businesses, now elaborate urban palaces sprawled, and the luxurious coaches of the new urban nobles trampled the pauper mobs of ex-citizens underfoot.

In some cases, cities were simply seized by princes. Even though rulers now had artillery that could always break the city walls, the citizens did not surrender easily. In 1428, Duke Casimir of Pomerania met ferocious resistance when he sought to enforce taxes on the city of Szczecin (Stettin). Once he won, he ordered the ringleaders' bones crushed and towering castle to be raised to control the city. Margrave Frederic of Brandenburg, after he came to power in 1440, refused to swear the traditional rights of the city of Berlin. Soon his army appeared at the gates, his mercenaries seized the city hall, and Frederic ordered construction of a formidable, overawing castle. The citizens fought back, setting mines to the castle foundations, and burning the archives. After Frederic prevailed, he subjected the city to absolute control. He was the one to appoint aldermen, siphon off revenues and confiscate individual citizens' property[144]. Where urban democracy used to rule entire regions, like in Italy, the richest bankers or clans of mercenaries gradually usurped all power, turning themselves into new urban princes. In the year 1400 in Milan, once a metropolis of manufacturing and trade, democracy was overthrown by the Visconti clan of mercenaries. The Viscontis styled themselves "princes" and promptly replaced the old-fashioned term "citizen" with a more modern one: "subject." In 1434, once-democratic Florence became a de-facto principality ruled by the rich coinchanger-turned-banker Medici family. In Renaissance cities, banking and parasitic urban 'politics'—the profitable business of ruling—became the staples of the new system. And politics paid handsome dividends: new studies show that Lorenzo Medici financed his shaky bank with stolen public funds of the city he controlled. "In this way," writes historian Huppert about what happened in the Renaissance, "the leading families of many cities tended to divorce their own interests from those of the communes which they had served and led in the past." [145]

The decay of democracy was accompanied by and related to the steady growth of wealth inequality. In 1427 Florence, 10 percent of families came to control 68 percent of the total wealth; in 1545 Lyon, the similar elite controlled 53 percent of the total wealth. Ownership of grain reserves, a speculative commodity with wildly fluctuating prices on which quick fortunes could be built, was even more skewed: In 1555 Pavia, a mere two percent of families controlled 45 percent of all grain reserves. In these new Renaissance cities, once bastions of equality, 50 to 60 percent of the population was now classified as very poor, and 10 percent were beggars[146].

We are now coming again close to these percentages.

In England, the municipal offices of the city of Leicester, before staffed by master craftsmen and merchants elected by the urban commune, gradually became reserved for a handful of families. While in theory all citizens (or "subjects") were still eligible for office, in practice the councilmen so manipulated the constitution as to perpetuate the control within their own circle. The decline of urban democracy coincided exactly with the Renaissance. In 1467, access to the Leicester city council meetings was forbidden to the average city folk. Eventually this extended to the City Hall itself. By 1580, when Renaissance was becoming Baroque, there was not a single master craftsman on any city council across all of Europe[147]. They were all controlled by ex-notaries, lawyers and bankers turned into aristocrats.

The beginning of the Renaissance was marked by a sharp change in social behavior. Arguably similar to the onset of the 1970s in our own reality, there was a dramatic rise in casual cruelty, brutality, coarser mores, and a hardening of hearts. Burning at the stake, practically unknown in high medieval civilization of the 1250s and introduced only with the Inquisition in the declining stage of the Middle Ages, now with the advent of the Renaissance achieved the popularity of Roman gladiator games, claiming thousands of victims, killed in front of screaming urban mobs. Breaking on the wheel, particularly horrible, was a Renaissance invention. Victory in a Renaissance family feud was routinely celebrated by raping and castrating the victims, ritual gnawing at the dead bodies, and playing football with severed heads[148].

Inquisition was the true child of the Renaissance, acquiring its terrifying powers only in the 1480s.

Some analysts specializing in the Renaissance assert that the age had a unique "twist of sadism" exceeding even what was seen in the later Baroque decline. This was the age when every year, during a huge ceremony in Paris presided over by the royals, few dozen cats were burnt alive for the enjoyment of the populace listening to their screams. Many of the Renaissance scholars we so admire today were employed to invent weapons for their princely sponsors. Curiously, many such weapons were designed more for refined torture than for mere killing. Leonardo da Vinci, considered a prized weapons expert, recommended to the ruler of Milan to poison fruit trees on the enemy's line of advance. But even Leonardo, bastard son of a lawyer and a peasant girl, complained of the haughty contempt shown him by the officials and the literati. "They go about puffed and pompous, dressed and decorated with the fruits not of their own labor, but that of others," wrote Leonardo. " . . . They despise me, an inventor, [because I am not a literary man]."[149] To many Renaissance noble officials, with certified degrees from top universities, Leonardo was a mere hired hand, almost a craftsman, a manual worker.

During the Renaissance, attitudes hardened and became openly selfish and pragmatic. As in the Late Roman Empire, the growing mobs of urban paupers of the Renaissance were treated to a diet of violent shows, mixed with haughty contempt from their betters. In this 'Age of Humanism', contempt and cruelty toward the poor became openly professed. Renaissance rulers like Duke of Burgundy Charles the Bold and emperor Charles V both laughed off the slaughter of their own foot mercenaries in the battle of Murten and the siege of Metz. The emperor compared his dead infantrymen to caterpillars and grasshoppers, saying that it did not matter if they lived or died[150]. New hires could always be found among the growing masses of the poor—just like with 'contractors' in some of our new wars, once mercenary system prevailed, these people became fully disposable. One scholar remarked that 'unnatural anonymity marks Renaissance battlefields and trenches'.[151]

In an eerie déjà-vu of the evolution of attitudes we have witnessed in our own reality, at first, the growing poverty around them was shown cynical indifference by the Renaissance newly rich; soon they came to flagrantly ridicule such medieval concepts as giving alms, showing compassion, redeeming sins, or ultimate equality before God. The new information professionals began describing the poorer ex-citizens as "insects" and "grubs". The new reality was given a 'humanist' spin.

With the new 'national' expediency of the bureaucracies, ends now fully justified the means. Any pretences of the Christian unity of old totally evaporated. Nothing symbolized it better than the construction in 1534 in Toulon, France, of a mosque and the setting up of a slave market serving the needs of the new naval base of France's Turkish allies[152]. Not just restricted to Turks, white slavery made an amazing comeback in the midst of Renaissance and Baroque Europe. Trade in slaves, during High Middle Ages a rare event, gradually grew in importance and by Baroque times was a huge global business, one of the principal money earners for many a merchant and the foundation of many a noble fortune. As the slave industry grew rapidly and their supply ballooned during the Renaissance, 10 percent of Lisbon's population in the 16th century were slaves.[153]

The fall of real wages that began with the onset of the Renaissance was paired with a rise in crime. Evidence seems to indicate that attacks against property rose sharply. There was a wave of frauds, thefts, muggings, gang robberies, and burglaries, reflecting both the growing cynicism of the age and the growing size and desperation of the underclass. This was matched by rising crime within the elite. It now became socially acceptable to kill a rival by poison or by firing a hidden handgun at someone's back. Poisoning in general became so popular that whole scientific volumes were written on the subject, and there were even schools that taught the art. Adriano da Corneto, a famous intellectual and humanist, author of many books, a rich patron of art and a cardinal, also had a habit of poisoning his rivals. He ended up killed by a servant for a small sum of money during a robbery. Adriano was a typical Renaissance figure: a highly educated bureaucrat, completely corrupt, without a hint of scruples or higher goals, a perfect mirror of a society that fully turned to unscrupulous pleasures of life.

As the famous medieval "Mirror of Princes", a study of life and governance style of the 13th century medieval king Saint Louis by Joinville, widely held as role model to medieval monarchs, was replaced with equally famous Machiavelli's guidebook "The Prince" advocating unscrupulous and callous "politics" where the end fully justified the means, the contemporaries did not have to reach for a book to see how reality evolved. The daily fare—excesses of the papal court under the Borgias, where murder, incest, nepotism, fraud and sexual orgies were the new normal—showed how far things changed since the 12th and 13th century medieval peaks, when the papacy still could claim the moral leadership of the civilization.

TAX, DEBT AND FORECLOSURE

"Many Americans are broke, or barely scraping by, so the only way they can make it is to charge it, running up balances on credit cards that are structured in a way that makes it harder and harder to pay them off."
—Arianna Huffington, Third World America[154]

THE EDUCATED "RENAISSANCE MEN" were interested in many things—arts, science, astrology, cartography, design (of everything from cities to fortresses to weapons)—but most critically they were interested in money. Just like our own elites today, virtually all of them were active, aggressive investors, and they and their times changed our approach to money. It now became a value in its own right, no longer just the means of exchange for merchandise, no more a practical tool to be hidden as hoards of coins in garden pots until needed. In fact, one no longer needed to be engaged in trade or manufacturing, or even land ownership to be wealthy. Now, money could be created just like today, from paper—through instruments of finance, through stocks, bonds, loans or letters of credit, or timely speculation. It was now supposed to continuously circulate as capital, to beget new money.

In the hands of the new educated investor class, there was a massive concentration of capital. This was especially visible in Italy—the result of a steady accumulation of wealth from hundreds of years of profits from trade and manufacturing. This massive accumulation, no longer reinvested in commercial activity but now seeking purely financial returns, was a typical Renaissance phenomenon. It drove the new reality: spectacular government debts, asset inflation, the rise of *rentier* classes, and increasing over-exploitation of agricultural resources in order to maximize yields.

Mirroring the trends we increasingly see surfacing today, the global investor class resided in few iconic cities. During that time, these were places like London, Milan, Naples, Paris, Venice, Genoa, Lisbon, Palermo, Valladolid, or Madrid. These were the places that could supply the entertainment, décor and services that the urban wealthy would now expect as part of their lifestyle. Smaller towns, abandoned by both business and *rentiers*, fell into ruin or froze in their medieval form, half-abandoned. Countryside inhabited by ex-farmers, now turned destitute farmhands or vagabonds and homeless, gradually became bandit-ravaged wastelands, haunted by dispossession, destitution and desperation. It was a peculiar, timeless process of social unraveling, little studied or understood, but typical for every historical cycle of decline[155]. Such social unraveling is an integral part of the Baroque Syndrome, and a visit to Detroit or any American inner city, or immigrant suburbs in Europe, or to thug-ruled countryside in Russia or China can give us a good taste of it.

The foreclosures rolling through America's cities and towns today mirror the Renaissance process of dispossession. Foreclosure was the true Renaissance hallmark. Its mechanics were very simple. Increasing populations meant that inferior soils were once again being farmed, so bad harvests were more likely. One bad harvest—or as little as a 10-percent production shortfall—was enough to force those peasants who still owned land into debt. Village records of the time are so repetitive that they would be almost boring if they were not talking about real people and real tragedies. They all report the same thing, across the entire continent. They talk about farmers in debt who, even if they had a good harvest, still could not repay the debt owed to lawyers and officials in town. They could not repay it because they also had to pay a new burden—state taxes. Regular and heavy taxation of peasants appeared with the Renaissance and rose, along with increasing land rents, to put an unprecedented squeeze on producers. As the elites invariably shifted the tax burden away from themselves, it fell almost exclusively on the peasants. Between 1400 and 1600 this combined tax/rent burden rose from 25 to 50 (or even up to 75) percent of the harvest value, and to this was often added an interest burden on debt.

Debt was easy to contract from lawyers, landowners and merchants in town, at loan-sharking rates, as long as land was used as collateral. The lenders ran no risk—the law was on their side, since they wrote it, and they would get either the land or fat interest back when the loans matured. On the other hand, the borrowers ran a high risk. Most of them could not specialize in cash crops—orchards, vineyards, fishponds, sheep pastures and the like—because the next grain shortage would starve them. So, regardless of what their land was suited for, they had to grow grain and raise pigs in order to be self-sufficient and survive. The lenders who foreclosed on their land did not have the same limitations. They could afford to specialize, study the soils, choose appropriate cash crops, rotate them for best results, sell crops forward through hedged contracts, invest in drainage, hire professional property managers, and implement agricultural innovations they read about in books.

The Renaissance "information highway," courtesy of the key invention of the era, the printing press, meant that the literate investor now had advantages of capital, law, and knowledge over the illiterate peasant. A grain shortage would wipe out the investor's tenants, not him, and he could always find new tenants among the eager and growing underclass of paupers. This polarization of wealth based on education levels and access to information and (increasingly available and international) capital was—exactly like today—the key breakthrough of the Renaissance Information Era.

Land records from the time of the medieval boom, the 11th through 13th centuries, show land parcels of roughly equal size, owned by a relatively egalitarian class of peasant-farmers, all property owners. This situation changes drastically with the Renaissance: Sixteenth—century land records typically show the top 10 percent of population now owning more than half of all the land. The bottom 20 to 30 percent of the population owned nothing except debt. In the Languedoc region of France, as late as 1450 the area still contained mostly middle-size holdings. Virtually no such holdings were left by 1700. While in 1450 very rich investors-landowners or landless poor were still a rarity, by 1700 the rich owned virtually all of the land and landless poor were everywhere[156].

Even in England, where the middle classes were relatively the most prosperous in Europe, the trend was the same. In the English community of Chippenham, studies show that the number of landless people increased steadily. In 1544, 30 percent of the population was already landless; by 1712, that category had jumped to 60 percent[157]. Many historians have found evidence that the rapid spread of Protestantism during the Renaissance and the phenomenon of Germany's Peasant Wars were closely linked to growing economic stress, as both peasants and the urban poor vented their anger at the elites by attacking castles or Catholic churches and abbeys[158].

Despite contemporary hype—so reminiscent of our era—the basis for the economic buoyancy of the early Renaissance was not science or education, but rather a massive population increase. Same as in our reality, rents and labor supplied by the ever-poorer, ever lower-paid newcomers into the economy sustained upward move in asset values owned by investors. Expansion was accompanied by the reclamation of empty land. Freed from recurring plague, people began to settle the land left empty or overgrown with forest after the Black Death. In just 70 years preceding 1530, arguably Renaissance's peak, the populations of many regions had doubled or tripled. By 1550, the population of Europe was reaching again for the medieval peaks, but its distribution was now very different. In line with the new efficiency of the era, instead of a uniform cover of grain fields and uniform overpopulation, people now concentrated in prime agricultural regions or large cities. While Tudor London grew much bigger, most of England's North became depopulated and turned into sheep grazing land. Grain was produced more intensely, on the best soils. The dispossessed, the impoverished, and those seeking their fortunes flocked to the cities to swell supply of cheap labor. Cities grew larger—the urbanization level of the Netherlands reached a near-industrial level of 51 percent[159].

The event patterns of the Renaissance were very similar to those we have been seeing over our last few decades. Through the phenomena we today would call "globalization" or "information revolution," or "service economy", the Renaissance civilization, searching for cost efficiency, optimized its wealth production. Same as today, this improvement in efficiency was accomplished without any real technological progress, no new machines, no revolutionary energy sources. It was done by expanding the footprint of the cash-crop system into new lands, cost-cutting, trade globalization, restructuring, financial engineering and effective use of widely available information to intensify productivity of assets; all these factors together wrung efficiencies out of the pre-existing energy system. But as the system efficiency was reaching its limits, the room for error or any instability grew dangerously narrow.

In an exactly the same process as today, where laid-off manufacturing workers find new Macjobs in the 'service economy', delivering pizza, fixing swimming pools, or providing home care to wealthy old people, the dispossessed Renaissance farmers flocked to the cities to become servants of the new investor class, providing a variety of services that were unheard of in the medieval communes. Even the Renaissance 'globalization'—the global search for spices, gold and silver, and other resources at the expense of Arab or Indian middlemen could be compared to today's corporate exercise of cutting out the cost of a middleman. Efficiency of foodstuff production was way ahead of the medieval averages. Just like our last few decades, it seemed to be a golden era.

Yet, in the long run, Renaissance's efficiency drive proved to be a false solution. A massive increase in population eventually outpaced efforts to squeeze efficiency out of the pre-existing energy regime.

Just like today, basic technology was stagnant. Increasing wealth polarization—typical for such periods—eventually pushed productivity down by de-skilling, de-educating, disincentivizing and impoverishing the basic producer: the farmer turned farmhand or urban manservant, the urban apprentice turned subsistence-wage laborer. This wealth polarization was the proverbial straw that broke the camel's back. By the 1580s, the Renaissance had ushered in the disastrous era that was the Baroque.

*

IF YOU EVER visit the Louvre Museum in Paris, make sure that after spending some time in front of the glorious paintings of the early Renaissance—essentially, everything produced before 1510 or so—and breathing in their joy, luminosity and intense color, walk to the Baroque section and compare these paintings to the somber, dark oils of the calamitous 17th century. Among these, make sure that you see the stunning paintings of Georges De La Tour, interiors of absolute darkness, illuminated by a single candle. Realities brought down to their very essentials, in the time of the darkest of nights that was the Baroque.

The features of the Baroque began to manifest themselves inside the Renaissance very early, as soon as the successes of the boom cycle began to fail. From the very beginning, the Renaissance efficiency boom was strangely uneven, in terms of timing and geography. It did not resemble the previous broad, uniform, and evenly-timed medieval boom. Characteristically, the faltering of the Renaissance boom first began in the most advanced civilization in the world, the country that had been the first to recover after the trauma of the Black Death: Italy.

Italy led Europe in recovery from the chaos of the Black Death. Starting as early as 1400, Italy already saw its population and commercial activity rebound, and by 1490 it had already reached its Renaissance peak. The leading economy of Europe, it enjoyed unprecedented prosperity. Since its medieval bulk trade was no longer profitable, Italy had turned from a merchant middleman into a manufacturer of luxury textiles, armors, gadgets, and art. This new activity gave the country a polish of luxury and success. Italy's industrial engine became Milan, a city producing superb armors, woolens, and silver—and gold-embroidered cloths. Venice found a different route—previously a merchant city, now it turned landowner, extracting from its farms and plantations stretching from Verona all the way to Cyprus a public revenue of a million gold ducats a year, plus considerable private income. In Florence, an industry of silks and woolens flourished, luxury artwork prospered, and even banking—in the form of the Medici bank—seemed to have returned (although far below its late 13th century peaks). Urban wages were high and stable. Even though basic industrial production was increasingly farmed out to the low-wage countryside, and even though old-fashioned urban democracy had faded in favor of cronyism manipulated by the richest merchants and bankers, life in 1490 still seemed good.

Yet Italy's 1490s peak was followed by a rapid, almost cataclysmic decline. A mere generation later, by the 1530s, writes historian Fisher, "the proud republic of Florence became a dark and wretched despotism that called itself the Grand Duchy of Tuscany[160]." The night of the Baroque first descended not on the trailing, but on the leading countries of the Renaissance civilization.

"[Damage wrought by wars and political disruptions] interacted with the more deep-seated causes of decline linked to the ageing process of the Italian economy," writes historian J.K.J. Thomson trying to understand the drivers of this dramatic and breathtakingly swift collapse. "From the late fifteenth century economic performance at all levels—agricultural, industrial, and commercial—began to flag. [Italy's] prosperity depended ultimately on the continued relative scarcity in Europe of technical skills as well as of privileged access to certain key raw materials . . . . However, from the late 14th century onwards, the skills and the raw materials were percolating [elsewhere]"[161].

Why did the leading engine of the Renaissance civilization collapse so quickly and so utterly? In the ominous deja-vu, through a process very similar to the one being widely discussed today in America, the economic driver of Italy's decline was the loss of its competitive lead first in manufacturing and then in technology; the decline's visible signs were the collapse of civil society, democratic façade, and liberty.

After the 1490s, it was as if a dark veil had rapidly descended over the country, affecting everything from people's minds, to their institutions, to their art. In Florence, the speed of descent was breathtaking. Most contemporaries placed the first signs of the city's decline in the year 1494, when, following French occupation and a brief resumption of republican liberty, Florence came under the control of the demonic monk Savonarola. As early as the 1530s, while countries like England and Poland had barely begun to savor their Renaissance peaks, Italy was already sliding into an abyss. In Italy, the descent from the Renaissance peaks into Baroque darkness took little over a generation.

One of the contributing factors of the Renaissance distress seemed to be the buildup of state bureaucracies and growth of the parasitic sector and taxation. Just like in the 20th century, and for the first time since the collapse of Rome, the Renaissance saw a massive rise of government bureaucracies, made possible by appearance and rise of state taxation. Easily enforceable now—thanks to centralized governments supported by mercenaries with cannons—taxes rode the Renaissance boom wave, stripping the surpluses, squeezing the peasants and small towns, offering fortune and advancement to the new class of civil servants, and spinning wealth off into growing liquid investment pools and into the emerging and expanding "service economy" of urban luxury. Increases in tax and rent revenues were phenomenal: In England, profits from royal tolls and estates doubled in the 16th century; the income from the duchy of Lancaster alone increased ten times.

But just like today, soon tax revenues could not match rising expenses—today social spending, civil servants' salaries and military budgets consume most of state revenues; during the Renaissance, while civil servants salaries escalated all the time, the bulk of money went to cover the cost of artillery and the new mercenary army. With artillery and mercenaries, no king needed to depend any longer on unruly barons and their retainers, or on arrogant cities. But costs of deploying cannon power were prohibitive. Ninety horses, consuming tons of fodder, were needed to move one large Renaissance siege cannon across the countryside, at a price that, including maintenance and gun-crew wages, could exceed 10,000 ducats a year. Gunpowder cost a fortune—its stockpile in Venice Arsenal was worth almost double the city's yearly income. War costs also increased because of the frenzy of fortress redesign. Since medieval castles could not resist artillery, princes now poured money into new scientifically-designed fortresses with angled walls and fancy earthworks. Cannons and handguns massively increased the costs of equipping an army and the size of armies also increased dramatically in these years, often tripling or quadrupling, as supply of cheap human cannon fodder kept increasing.

Just like today, increased revenues could never cover expenses. In Spain, the expenses of its first-ever world empire were financed only in part by the flow of silver from its American mines; the shortfall was met from increased foreign and domestic borrowing, and by raising taxes in Castile. "The requirements of state finance increased at a higher rate than the inflation rate," writes historian Treasure. "Between 1554 and 1566 the budget doubled. The Castilian peasant was called to pay. Ironically, those who really profited from the inflation, the merchant elite and the landlords, escaped the burden: though taxes became far more burdensome under later Habsburgs, already the gap between the rich and the poor was widening inexorably."[162]

As taxes were being raised, while population and tax bases began to shrink during the Baroque decline, so financial burdens—in an eerie echo of today's creative taxation 'solutions'—were 'devolved' down to lower government levels, to let them, same as today, 'deal with the problem'. Cities were forced to get into debt themselves just to fulfil their crown tax quota. "The debt of Cordoba in 1580 stood at twice the annual yield of the alcabala [sales tax, the city's main source of revenue]," writes Thomson. In a language recalling today's sovereign debt crisis, he says "In the space of a century there had been a shift from exceptional monetary abundance to general discredit. The damage to the country's credit system was another reason for the depth and duration of the [Baroque] crisis[163]."

Renaissance was the first era that saw government bonds, this symbol of our problems today, issued on a massive scale. The government of Castile, having issued its first bonds ever in 1489, was by 1504 already heavily dependent on borrowed money, with regular tax income as implicit collateral. After that, the government's debts grew every year at an alarming pace. It was a circle: Not only imperial foreign wars—like today's imperial adventures in Iraq and Afghanistan—consumed huge sums of money. In addition, to collect taxes effectively, the government needed artillery, but the prohibitive costs of artillery warfare drove up the need for cash. The failed siege of the city of Metz cost emperor Charles, King Philip's father, 2 million ducats. In February 1544, when the cash at hand was only 750,000 ducats and the deficit well over 3 million, prince Philip reported to his father: "We do not know from where or how to meet (the deficit), since income from the Indies is committed for several years . . . ."[164]

Today's USA is inflicted with many of the same illnesses that were ravaging Baroque Spain. It has massive military expenditure, runaway debt, oversized and overpaid civil service. Just like in the previous Baroques, over the last few decades compensations and benefits of the civil service kept growing, far outstripping the real economy. By 2010, as per U.S. Bureau of Economic Analysis, average salary of a U.S. civil servant was around $81,000, plus around $42,000 in benefits, versus private sector's $50,000 in salary and $11,000 in benefits. At the same time, U.S. federal government debt alone was $14.3 trillion, roughly 100 percent of the GDP; it has increased more than fourfold since 1990. "We are accumulating debt burdens that will rival a third-world nation within 10 years" said in 2010 David Walker, former chairman of the Congressional Budget Office.

And he warned about a possible bankruptcy scenario: "Once you end up losing confidence of the markets, things could happen very dramatically and very suddenly. We've seen that in Greece, we've seen this in Ireland, and we must not see it happen in the United States[165]." Just like in Baroque Spain, one of the key sources of debt was runaway military spending. By 2010, 20 percent of the U.S. Federal Government spending was going to the military. The defense budget has grown by 80 percent since 2000[166].

Just like in Baroque Spain, the lethal combination of huge military spending, bloated bureaucracy, and effective exemption of most of the richest earners from taxes was bankrupting the country, even as it could not work its way out of debt, thanks to its loss of competitiveness and de-industrialization and thanks to supporting—on credit—its population's illusion of prosperity.

Nor was it likely the size of the government could be reduced. Lawrence Summers, Harvard University professor, argued that the costs of U.S. government will continue to go up, no matter who wins the 2012 presidential elections. One of the reasons will be the rising numbers of elderly on government support, as American society ages; the other doubling of costs of debt service as interest rates return to normal and more money is borrowed. But another major contributor will be the escalating costs of what the government buys: high-end services. Cost of such services, whether drafting banking regulation, providing medical care, accounting or legal costs, scientific research, and especially education, have dramatically risen compared to costs of industrial goods, produced either by cheap overseas labor or in highly automated factories, or both. "The price of hospital care has risen more than 100-fold relative to that of TVs" was the article headline, dramatically illustrating the inefficiency of services, the biggest segment of the economy and one of the major contributors to our malaise.[167]

Similar to eurozone's dramatic illness, Spain's financial distress made and broke the fortunes of speculators and bankers. As the deficit kept deepening, the Spanish government supplemented long-term bonds with short-term borrowing in Genoa, at rates that would shame a loan shark. In the 1510s Spain paid 10 percent interest on its debt; in the 1520s this rose to 18 percent; in 1556 the rates charged by Genoese bankers hit a stunning 49 percent per year. At that level, Spain's debt service as a percentage of regular revenues reached 68 percent, up from 36 percent a generation earlier. In April 1557 king Philip declared his first ever national bankruptcy. All debt payments were suspended, with most of the balance rolled over into long-term bonds paying just five percent.

The rise of bureaucracy was closely related to and fed by, a massive rise of warfare. In an otherwise relatively stagnant economic reality, war whipped up a whirlpool of fast, messy and enormously profitable activity. Away from the battlefield, benefits accrued to courtiers and bureaucrats, tax collectors, army contractors, notaries, bankers, spies, speculators, officials selling officers' commissions and bondholders. Closer to the war theater, army officers, agents and suppliers all skimmed the cream from the loot, stolen funds, substandard supplies, and non-existent troops. Contractors who could recruit and bring thousands of mercenaries on call to a war theater made fortunes and often made a quick jump to the ranks of the nobles.

Since it was in the financial interest of the elites to keep the wars going, they went on for generations—or until the money finally ran out. The titanic struggles of the Habsburgs for the continental empire were terminated only due to sheer financial exhaustion.

*

WHEN INCREASED BORROWING and taxing failed to match the runaway spending, Renaissance governments began to privatize national assets. Land, buildings, state monopolies, tax collection, collection of road tolls, customs and duties—the more government got into debt, the more of its assets, so cunningly accumulated by previous kings, had to be shed. Same as today, both government debts and privatizations were creating and enriching a growing new social group—investors, lawyers, bankers, *rentiers*, bondholders, speculators, corrupt bureaucrats, all top-level 'information professionals'.

In Spain, privatization arrangements called "asientos" (contracts between the government and private business) leased out public assets to allow shady private profits. The Fugger banking family, for example, were granted tax farms covering huge territories of three great Church orders in lieu of loan interest. Under emperor Charles, in the four decades after 1519, more than 500 such *asientos* were contracted, for the total value of 59 million ducats—an enormous sum worth many years of state tax revenue. Yet this figure was already topped by 1575, in less than 20 years of king Philip's reign[168]. Sale of tax exemptions, state offices, crown lands, tax farms, customs farms, road tolls and state monopolies brought in large and immediate cash injections, but at the cost of undermining future revenues and—more importantly—sanctioning the convoluted and often corrupt alliance of private business and official power.

Privatization of government business reached across the entire society. On the village level, in return for their acceptance of a new excise tax, government gave village leaders a free hand in deciding what to do with village resources and how to produce the tax money. The result was accelerating wealth inequality inside villages and the rise of local mafia-like "bosses," men who controlled villages—lending money, animals, or seed to the less fortunate at extortionate rates, and concentrating foreclosed property in their own hands[169]. We see examples of similar crude privatizations resulting in semi-feudal fiefdoms beginning to operate at the village level in countries like China or Russia today.

Renaissance privatizations gradually began to involve not just the selling of tangible public assets, but also any profitable aspects of the business of governing. This was accomplished, just as in today's China, by selling government offices to private investors, thus turning them into private licenses to make money in a myriad of ways—squeeze the taxpayer, collect bribes, cut corners in supplying· substandard materials, collude in public contracts, and extract war loot. Investors paid premium prices to buy the most lucrative license to squeeze or to loot. Army officers' commissions sold well, considering the large loot shares allocated to senior officers, but the best sellers were tax-collection offices, which provided first-hand access to vulnerable taxpayers. One contemporary Spanish *procurador*, or court attorney, openly attributed the general misery of the time to " . . . the weight of taxation and the oppression of tax collectors."

Just like privatizations of today, privatization of Baroque Spain was a deep-seated movement, reflecting both the neo-conservative face of the Renaissance, and the related financial distress of the governments. Anything that could be privatized, was privatized.

Even empire building tied neatly into this pattern: The ease of the Spanish conquests in America depended to a great extend on the collaboration of Indian elites. They became, says historian Charles Gibson, the middlemen in the subjugation and religious conversion of their own tribes, selling their loyalty to Spanish Crown in return for grant of tribal land as inheritable landed estates. "By the eighteenth century there had emerged a small group of extremely wealthy and aristocratic caciques [Indian elite members] who were owners of slaves, cattle, and large propertied estates and who made a transition to Hispanic life at an affluent social rank[170]." Money counted more than racial background during the Baroque, same as it increasingly does today.

The explosion of "nobles" during the Renaissance/Baroque era that has so perplexed modern historians had little to do with nobility, but everything to do with money. "That the richest merchants focused their ambition, single-mindedly, on the acquisition of noble status is entirely understandable. From the sixteenth century onward, when regular royal taxation was becoming a fact of life, nothing could be more valuable than to find a way of reaching tax exemption[171]" says historian Huppert. Securing a grip on rent-producing real estate assets with a view toward buying a tax exemption wrapped in a title of nobility was the means to this end. By 1600, virtually everyone who could afford it bought such tax exemptions. By 1650, the richest ten percent of the entire Spanish population were all "noble" and tax exempt. This record number of nobles was almost matched by the number of civil servants—six percent of all employed, a stunning percentage for a low-energy, low-surplus society, where vast majority of people had to work on the farm to feed the rest.

Now, entire 'noble cities' came into being. Valladolid, the one-time capital of imperial Spain, was not unlike modern Washington, D. C.: In 1510, a full 80 percent of this imperial capital's population was composed of civil servants, lobbyists, hangers-on, *rentiers*, domestic servants, and unemployed[172]. The city's productive sector had virtually vanished. By the time of King Philip II's reign, writes Huppert, "The *rentiers* of Valladolid were in good position to exploit the entire Spanish Empire . . . . No more than 40 percent of inhabitants could be described as working, in one way or another. Their wealth was typical *rentier* wealth" based on income from bonds and property.[173]"

By the early years of King Philip's reign, the Spanish government had essentially become a gigantic wealth recycling machine, turning upstart property investors, legal clerks, and junior civil servants into future nobles, allowing them access to the tax money trough and to the levers of the entire 'squeeze machine', precipitating the onset of the Baroque reality. The other state machines in Europe behaved exactly the same. "Those bureaucrats, once in state service, could hope to found their own dynasties," writes historian Henry Kamen. "The elite became self-perpetuating as sons followed fathers into *collegios mayores* and then into the chief administrative offices of the country." [174]

And—same as today—for all those Renaissance elites, the key means of entry into that polished world of serious money was a top-notch education and access to information.

KINGS OF INFORMATION

A S THE SCOPE of Spain's imperial delusions grew—as measured by the size of armies, debts, taxes, and bureaucracy—it required enormously expanded processing of information. The increase in paperwork was staggering. King Philip was reported to have personally read and answered in one month alone (May 1571) well over 1200 documents—around 50 a day. This era of desktop bureaucracy and its overflow of paper information were light-years removed from the time of medieval simplicity just two generations earlier—the time of Ferdinand and Isabella, who would travel across the sierras in wind and snow to personally meet their nobles and burghers and dispense simple justice. But even they began—at the onset of the Renaissance, in 1476, to use the printing press to broadcast the growing output of laws and regulations.

By Philip's time, every day of added complexity created more bureaucracy, and more bureaucracy created added complexity. Law and bureaucracy combined to form a vicious, self-feeding circle. In Baroque Spain, as in today's America, law was the preferred background for bureaucrats and prospective nobles. As the society grew more and more conservative, with officials increasingly looking down on small business's "dirty hands" ways of making money, the ability to pull the strings that made this new money-making machine work became all important. For that—same as today—the best study choice by far was law.

By the pivotal year 1600, at Valladolid and Salamanca Universities, law students outnumbered those of theology, the medieval career of choice, by 20 to one. (In our own time, law students in the U.S. have come to outnumber those in engineering, career choice of the high Industrial Era, by 10 to one.)

Few people noticed that face of learning has dramatically changed with the advent of the Renaissance. Even as the numbers of schools and students exploded, universities turned from research and quest for understanding the world into mass-production of elite members of the establishment. "By 1595 nearly three-fourth of all students were taking courses that promised them a career in the bureaucracy . . . in turn the universities, from being places of research and learning, decayed into the training grounds for *letrados* [law graduates]. Faculty chairs became stepping-stones to high office..." [175] During the Baroque, universities became copy machines, replicators of pre-existing societal systems and concepts with all their achievements, but also with all their fallacies and mistakes. "The universities' systemized, authoritarian pedagogy made them custodians of pre-established knowledge" writes historian Gibson. "The parading of knowledge became the scholar's goal. Scholarship depended upon intellectual intensification and memorization and verbal manipulation rather than innovation or investigation of any kind . . . Writing became complex, stylized, lavish and involuted . . . preoccupied with cryptic ways of disguising that it had nothing to say . . . Trivialities were exalted. Everywhere prominent issues were petty ones[176]."

In decline eras repetition of politically-correct and well-worn clichés tends to substitute for any innovation or true discovery. This was the case of the Baroque, and it is increasingly the case of our education system today.

Spain in its decline cycle produced lawyers by the thousands, breeding them to fill the needs of its state bureaucracy. It was a deliberate policy: Every year's scores of decrees regulated in minute detail study programs, contents of textbooks, test questions, lecturers' salaries. And just like today, the future legal stars were recruited right at the universities.

When we flip today through the endless volumes upon volumes of this useless legislation, printed on the finest paper and bound in the finest leather for and by people totally ignorant of real life, we can only marvel at the recurrent folly of the human mind that believes life's problems can be solved by legislating from the desktop, and that the symptoms of societal ills can be cured with more paper or overflow of information. Throughout time, such educated elites have failed to perceive that their own parasitism, interference, and polarization of society based on wealth and education—what they often see as the solution, or at least a God-given right—may in fact be one of the main roots of the problem.

Analysts studying Spain's decline all agree that the bureaucratic diseases—escalating government costs and taxes, corruption, collusion, and privatization of public assets into huge private fortunes, plus the flood of restrictive regulation—created as their byproducts growing poverty, crime, tax evasion, business closure, and vagabondism. As early as the 1560s, some roads in Aragon, always considered safe before, were now declared unsafe at all times, as banditry re-appeared in the region. The response to that was, just as it is in our time, more fines, more police, more prisons, more guards, more work-creation programs, more judges, more regulations, and more plum bureaucratic jobs "to deal with the problem"—all supported by more taxes and deficits. Then, same as now, nobody seemed to be asking the essential question: why are real wages declining? How can we do more than just to give the poor a job—how can we actually increase their incomes and stimulate genuine economic growth?

*

"THE FINAL STAGE of urban prosperity, which coincides with growing economic distress, can be called 'parasitic' rather than productive or 'generative,'" wrote historians Hohenberg and Lees about the eve of the Baroque. "Property incomes take an increasing share of a no-longer rising surplus. Even in the city, the contrast between the rich *rentiers* and the inflation-wracked poor is heightened. Recipients of rent, including church and state, not only consume ostentatiously but take advantage of the flood tide to commend themselves to the posterity in stone. [Monumental construction and public works] tend to rise immediately prior to collapse, part as reflection of elite consumption, part as state legitimizing effort and job creation for the growing restless masses[177]."

As the Renaissance wore on to its inevitable conclusion and began to turn into Baroque, the outlines of the endgame began to show. Foreclosed Burgundian vineyards were bought up so fast by urban investors that by 1650 there was not a single independent owner there—they had all been transformed into miserable hired hands working for absentee owners. The pauperization of what used to be the middle class—bakers, drapers, smiths, small-and-medium entrepreneurs, millers, vineyard owners, small manufacturers, and middling merchants—once the backbone of the medieval society, resulted in an ongoing simmering of social discontent, often translated into open rebellion but most often resulting in a malaise and apathy that affected the whole society.

All new studies show that the frequent peasant rebellions of the Renaissance were not led by the dregs of society, as the biased officials' records would lead us to believe, but by those formerly-affluent farmowners-turned-farmhands, often allied with the impoverished urban craftsmen, now locked into apprenticeship for life. Even by 1550, these people were still used to the old medieval freedoms, to carrying arms within the city militias, still considering themselves to be free citizens deciding their own fate.

Now they rose, as Huppert says, "driven to despair by tax collectors, money lenders, tithe collectors, lawyers, court clerks, small-town officials, all those sleek fat personages who were so quick with pen and paper and who operated behind the closed doors of the city, cloaked in the power of the law[178]." All the Renaissance upheavals, from the Reformation to the great peasant rebellion that shook Germany in the 1520s, were essentially directed against both the growing control that the financial and legal elites (including Church elites, who were easier to denounce because of obvious hypocrisy) exercised over their lives, and against the growing corruption of this entire establishment. "For hundreds of years, men, women, and children suffered, fought, and died to defend their livelihood against the depredations of the mighty. The "army of suffering," as the rebellious peasants of Normandy called themselves, always lost its wars. Peasant fantasies of easy triumph were never realized[179]."

By 1550, noble officials and their families controlled both the city and the countryside. They controlled the laws, the taxes, the land rents, the interest rates. They had the law and royal mercenaries behind them, since they wrote the first and helped fund the latter. Records show that peasant attacks on Frankfurt or Bordeaux were aimed at replacing those venal city elites with new people, "who," say the records naively, "will render equitable justice[180]."

When free market systems entered developing countries in the last decades of our own era, replacing traditional social arrangements with the raw power of money in societies where peasants still live off the land, peasant rebellions resisting land grabs and corruption of the elites began to multiply, from China to Brazil to Mexico. The famous 1994/95 Chiapas rebellion in Mexico was directly related to the globalization-related opening of the Mexican economy. Starting in late 1980s, agricultural subsidies and protections, including the state's regulation of the coffee crop, were reduced, dismantled, or abolished by the government of President Salinas, exposing peasant livelihoods to the vagaries of open markets. The trigger to rebellion seemed to be a 1992 constitutional amendment allowing communal lands to be sold to anyone, exposing their communes to strong-armed landlords and developers[181].

These kinds of uprisings had plenty of Renaissance antecedents. One of the key features of early Renaissance was land becoming a commodity that anyone with cash could buy. Only recently have the first-ever attempts been made to objectively reconstruct some of the

Renaissance rebellions, painstakingly piecing them together from various records rather than relying on official noble historians. One such reconstructed story is that of the rebellion in the French town of Romans. The story was quite typical for its time. The city was controlled by Judge Guerin, well entrenched within the governing elite of the province. Controlling both city councils and courts of law, people like Guerin bought land, lent money at loan-sharking interest, foreclosed on properties, and arranged strategic marriages, the goal of which was always to gain noble status which would bring tax exemption to their estates. In the nearby region of Valence, there was a virtual explosion of such nobles; between 1523 and 1594 their numbers shot up by 50 percent, just as the taxes were rising and economy stagnating. In the province of Dauphine, writes historian Huppert "land was changing hands at alarming rate. About one third of the real estate in the province was sold to new owners in the course of a single generation. Even though taxpaying commoners were still holding on to a respectable 60 percent of the farmland, they were on the defensive[182]" as urban investors bought land and then exempted it from tax.

Guerin was so hated by the people of Romans and the surrounding region that repeated rebellions were aimed just at removing him from office. At one moment the rebels—farmers and city craftsmen—managed to get hold of the city of Romans, sending petitions to the queen to remove Guerin and change oppressive tax laws. On July 18, 1579, the queen of France visited the "rebel" town and was presented with petitions. She refused to listen. Unlike in the Middle Ages, the strengthened crown no longer needed to listen to grievances of the urban folk, appease them, or respect their old-fashioned rights. With artillery and enforceable taxes, Renaissance governments no longer needed popular support, urban democracy, old-fashioned parliaments and their squabbles. Instead, they needed tax money for their cannons, mercenaries, and court luxuries. They needed people like Guerin—elite bureaucrats, taxmen, and lawyers who were helping to enforce the squeeze. On the evening of February 15, 1580, during Carnival, Judge Guerin and his supporters disguised themselves in the costumes and masks of a Carnival crowd and took over Romans, staging a bloody massacre. Soon mercenary reinforcements were hunting people down, confiscating property at their whim and staging improvised trials. Hundreds of small landowners and craftsmen were killed in cold blood[183].

"Bowing and scraping, insisting on their prerogative to remain seated or to keep their hats on, attended by servants and pushing their way into the place they felt entitled to on public occasions, hordes of men and women insisted on their various and conflicting positions in the world of privilege. They came to blows, in church, over the right to be seated on the front benches[184]." Thus wrote historian Huppert about the new class—the noble investors and bureaucrats of the Renaissance. Around the fateful year of Carnival at Romans, 1580, when brilliant Renaissance was turning into dismal Baroque, this new, top-educated investor nobility derived from lawyers, bankers, notaries, doctors, civil servants and ex-businessmen was well on its way to owning virtually all the income-producing assets of the civilization.

It is hard to speculate whether it would make a difference what such assets were—land, urban real estate, bonds, or corporate equity. All we know is that—just like in all previous decline cycles—it was precisely at this moment of final triumph of wealth, education, and social inequality that the prolonged economic and societal decline set in, when, literally, the darkness came.

*

"Along the roads to Madrid moved a steady procession of poor travelers, civil servants without posts, captains without companies, humble folk in search of work, trudging behind a donkey with empty saddle bags, all faint with hunger and hoping that someone, in the capital, would settle their fate."
—Fernand Braudel, The Mediterranean and the Mediterranean World in the Age of Philip II[185]

LOOKING ACROSS THE river Tagus, the city of Toledo seems to be frozen in time. It is not only the effect of a cold, Christmas Day morning, with light snowfall in the air: Toledo, with its stone ramparts, towers and the ancient stone bridge across the shallow but turbulent Tagus, with its enormous royal castle crowning the hill, is truly frozen in time. Once it ceased to be a royal capital, once its industry collapsed during the Baroque, the city virtually ceased to be. Now essentially a museum, its fate serves as a chilling reminder that progress is hardly a linear affair.

Four hundred years ago in Toledo, and across all of Europe, there came a time of a haunting, inexplicable decline. It was a time when poverty, corruption, and un–and underemployment soared and when real wages plummeted, when the numbers of the hungry and the homeless exploded and when the underworld took over entire city sectors. It was a time when wealth gaps opened wide, wider than ever remembered, and the middle class shrank and then withered and died. It was a time of near-continuous war, of resurgent long-forgotten diseases, of returning slavery and piracy–a time of absolute despair.

They all arrived along with, and seemingly in spite of, triumphs of education, reason, logic, and science. Oddly, the decline began to take shape at the very moment that the new information technologies–mass printing, newspapers and mail–began making the civilization better and faster informed. Collapse took place amidst the rising numbers and exploding wealth of the new university-educated elite. It coincided with the triumph of sophisticated global finance, efficient management of assets and privatization of public property, with the supremacy of law and elite-educated bureaucracy.

The story of the Baroque is a chilling reading.

The first signs of the incoming Baroque showed in the growing numbers of the urban poor. Same as in the last decades in the U.S., the averages climbed fast. From the usual 10 or 15 percent they rose, within a single dramatic decade of the 1590s, to a quarter or even half of all the urban populations of the Spanish empire and across Europe. Most of these poor, sometimes as high as 80 percent, were single women and children, a chilling precedent for today's statistics. Between 1590 and 1595, the number of desperately poor in Salamanca (as measured by the number of abandoned newborn children) almost quadrupled,[186] despite falling population.

Amazingly, we can pinpoint exactly when the bottom fell out of the late Renaissance–early Baroque reality. It was 1588, when, as if by magic, the birth rates started to fall simultaneously in all Spanish cities–and then just continued to fall. They kept falling for more than a century. In the Toledo cathedral, clergyman Sancho de Moncado, studying baptismal registers, found that the number of births dropped by half between 1550 and 1617. He observed that this drop happened not because of plague or migration, but because people could not support themselves and raise families[187].

The 1590s were the first truly horrible decade. Contemporary records convey a haunting vision of half-deserted towns populated by starving widows, beggars, and cripples. Travelers reported towns full of boarded-up businesses and empty houses, as if touched by plague or disaster. In some of them, half of the families ran away because they could not pay the hated poll tax. They joined the growing underworld of pimps, beggars, hawkers, thieves, homeless, crooks and prostitutes, living in decaying urban centers. In some cities, the homeless took over entire abandoned city sectors. The Spanish Council of Finance was inundated with *memorials* about deserted villages. In Germany, Belgium, and Switzerland, cities were flooded with refugees from the starving countryside. The ruling elites frantically tried to invent public works, usually the building of fortifications, to employ these unruly crowds[188].

In Italy, previously the richest manufacturing economy on the continent, the 1590s were a time when a feeling of some horrible, imminent disaster permeates all records. Entire provinces were controlled by brigands and bandits or were tormented by hunger. The list of calamities in contemporary records included "an endless succession of thefts, arson, murder and atrocities, comparable to those committed by pirates at sea."[187] Rebellion became an almost daily occurrence, so common that it was taken for granted and often not even mentioned in the records. In decaying urban centers, the growing abyss between the rich and the poor festered into permanent social hatred. The dramatic increase in poverty, injustice, social parasitism, and oppression resulted in some cases—for example in Naples, one of the biggest cities in Europe—in a wave of crime on a scale resembling a continuous civil war.[189] Government of Naples ordered watchtowers erected and watchfires lit on the hills over the city to warn of the approaching bandit mobs. Emigrants fled once-prosperous Italian cities by the thousands.

To the readers of today's newspapers reporting the virtual civil war in Rio de Janeiro, this must feel like a déjà-vu. In November 2010 an all-out battle erupted there between the authorities—thousands of heavily armed police supported by helicopters and armored vehicles—and drug lords' militia. As the authorities tried to take over some of Rio de Janeiro's *favelas*, hundreds were left killed or wounded in one day alone. In Mexico, rising drug violence between drug cartels and police claimed over 60,000 lives in just 6 years to 2012. Entire US-Mexico borderland became full of deserted towns as tens of thousands of families fled. Riots that swept through London and other British cities in the summer of 2011 signaled the deep discontent festering among the alienated youngsters and low-income people not only in out-of-sight poverty-stricken townships like Tottenham, Croydon, Bromley and Clapham, but across the whole country.

As the Baroque set in, real piracy, long forgotten, returned to torment the seas. Thousands of travelers were captured and sold into resurgent slavery. By 1600 the Mediterranean, in medieval times a prosperous sea of commerce, was once again surrounded by backward, agrarian, neo-conservative kingdoms. Increasingly, its waters became a firm domain of pirates and slavers, businesses often colluded in by noble officials. From Algiers to Albania, pirates, brigands, and corsairs now preyed on the weak and the poor of the decaying reality, as did the bureaucrats themselves.

Unlike in Toffler's rosy visions, the transition from the industrial to the post-industrial economy was absolutely frightening for most. The Baroque reality of the black market, the vagabondage, rising crime and prostitution mirrors some of the starker forecasts of our own future—or perhaps a reality emerging right in front of our eyes. "Increasing number of unemployed and underemployed people will find themselves sinking inexorably into the permanent underclass. Desperate, many will turn to the informal economy to survive. Some will barter occasional work for food and lodging" so painted author Jeremy Rifkin the coming decades. "Others will engage in theft and petty crime. Drug dealing and prostitution will continue to increase as millions of able bodied human beings, stranded by a society that no longer needs or wants their labor, try to better their lot in life. Their cries for help will be largely ignored as governments tighten their purse strings and shift spending priorities from welfare and job creation to beefed-up police security and the building of more prisons." [190]

As the Baroque set in, all over Europe, the former "middle class" descended into poverty. Squeezed by growing taxes, underemployed, deprived of incomes when their small businesses failed, they quickly morphed from merchants and well-paid craftsmen into denizens of the new service proletariat, and the underworld. Millions of people went hungry every day, as wages kept dropping. Wherever business declined, crime made an instant appearance. Travelers' accounts from 1590s Venice—a hundred years earlier the richest city in Europe, and possibly in the world—now conveyed an atmosphere of abandonment and physical danger. Muggers and hired murderers lurked under the arcades and bridges, daggers concealed in their cloaks. Along the canals, fights, muggings, and murders were now a daily occurrence; everybody carried a weapon. Stabbings, even in open daylight, became commonplace. As neo-conservative, radical outlooks gained currency, contempt for human life was professed as openly as contempt for the poor.

In Baroque paintings, we see empty piazzas where businesses have shut down, with beggars in rags lounging endlessly on the steps of churches, children playing around hovels and piles of garbage, an overwhelming picture of desolation, hopelessness, and decay. The new, post-Industrial Venice was like a modern disaster area, almost a Baroque Detroit. At the very bottom of the recession, the business of the Arsenal, once the continent's biggest shipyard, fell to almost zero. There were days when no ships at all came to or left Venice harbor.

Whenever society decays, horizons rapidly narrow. The 1590s—and late Renaissance and Baroque in general—saw a dramatic decline in art and philosophy, and a dearth of mechanical inventions, accompanied by narrow-minded visions of reality, and tormented and obsessive concepts. As decline accelerated, it brought fear. In Venice, in the frightening decade of 1600-1610 when the city virtually went bankrupt, fear became a total obsession: Spies of the Council of Ten, the ruling body of Venice, were everywhere, sniffing out real and imaginary conspiracies against the establishment. At the peak of the fear frenzy, every day horribly mutilated bodies, victims of torture and secret executions, were displayed daily in front of the Doge's palace. As in recent witchhunts and fear paranoias during the 'War on Terror' frenzy, it seemed that the world had gone mad.

Populated by thousands of lawyers, civil servants and other information professionals, one city grew amid the emerging Baroque reality—the imperial capital, Madrid. It was a city built exclusively from tax and rent revenues, a brilliant city of pure display. Buoyed by an abundance of tax and rent money, Madrid quadrupled its population within a few decades, even as old industrial and commercial centers began to collapse. It was a city where, according to Braudel, "the rich were extravagantly rich and the poor miserably poor; beggars sleeping on street corners, rolled up in their cloaks, bodies over whom the nobles had to step to reach their palaces, serenos guarding the doors of the rich, the disquieting underworld of ruffians, soldiers, hungry valets, gamblers fingering their greasy cards, cunning prostitutes . . . . [191]" Madrid of the 1600s was a phenomenon not seen in Europe for 1500 years—the first tax city to emerge on the continent since the collapse of Rome.

*

ONLY A DECADE earlier, the signs of the coming collapse were hard to see. In the summer of 1581—the time roughly identified as the advent of the Baroque, and seven years before the reality began to fall apart—to all people in the world the star of the Spanish Empire seemed to stand at its zenith. That summer, in a small house overlooking the river Tagus in Lisbon, King Philip II was reviewing the affairs of the newly conquered Portugal and writing loving letters to his daughters. The first ever global empire seemed firmly in control of the world. The King's missionaries were gaining thousands of converts in Japan. Viceroy De Toledo was strangling Inca resistance in Peru. Spanish armies were marching across France, Belgium, Holland, Germany, and Italy, and the King's fleets routed the Turks once again in the Greek seas. As other Spanish armies were completing the conquest of the Philippines, and as Portuguese outposts in Brazil, Africa, India, China, Arabia, and Malaysia were now firmly under Spanish control, the crown's shipyards around the Mediterranean were working on an immense fleet to conquer England.

While timber for these fleets was being marked for felling in the forests of Poland and Indian miners in Bolivia were extracting silver to finance the very existence of this first-ever global empire, even the most daring of dreams dreamt by the King's viceroys—that of conquering China—did not seem impossible. After all, the apocalyptic prophecies of a Franciscan friar in Mexico, Toribio de Motolinia, were still echoing in the hearts of believers, announcing the arrival of an empire that would encompass the whole world, subjugating the infidels and the barbarians, a universal empire that would have no end[192].

In the summer of 1581, few would expect the coming disasters. Europe still seemed in the midst of what was the greatest boom in centuries, and in the middle of its own Information Era.

Books—handmade, expensive, and focused primarily on religion during medieval times—were now printed by the millions and were available to any and all of the new-fangled information professionals. By 1500, 20 million printed books had already been sold. Just like today, progress was there for everyone to see. Advances in education, masses of college graduates, spanking new schools and universities, improvements in information and money flow, globalization of trade, financial engineering, improved asset yields, and management efficiency—not to mention military technology—were there as proof, if anybody would doubt. The elites were getting richer by the day and displaying their education and opulence. Populations continued to increase rapidly, and by 1550, a mere generation prior to the onset of the collapse, growth had reached an almost euphoric stage.

Just as the case of today's iconic 'global cities', Baroque's tax capitals, the only ones growing during this time of decline, were more magnificent than the old medieval cities of trade and industry had ever been. They were built when the investment incomes were taking the maximum share of the shrinking pie. "Paradoxically," write Hohenberg and Lees, "the phase of urban decline was often a time of architectural brilliance when baroque extravagances were added to the cityscape . . . . The money that financed this growth came almost exclusively from passive property incomes rather than profits from commercial activity . . . . As the model shows, rents increase past the peaks of production. Rentiers, therefore, are at their most affluent during times of declining output and low wage incomes. Ancient glories and grandeurs were reworked in an aesthetic that served the absolute power[193]." During the Baroque, the scale shifted from human to grandiose. Baroque city became a theatrical stage set, a backdrop for the glamorous life of the ruling elite.

In Baroque Florence and Augsburg, in Lyon, Venice and Burgos, marqueses and dukes—members of noble dynasties sired by lawyers and bankers a generation or two earlier—would now stir all the action with partying and gambling where trade and manufacture used to be the lifeblood of the cities during the Middle Ages.

As in other historical cycles in which civil servants and information professionals grew rich and influential, the Baroque created a vast 'service economy'. Unlike the rustic warlords or staid burghers of the medieval era, these new educated investors wanted a fancy urban living, and so they needed servants, specialized in 'service professional' type jobs that generally did not exist in the medieval times. The investor class of the Baroque 'plutonomy' found that they needed butlers and pastry cooks, interior decorators, salespeople staffing new luxury boutiques full of latest fashions, music composers and musicians, hatters, chefs, actors, lackeys, coach drivers and gardeners, librarians, sculptors, painters, piano and drawing tutors, tailors, dentists, seamstresses, jewelers, and opera singer-mistresses. They need them all, at their fingertips, to serve their daily needs. They needed real estate agents and property managers, investment advisers, and specialized lawyers to grow and protect their investments and foreclose on their debtors. They needed artists to preserve their features for posterity. The Baroque 'service economy' was virtually undistinguishable from ours.

For the lowest of service occupations, the domestics, drivers, grooms, wetnurses, chambermaids or gardeners, the investors might hire among the dispossessed farmfolk on whom they had foreclosed. The more skilled and articulate of the servants became their provosts, butlers, cooks, clerks, estate managers. The most talented 'service professionals' were commissioned to make pictures or sculptures immortalizing the investors, warmed their beds, played piano, sang or composed opera, pulled their teeth, or managed their assets, often making enough money to send their own children to universities to join the ranks of the establishment. The uneducated, the unemployable, the unskilled, the untalented and the unlucky dropped out into the new urban slums, an underworld of pickpockets, prostitutes, pimps, burglars, conmen, and cannon meat for the growing mercenary armies.

Increasingly, as the middle class universe and its obsolete work ethic collapsed, success became, just like in today's reality show, a game of chance—access to brand-name academy, or wizard talent, or perhaps a lucky scam, chance encounter with a rich patron, or some other timely break was what brought patronage and riches. Simple hard work and adherence to society's principles no longer delivered success to ordinary people.

This was the world of the Baroque—brilliant, rational, and practical to the utmost. Every special skill employable was employed to serve in a simple society divided between those who had elite education and used their smarts and contacts to acquire income-producing assets to live the charmed life and distribute favors and scraps of wealth to the less fortunate, and those who had no smarts, contacts, elite diploma or lucky break and therefore were forced to serve those who had. It was this rationality—so eerily similar to ours—that was glorified as the "Age of Reason."

Baroque was an explosion of a world of convenience, aesthetic luxury and artistic sophistication never seen before and—as some culture historians tell us—never matched since. The urban theater of the Baroque service economy was animated by the money that came from the productive sector, which at that time happened to be agriculture. But from the socioeconomic point of view, it might have mattered little what the income-producing asset was. Baroque's positional asset—a bond, a tax farm, a land rent, a government or army office yielding an income—was not much different from today's shareholder claim on a stock in some never-seen company holding some never-seen assets. Just like defunct Lehman Brothers, the investors of the Baroque bought a claim on the productive sector; improved, commoditized, securitized and rationalized it through management and financial engineering for maximum efficiency; but otherwise contributed nothing.

*

THE DECADES BETWEEN 1590 and 1620 witnessed chapter one of a major economic collapse. All statistics began dropping at the same time. The number of ships passing Danish Sound in and out of the Baltic began shrinking in 1600. The tonnage of ships passing through the port of Seville reached its peak in 1610 and fell sharply thereafter. From Venice to Dubrovnik to Marseille, all shipping volumes began to drop rapidly after 1600, as economies began to collapse in tandem. Manufacturing of textiles, whether in England, Italy, or Spain, peaked during the 1610-1620 decade, and then fell, the collapse lasting for over half a century. In many places, it lasted for 200 years or longer, usually until the onset of the Industrial Revolution. Manufacturing in Amsterdam and Rotterdam, the most prosperous industrial cities in Europe, dropped rapidly after 1620[194].

Dropping commercial activity, rising taxes, growing inequality, and rising poverty all went hand in hand. Between 1560 and 1600, the tax burden on an average taxpayer in Castile rose 430 percent, while wages (both unadjusted for soaring inflation) rose only 80 percent. Even so, the reign of King Philip II ended with a crushing mountain of debt. Every year, more and more public income sources were pledged for the payment of debt interest. Tax rates were going up, while the taxpayer base was being eroded. Despite that, the bureaucracy was spending as if there were no tomorrow. Under Philip III, in the first two desperate decades of the 17th century, the already huge civil service had doubled. But the cost of their salaries virtually exploded—an increase of 500 percent. Almost every year, the bureaucrats awarded themselves hefty pay raises.

Yet the officials' salaries were only a tip of the proverbial iceberg. Unprecedented corruption permeated the whole Renaissance and Baroque government system. Cosimo Masi, secretary of the Spanish commander-in-chief in the Netherlands, accumulated almost half a million gold florins in stolen public funds, enough money to field an army. In Shakespearean England, the Queen's Treasurer, Sir George Carey, embezzled the fantastic sum of 150,000 pounds sterling. The money, whether obtained by bribery, extortion, or fraud, financed extravagant aristocratic lifestyles of the bureaucrats. They built palaces, bought castles, commissioned art, jewels and paintings. "Venality, graft, peculation, and personal use of public funds attended the operation of government at all levels," writes historian Gibson. "Tax funds were regularly dipped into by individuals authorized to make collections. The distinction between fees and bribes became blurred . . . The crown's extravagant use of public money was imitated at all subordinate levels of hierarchy[195]."

*

STRANGELY ECHOING TODAY'S worries about climate change, what helped to turn the economic decline into depression was a sudden change of climate, resulting in lower crop yields. Beginning around 1570, there was a sharp drop in food available across Europe. The weather turned increasingly cold. Before, it hardly ever snowed in Venice, but the winter of 1603 was atrocious. "All the houses were coated with ice so that they shone like mirrors," according to an eyewitness, "The snow on the roofs was [very] thick . . . Numbers of boats were out breaking the ice [on the canals] with hammers[196]" so that supply ships could come into the city. The 1590s were so cold the Alpine glaciers began to send rivers of ice through populated valleys, burying villages in Grindelwald, Chamonix, and Aosta valleys[197]. While similar natural disasters had happened before, in the 1590s they hit an overstrained economy that was ready to break. In 1603 Seville, the great Guadalquivir river froze during the winter. Around Marseilles, even the Mediterranean Sea froze in 1595, trapping galleys in the harbor.

In Sweden, parish registers from Osterlosa paint a graphic picture of the terrifying year 1596: "Many died of hunger and starvation . . . People were found dead in the houses, under barns, in the ovens of the bath-houses and wherever they were able to squeeze in . . . though dogs ate many corpses. Children starved to death at their mothers' breasts, for they had nothing to give them to suck. Many people were compelled in their hunger to take to stealing . . . Gallows were built in our district and hung full. Women were flogged and had their hair and ears cut off at the gallows."[198] As far away as China, great lakes of the Yangtze River froze repeatedly, during the coldest winters ever recorded. The average cloudiness, painstakingly reconstructed by meteorologists from thousands of paintings, increased from 33 percent to a depressing 82 percent from the 15th to the 17th century. In pictures painted after 1590, the sky is almost always dark gray, even art reflecting this atmosphere of pervasive darkness. It has only recently been discovered that the famous painting "Night Watch" by Rembrandt is actually a day scene. Melancholy permeates Baroque paintings, whether of Rembrandt, El Greco, or Georges de La Tour, where only a single candle sheds light onto a bleak reality of total darkness. Darkness permeates all the works of Shakespeare written after the pivotal year 1600.

Almost all countries registered widespread crop failures and famines. Starvation reached massive proportions, especially in the overpopulated Mediterranean regions, from Spain to Turkey. Even traditional breadbaskets like Sicily and Egypt were hit; after 1560 they stopped exporting grain. The 1590s and the following decades of the Baroque witnessed the buying of massive quantities of grain, mostly from the Baltic, by Spain, Italy, and Turkey. Vast areas of the Balkans were starving. The giant city of Constantinople was repeatedly without food during that decade.

Millions of people got caught between the relentless squeeze of rising taxes and rents and falling wages, and the cyclical turn of the climate. Just like today, those without assets or government jobs, those who relied on their income from small farming or small business had nowhere to hide. Every new tax, every income drop, every attack of cold winter left more of them starving and dead by the thousands. Epidemics, which disappeared during the relatively prosperous decades of 1460-1560, now struck with a vengeance. The great plague of 1596 killed 15 percent of Spain's population. Some towns were completely emptied by the plague, and many productive areas turned into desert. The great famine of 1606 (the worst ever recorded in Spain, according to eyewitnesses) turned out to be a mere prelude to a series of devastating plagues, revolts, and starvations. A revolt in Cordoba started spontaneously when a young mother went weeping through a street, holding the body of her child who had died of hunger. Another attack of plague in Seville in 1652 killed half the population. In Amsterdam, a city of a hundred thousand people, a rampant six-year plague in the 1620s killed 35,000. It was no different in London, Venice, Paris, or Florence. During the plague, people were too afraid to go out; hiding in their houses behind shuttered windows they participated from home in religious services celebrated on a street corner by a priest.

Plague would kill the poorest, the undernourished, those crowding in miserable hovels. During the 1631 plague attack in Florence, it was found during inspection that 72 people lived in a small tower in the courtyard of de' Donati; 94 people lived in a single house in via dell' Acqua, and 100 in another small house in via San Zenobi, with an average of ten people per room. If just one of them got infected, hundreds died.[199]

Across virtually all of Europe, travelers of the Baroque reported conditions of unprecedented poverty in the countryside, de-urbanized provinces, devastated and semi-abandoned towns, unbelievable rural depression, peasants literally living in holes in the fields, like animals—all this desolate reality seemingly existed just to supply rents and tax revenues to feed the theatrical opulence of the Baroque elites living in a handful of cities—the iconic tax-and-rent capitals. This was the time of extreme parasitism and cynicism, a world in which membership of the elite, top education, special skill or talent, chance and cunning, and lack of scruples were the key instruments to get money and then rent-producing assets. Gambling reached records. As the Baroque decades went by, money became the only focus of life—how to win it, steal it, loot it, scam it, invest it, multiply it, defraud it, in short—how to squeeze it from others was the only thing that mattered. This decaying reality simplified, stupefied, and coarsened with every passing decade. *The only measure of people of the Baroque, all the way to the Industrial era, was how much they were worth in annual rent income.*

In this world, the only growth industries were the perverse 'businesses' of law, debt, tax enforcement, privatization, warfare, insider information, and financial speculation. The elites of 'information professionals' who had created and fed on this self-destructive system were continuously recycling the society's wealth to the top participants of the Information Society game. And the master in this game of information and wealth recycling was the New York of the Baroque, the first-ever truly global financial metropolis: Genoa.

BAROQUE NEW YORK

"The financial sector seems to be a machine to transfer income and wealth from outsiders to insiders, while increasing the fragility of the economy as a whole."
—Martin Wolf, Financial Times[200]

"In 1950, manufacturing accounted for more than 30 percent of non-farm employment. As of last year, it's down to ten percent. Indeed, one third of all manufacturing jobs disappeared since 2000. This devastating downward trend has contributed greatly to the erosion of the middle class."
—Arianna Huffington, Third World America[201]

ON JUNE 20TH, 1584, twenty galleys arriving from Spain under the command of Admiral Gian Andrea Doria dropped anchor in Genoa harbor. Their cargo was an enormous load of gold and silver, equivalent to three or four million gold crowns. This shipment was only part of a river of money just starting to flow into Genoa. It came from Potosi, the silver mountain in Bolivia, and was transshipped through Seville, to be exchanged in Genoa from silver to gold coin, and then to be carried over Alpine passes to pay Spanish mercenary armies in the Netherlands.

During the 1590s decade, around six million ducats in cash alone passed through Genoa. In 1602, the Genoese bankers underwrote a single loan to Spain for an enormous sum of over nine million ducats. This sudden wash of money re-galvanized the moribund economy of the entire Italian peninsula. It paid old debts and allowed contracting of new ones. Converted into luxury purchases, houses, and investments, this windfall revitalized the luxury sector in a country ravaged by generations of wars and recessions. Amid this financial Indian Summer, Baroque Genoa found itself basking, just like New York or London today, in the flow of wealth originating far away. Financial center of half of the world, it found itself handling—for a hefty fee—loans, deposits, precious metals, commodities, debt settlements, credit notes, and bills of exchange. For the very last time in its history, Genoa's star shone, but with the most fickle kind of reflected light, that of a financial capital.

Just like today, as skills, capital, and investment were focused on and absorbed by high finance, Genoa gradually abandoned basic commercial activity. Just like in today's New York, as Genoa's most talented and educated turned to finance, the less talented, less educated turned into paupers and servants when commerce and manufacturing declined. As soon as the metropolis turned to finance, Dutch and English shippers took over Genoa's shipping business, even its local coastal trade[202]. Italy itself was by this time long hollowed out. Just like America's Indian summer of the two decades preceding the 2008-2009 crisis, early Baroque Italy's Indian summer was an illusion. Sky-high labor costs extracted by monopolistic guilds to keep *rentier*-like master craftsmen living in idle luxury, excessive taxes, stagnant productivity, receding technology, overregulated production, and focus on luxury goods—the seeds of Italy's economic collapse went much deeper than mere lack of Atlantic trading routes or timber. As profitability of commercial ventures declined, an appetite for high-yield, quick-profit investments grew, fueling financial and real estate speculation.

Just like today, earning investment income was becoming preferable to productive work: "The Spanish need for finance was complementary to the search by Italian investors for safe and prestigious (in that they involved no labour) placements for the capital accumulated over centuries," writes historian Thomson[203].

In a slow de-industrialization process similar to the one affecting today's America (prior to recent crisis, proudly hailed as 'post-industrial', presumed to be a sign of progress and modernity), Baroque Italy was visibly falling behind, out-traded and out-maneuvered by Dutch and English competitors who could manufacture more, faster, and cheaper. Venice, this old symbol of industry and entrepreneurship, which still managed to export 25,000 woolen cloth pieces a year to the Middle East in year 1600, barely exported 100 pieces a century later. Same as today's America, Italy had entered its Renaissance as the leading industrial power of the globe. During the Baroque, it began to acquire all the stereotypical features of an underdeveloped economy, increasingly an impoverished provider of agricultural commodities.

The amazing transformation of Genoa from a productive to a finance-driven economy seems to have been followed by Information-Era America. Between 1973 and 1985, financial industry's share of U.S. domestic corporate profits was at best 16 percent. Just before 2008 financial crisis, it stood at incredible 41 percent.[204] Just as during the last Baroque, instead of merely supporting economic efficiency, financial industry seems to have developed an appetite to feed on the real economy. In the end, it almost ate it away.

Genoa's own evolution set the standard. At the end of the 15th century, the city began to move from a trade-based to a finance-based economy. As it was losing its merchant colonies in the Black Sea and the Aegean, it began opening banking houses in the western Mediterranean, especially in Spain. Whatever was left of Genoa's old democratic illusions was suppressed early in the Renaissance era: in 1528 the financial "aristocracy" strangled the city commune. From then on the bankers maintained power, despite bloody uprisings by mobs of impoverished ex-citizens. The commercial decline of the mid–to late-Renaissance period hit Genoa hard. Its commercial and industrial base completely vanished. By the 1580s the wretched unemployed were dying in the streets whenever the price of imported bread took a jump. And yet, the city was still wealthy. It benefited from the misfortunes of others—for example, the collapse of the merchant and financial center of Antwerp, soon followed by the bankruptcy of French banks in Lyon. The contracting Baroque reality forced the global finance of Spain to defer to Genoa[205].

By the 1580s, all the wealth of Genoa—and, indirectly, a large part of the wealth of the Spanish empire—was concentrated in the hands of a few financier families, all descended from merchants. The tall, fortified palaces of Genoa's bankers were said to be the most splendid homes in the world. Just as in today's Manhattan, some of the richest people of the world led charmed lives above the squalor and homelessness of some of the most destitute.

In the world around Genoa, other old trading and industry cities simply died. In 1577, grass was growing again on the Place des Changes in the center of Lyon, the very spot that 50 years earlier had been hailed as the industrial and merchant heart of the continent. Along with Lyon and Antwerp cities like Nurnberg, Lubeck, Milan, Florence, and Augsburg—all symbols of industry and commerce, all wilted and faded away by the 1580s. South Germany, barely two generations earlier the hub of manufacturing, faded into obscurity. Venice, once the commercial capital of Europe, was now scaring off visitors with boarded-up businesses and an ominous aura of gloom and decay.

Only Genoa, for a few decades anyway, entered the voodoo world of the post-industrial economy—a world in which fortunes could still be made on pure information, if one only knew how.

*

LET US STOP here for a while to see if we can detect a pattern of similarities between the decline cycles: our own era and the Renaissance/Baroque one—and also similarities between peak cycles: High Middle Ages and 19th century Industrial Era. The medieval cycle of expansion was eerily similar to our own high industrial era of 1850-1960 not only because of innovation, new machines, and new energy sources driving both realities. Both eras shared more than that. Neither was yet an 'information era' or 'post-industrial', or 'service economy' era. In both, money was invested in trade, manufacturing of mass-produced goods, in expansion of infrastructure, shipping, massive urban construction programs in support of explosive economic growth, or in support of dramatic increases in the productive capacity by building new factories and machines, in exactly the same way China and India are growing today. Long-term, predictable investments in basic capacity expansion yielded long-term, solid and predictable returns. This wasn't yet the time when chance could turn someone into a high-paid "celeb" while someone else, perhaps with similar capabilities, would continue waiting tables, with little other career avenues in between. The peak eras were invariably times of the triumph of the middle class, when average people were prospering and their numbers growing, with steady increases in employment opportunities and strong increases in wages. Speculation, luxury industries, or high finance were not yet the core business; relatively high degree of equality went hand in hand with widespread ownership of assets, such as small land holding or small business. Destitution, unemployment, homelessness, asset bubbles, financial crises, bureaucracy, extortionate taxes, rents or property speculation were not yet the household words.

But during the two Renaissances we are comparing—the original one in the 16th century and the recent one that started in the 1970s—things changed dramatically. Both eras lived off legacy technologies—the first one off medieval mechanics, the recent one off the inventions of the Industrial Era. While hardly any new machines or productive technologies were invented, the breakthroughs that were made, were in both cases made in warfare, information technologies (mostly in the speed, volume and ease of processing and distributing information, rather than any content quality), and, above all, in finance and money. In both eras there was a dramatic increase in human numbers, putting pressure on resources and dramatically driving up prices. In both average wages declined, pushing what used to be middle class into or close to poverty. In both conservative ideas triumphed; in both there was a dramatic widening of the gap between the rich and the poor. In both, mass-distributed, easily accessible information and mass-entertainment (often violent and crude) triumphed; in both human life seemed cheaper and contempt for the poor replaced the old-fashioned ideas of equality.

Both Renaissances were the eras of triumphant global capital. In the 16th century Renaissance, concentrated cash capital began to operate on a massive, highly sophisticated, and global scale. This had never happened in such a way before—not in Rome, not in China. In medieval Europe, cash had been spread out among many different merchant ventures, city communes, local churches, warlords, wealthy republics, and affluent middle classes, and was simply non-existent in the countryside where life operated largely on self-sufficiency or barter system. Cash was something to hoard rather than a commodity to invest in. Investment information was limited and unreliable. Banking focused mostly on servicing trade in physical goods or lending to monarchs. The medieval world was akin to pioneer America, with its simple but massive and ever-expanding manufacturing and trade of foodstuffs, clothing, and household and farm basics.

The Renaissance changed all this. With the countryside now fully incorporated into a cash-based *rentier* system, increasingly covered with cash crops and taxed to maximum, with new mines in Germany and Bolivia producing silver in abundance, with cannon-enforced taxation draining this silver towards treasuries of newly integrated nation-states, with speculation, inflation and privatizations providing added liquidity boosts, extremely liquid investment pools and flows appeared. Fast, cheap and reliable mass-printed information in the form of maps, books, atlases, and soon newspapers for educated investors appeared as well, complemented by insider networks of correspondents keeping each other informed through e-mail-like massive daily message writing, allowing investment and speculation bonanzas to begin. Massive liquidity combined with pressure on resources and living space to create inflation, bubbles and speculation that impoverished many but helped to quickly enrich a few. Just like today, speed of exchange of information enabled the educated and cunning insiders to rapidly become rich by playing, rigging, and refining this system. Privatizations of state assets, massive growth of corruption, ability of the new investor class to exempt itself from taxation, all worked to build fast, speculative fortunes, quickly re-invested into new income-producing assets. In both eras, dropping average incomes, massive inequality, dispossession, and growing destitution of many went hand in hand with the luxury and sophistication of the educated investor elite.

Grain speculation was one of the favorite money-makers, and a quick builder of fortunes, not just for merchants but also for all well-informed members of the elite, including nobles and even kings. Times of financial instability and stress have always favored speculation of one sort or another, with invariable increases in the wealth gap. Whether in grain, politics, or money, speculation became a way of life in the 16th century.

State borrowing grew spectacular. Not only Spain borrowed; every single government did. England's Henry VIII, despite massive cash inflows amounting to two million pounds from confiscated Church assets (compared to Henry's annual 150,000 pounds income), in a single three-year period still had to meet his escalating expenses with an enormous loan of three million pounds from German and Italian bankers. High-paying government bonds, privatization opportunities, grain and currency speculations, banking transaction service fees, and tax farms—all could yield spectacular returns for ruthless and educated people armed with insider information, the right timing and the right contacts. Early knowledge of imperial elections or battle results could make or break fortunes. As the general economy turned increasingly bleak in the later part of the Renaissance, and the investment environment increasingly speculative, information—just like today—became the most valuable commodity. The very rich, like the Fuggers of Augsburg, maintained their own post service on crucial routes, as well as spies in major centers so they could profit from first-hand knowledge of events: harvests, wars, battle outcomes, alliances, loan and forex rates, VIP births, marriages and deaths. While the uninformed masses were losing their shirts with rising prices and dropping incomes, the best-informed elites could and did make fortunes overnight.

The players sometimes lost their shirts, too, as their speculators' luck ran out. The Fuggers, third-generation peasants considered the richest bankers in Europe, went bankrupt in 1577. This was the information era Renaissance style, a time of cool heads, no scruples, and quick reflexes. Decade after decade into this era, reality revealed itself to be more ruthless, more raw and convoluted, more obsessed with money and gain, more grotesque in its cynicism, greed, and base passions—a world of wheeler-dealers, scam and rip-off artists, adventurers, lawyers, fake nobles, ghetto-dwellers, mercenaries, bankers, pirates, high-priced whores, spies, slave-traders, and bureaucrats. Its information professionals were more educated, more sophisticated, more informed, and more cunning than the rather bland medieval merchants, staid burghers, and rustic knights. They had to—just like the Wall Street sharks of today, they only made money on information and investment and speculation wizardry.

The bankers of Genoa were the best of the best. To pay Spanish mercenaries in Netherlands in gold coin, they would buy cheap Chinese gold in Egypt, then bring it to Italy and convert it to cheap Spanish silver from Bolivia. They would then send the silver to China through India, or later directly through the Pacific. It was a gigantic global circuit of cash exchanges, in which huge profits could be made from small variations of gold-to-silver exchange ratios in different countries of the globe, all based—just like today—on access to information and other people's capital. It was this ever-growing demand for information and resulting efficiency and competitive edge that was the driving force for books, maps, postal services, couriers, spies, and an avalanche of daily letters, all performing just as well—even if not as fast—as today's information superhighway. Ships were circumnavigating the globe on a regular basis and the post-industrial economy of the late Renaissance—just like ours—seemed to have nothing but a bright future ahead.

For 70 years of their financial dominance, a handful of banking families of Genoa—Grimaldi, Piccamiglio, Spinola, Doria—completely controlled the finances of Spain, and, indirectly, of half of the world. Cascading government bankruptcies hardly affected them. Unlike the Fuggers, they did not borrow money from investors to lend it to unreliable governments. Instead, the new knowledge professionals merely repackaged, for a hefty commission, other people's money, and passed on the risk in small print. When Spain declared bankruptcy again in 1595, they paid back the investors from Venice in low-yielding replacement Spanish bonds rather than cash, ruining many. Taking full advantage of and manipulating the follies of the decaying reality—"religious" wars, imperial dreams, bureaucratic corruption, ruinous taxes, greed or desperation of lesser investors and kings—the global bankers helped many part with a good part of their tax and rent wealth. They charged Spain up to a 35-percent "service fee," on top of an exorbitant interest rate, to exchange money from silver to gold and deliver it to the theater of war in the Netherlands.

And just like in 2008, the taxpayers paid all.

Eventually, in 1627, desperate Spanish reformers under Count-Duke Olivares switched to Portuguese/Jewish bankers centered in Amsterdam, and Genoa's career as a global financial center came to an abrupt end. While it retained some banking activity, it became principally a *rentier* city: bankers' income from debt interest amounted to fully half of Genoa's total income[206]. After Genoa's fall—paralleling Spain's freefall collapse—there was no global financial center for almost a century. Poorer and smaller late

Baroque civilization could no longer support financial sophistication on the previous scale. Amsterdam was merely a colonial trading centre, with restricted financial operations. A new global financial center would emerge only in mid 18th century—London, buoyed by new growth based on new colonial staples: sugar, tea, coffee, cotton, and tobacco, all supported by massive growth of demand. This growth of demand came from rising populations, now fed with potatoes, sugar and maize. Especially sugar and potatoes, new cheap energy sources, were very effective in replacing the previous, more expensive ones: meat and wheat.

Slowly, Genoa turned into an empty shell, serving no real purpose. Bankers' money, now invested in foreign landed estates, abandoned the city. Inhabited by a wretched mob of ex-citizens, the first global financial capital fell during the centuries that followed into poverty so desperate that, generations later, French army recruiters found local men unfit for military service. This was because centuries of malnutrition had dwarfed the population of Genoa. In 1792, more than three-quarters of the males of Genoa stood less than 1.5 meter (4'-11") tall[207].

REPUBLIC OF THE BEWITCHED

"The accumulation of capital has created a new elite, interested not only in wealth, but also in power. In the immediate post-war period politics was open to talent. Now families connected by blood, marriage and patronage are taking the place of the old aristocracy. The rise of the new establishment is most evident in the Diet, where about one third of the ruling LDP members are sons and sons-in-law of former politicians.

Political dynasties abound. Nearly every post-war prime minister has a son or son-in-law in the politics. The families of all but three of Japan's 17 post-war prime ministers also have in one way or another allied themselves by marriage to the imperial family . . ."

—Globe & Mail, 1989 [208]

B Y 1600, BAROQUE tax-and-rent capitals were emerging everywhere, the only growth industry among the decay. Madrid was not alone. In Istanbul, the Turkish noble bureaucracy could easily outshine Madrid in its own extravagant spending. As the dazzling opulence and lavish display of the Seray were increasing year after year, they were only matched by the growing displays of decay, wretchedness, banditry, and tax-and-rent oppression in the countryside, where the money came from.

Escalating costs of government combined with a flood of American silver to create a stagflation similar to the one of our own reality. Landowners from France to Turkey raised their rents, in some places by a whopping 1600 percent. The Turkish state, seeing tax revenue teeter, farmed out its collection business to unscrupulous loan sharks and strongmen. In its own peculiar "privatization" process, Turkey, like Europe, created a whole class of land-owning bureaucrats. They muscled away the commercial bourgeoisie–the people we would describe today as middle class.

By the 1590s, as the post-industrial reality took over, the middle class has been largely strangled. Millions of those engaged in manufacturing closed down shop. Those who worked for wages became servants or paupers. Those who did not make timely investments in land, government bonds or office, or 'noble' tax exemptions to shield themselves from abuse and enable them to abuse others, those who did not educate their children as lawyers–those people simply fell through the widening cracks into the teeming underworld of bandits, beggars, servants, and prostitutes. And as war, poverty, piracy, and plague came back to haunt Europe in the frightening decades that followed, traces of many families disappeared forever.

Just like in 1970s America, a flood of cheap manufactured imports began arriving into Spain in the 1580s and 1590s, when Bolivian silver was coming in like a torrent, driving Spanish wages and prices high above the European average, hollowing out local enterprise. The empire began to run a crushing trade deficit, as–in an eerie déjà vu of today's America–it started importing virtually everything, and especially most manufactured products. In an eerie echo of today's America, the trade deficit was financed by not just with Bolivian silver but mostly with foreign borrowing and rising taxes on the low income earners. But after 1598 the supply of silver from Bolivia fell off sharply. Military efforts began to suffer mutinies of unpaid troops. As the new century opened, a systemic decline became visible. By the year 1600, reform proponent Cellerigo de Celloro, calling Spain the "republic of the bewitched," identified the root of the problem–the fact that the government and the elites "have scorned society's natural foundations and . . . have adopted the destructive attitude of all commonwealths: the belief that richness lies only in money . . . Wealth has not sent its roots deep because it has never come down to earth."[209]

After the year 1600, things only got worse. The flow of silver from Bolivia dwindled steadily, from 83 million ducats (between 1590 and 1600) to 31 million ducats (1640 to 1650); at the same time, the growth of bureaucracy, debt, and expenditure all reached truly fantastic rates. By 1621 the situation had become untenable. The king was told that "the money for this year's expenses has not come from present revenue but from revenue anticipated up to 1625"[210]. Duly sobered, the government appointed well-known reformer Count-Duke Olivares to head a new Junta of Reform. The Junta promptly decreed an austerity program—the closing of brothels, prohibition of expensive clothing and other displays of extravagance and luxury, an anti-corruption drive, and restriction on foreign imports. As an object lesson, a strongman in the previous government, Rodrigo Calderon, was accused of various crimes and summarily beheaded.

In these exhilarating days of reform, Count-Duke Olivares and his colleagues worked around the clock to review the situation and seek ways to change things. The young king personally worked with dozens of commissions dealing with various reform proposals, reviewing laws and taxes. The Count-Duke managed to reduce the expenditure of the court, curtail corruption and set up a trading monopoly with northern Europe based in Seville, aimed at reducing the advances of the Dutch. His visions reached much further, proposing in secret memoranda a brotherhood of all Spanish realms—effectively a centralized, modern state.

What strikes one reading the countless reform proposals, law drafts, and memoranda of those years is how clearly—perhaps more clearly than today—people were aware of the reasons for the rot of their society. The sheer volume of reform proposals is stunning, and so is the similarity of the ideas to the "modern" ones we dream up today—promote immigration to counter population drop; restrict imports to protect domestic enterprise and employment; subsidize exports and create new state-sponsored export-oriented industries; promote technical education of the young; reduce government debt and cut state expenditure; simplify taxation; abolish internal customs; standardize laws and regulations; deploy anti-inflation measures. Virtually every single of these ideas you can find in the media today, as a remedy for the ills of our society.

Even the wealth gap, a near-taboo subject today, was addressed in 1616 by a Madrid magistrate in a way we might find too daring in our increasingly opaque and aggressively neo-conservative reality: "The maldistribution of wealth is very harmful," wrote Baroque magistrate Mateo Lopez Bravo. "It creates power, arrogance, and idleness among those who have it and misery, humiliation, and despair among those who do not[211]." Unthinkable today, moves against big accumulations of private wealth—such as partitioning of the great estates and giving land to the landless and the destitute—were being studied by the Baroque reformers.

Yet no reforms seemed to work. By the early 1630s, Olivares was complaining of bad health and insomnia, as the edifice he was trying to build was clearly crumbling. The mental strain made him lose control over state affairs. The collapse of the economy was proceeding at a breathless rate. Taxes were not cut; instead, new taxes were being introduced to meet escalating demands of war, bureaucracy, and debt service. By the late 1630s, the nobles stopped attending the government meetings. "Disenchantment and cynicism enveloped the country and paralyzed the efforts of those who tried to alleviate it or to reform," writes historian Treasure. "The repartition of estates was in itself no answer. There was little heart in the land, or in the cultivator, and the system told against him at every level. Agrarian misery points to the moral decadence of the Spanish upper classes content to draw their income from oppressed and hungry peasants[212]." By 1642, currency debasing went so deep that forced pricing was imposed, paralyzing all trade as people hoarded good coin. By that time money was in such short supply that no cash could be raised to fight rebellions in Catalonia and Portugal, to which bankrupt Castile tried to extend its rapacious tax system.

Thousands escaped starving farms to swell the urban underclass; it was among these unfortunate that the plague claimed a quarter of a million victims when it hit a generation later. Beginning in 1643, the king drew strength from the sole advice of Maria de Agreda, a mystic Franciscan nurse. Olivares was dismissed and became mentally deranged. By 1650 Spain, the world's biggest owner and importer of bullion, had virtually no gold or silver in circulation. Only copper stayed. A six-pound bag of copper coins would buy ten pounds of cheese. Many transactions reverted to barter, as a shortage of cash and wild swings between inflation and deflation completely paralyzed the economy[213]. In 1652, the third government bankruptcy was declared, and in 1662 the fourth, with payment of debt interest alone consuming 75 percent of current revenues; overall debt was equivalent to 18 years of revenue. "On many days," wrote the diarist Barrionuevo, "even bread cannot be had in the royal household" of Philip IV, king of Spain[214].

The 1640 revolutions that broke out in Portugal and Catalonia–in response to an attempt to extend to these regions the extortionate levels of taxation that were ravaging Castile–were just a sampling of the wave of revolts and rebellions that plagued Europe in response to horrible economic conditions. In England, the revolt against and eventual execution of King Charles I was triggered by the king's attempt to extract more money from the country. In France, a series of revolts between 1648 and 1654, called the Fronde, were triggered by money disputes between the king and his Paris parliament. From Sicily to Naples to Denmark to Poland to Scotland and Ireland, revolts and civil wars shook Baroque Europe at the bottom of the crisis, 1620-1660. Peasant rebellions took place in extraordinary numbers: in the south of France alone, there were 264 insurrections between 1596 and 1660, the largest such number in recorded history.

As wars and epidemics ravaged the continent, Europe's population dropped to around 60 million people, much lower compared to what it was during the medieval peak and not much more than in the year 1000.

*

THERE ALWAYS SEEMS to be a peculiar connection between a time of decline and the declining caliber of the people themselves. This link has often been observed but still remains essentially a mystery. From Italy to Poland, from Spain to Germany, not just the artistic quality of the portraits seemed to decline during the Baroque—so did the quality of the people portrayed. In portraits of low artistic value we look into the eyes of people obese and mediocre, conceited and narrow-minded, trivial and petty, pompous and mean, often ugly or deformed. Faces conveying vision, charity, wisdom, purpose, integrity, love, or compassion are hard to find. Writings of the time, expressed in the cryptic, convoluted, "baroque" language—obsessed with titles, hierarchy, academic titles and education and the constant distinguishing between "nobles" and "non-nobles"—convey to us the idiotic divagations of the Academia. In a trend eerily similar to ours, trivialities were exalted, any original ideas suppressed. Just as in other declining "information eras," from Hellenistic Greece to late Rome to late dynastic China, Baroque's over-abundance of information is overflowing with plagiarism, pettiness, trivia, repetition, and venality. These works reveal the general lowering of goals and interests—an absolute intellectual void lasting through the long Baroque generations. Against this dismal background, scientific discoveries of Galileo, Descartes and Newton had virtually no impact on the daily reality of the Baroque. Dwarves were a favorite subject of the time, and pencil sketches revel in the repulsive wretchedness of the poor. And always, the preferred background of the paintings is total darkness.

One by one, Spanish industries died, as the country entered the murky 'post-industrial economy'. The manufacturing of swords ceased in Toledo. As the industry abandoned the city, its population fell by more than half. Entire urban sectors were taken over by vagrants and thieves, and the city froze in time for centuries–a fact noted with amazement by today's tourists. As depression worsened, industrial production and trade in the biggest centers, such as Burgos, Medina, and Segovia fell to almost nothing. In the Basque country alone, the number of large merchant ships dropped from 200 to zero in mere 20 years. Castile, which had more than a thousand large merchant ships at the end of the Middle Ages, had virtually none by the end of the Renaissance. The number of cloth looms across the country fell by three quarters before the bottom was reached around 1660.

Decline in Spain's urban populations was stunning: From 1600 to 1650, the population of Burgos dropped by 77 percent; that of Medina del Campo by 79 percent; Salamanca's by 40 percent; Valladolid's by 62 percent; Seville's by 33 percent; Toledo's by 60 percent. Only the tax-capital Madrid grew, by more than 160 percent[215].

This dual collapse of both populations and industry affected virtually all of Europe. Between 1600 and 1650 Milan lost half its inhabitants; Cremona's population dropped from 37,000 to 17,000. The population of Lombardy fell by a third. In the near-century between 1606 and 1700, the number of Milan silk looms shrank from 3000 to 461; between 1600 and 1640, the city's wool production fell by at least 80 percent. Cremona, which around 1580 claimed 14,000 cloth industry workers, had only 100 people still employed in the business by 1650.

Within a very few decades, a process of near-total de-industrialization of North Italy reversed the growth trends of some 800 years. At the bottom of the Baroque depression, huge stretches of the region went completely out of cultivation, herds decreased in size, and rents and land prices that had soared for over a century finally, and dramatically, collapsed[216].

Thereafter, and for the next two centuries, until the advent of a new energy system, Milan and other post-industrial centers in Italy became "centres of consumption, feeding on a flow of agrarian rents and government expenditures. Between the urban economies of the late Middle Ages and the Renaissance, and their Industrial successors of the 20th century there is . . . a gap, a striking discontinuity"—tells us historian Domenico Sella[217].

By the 1650s, the process of wealth-accumulation by the new, educated investor elites that drove the dynamics of the Renaissance and early Baroque was completed. Then—once virtually all land in Europe became part of gigantic landed estates reminiscent of late Roman latifundia, once most independent producers have been turned into farmhands and servants, and once all those who could afford it became tax-exempt nobles—the civilization, its goal seemingly accomplished, completely lost its focus. For the dispossessed, there was no more hope. For the one-time 'cognitarian' or 'information professional' families, the lawyers and the bankers now turned into idle noble dynasties, there was nothing else to strive for. Around Rome, an enormous territory half the size of Holland was owned by six noble clans. In fertile Lombardy, noble investors' estates accounted for 97 percent of all cultivable land. On vast European plains, in Poland and in Hungary, individual family holdings rivaled the size of some German states. Baroque Europe's largest landowner, Polish magnate Lubomirski, owned more than a 1000 estates—dozens of towns, hundreds of villages—spread over an enormous territory bigger than England. This Baroque prince was a master of over a million servants, clients and serfs, almost 2 percent of Europe's population.

But as the civilization ate away its very fabric, at the decline bottom, even land incomes could not escape the all-pervading recession. Depopulation and land abandoning sharply reduced rent incomes and began to drive down property values. In 1643, the accountant of the Duke of Bejar reported that the estate revenue barely covered the administration costs and servants' wages. Even in Lombardy, in the estates of Ambroggio d'Ada near Milan, land yields dropped from a healthy 47 percent in 1608, at the onset of the Baroque, to a paltry five percent in 1632, eroded by an abysmal economic situation.

The growing incompetence of the elites seemed to mirror the general decline. By the mid-17th century, travelers passing through the interminable estates of the Duke Medina Sidonia in Southern Spain were dismayed by the overwhelming neglect and poverty they witnessed. This was because, as profits from land ownership kept dropping, the landed estates of the Baroque were increasingly being farmed not on a long-term, sustainable basis, as in the early Renaissance, but for short-term profits to fulfill the desperate need for cash. The squeeze on producers kept tightening, driving them not just into destitution but into extinction. Despite deflation, land abandonment and the dire poverty of the countryside, rent rates in many places still kept going up, squeezing the very last pennies out of the producers. Records of the time are all full of stories of mismanagement, corruption, stupidity, and waste.

By the mid 17th century, in shrunken, dilapidated cities, in countrysides depopulated by plague and recession, people of the Baroque lived out their lives as if caught in a bewitched reality where time stood still. Visitors to Spain "were dismayed," writes historian Treasure, "by the ignorance of the men, the withdrawn behavior of the women, the longueurs of the tertulia, or the evening gathering, the endless lounging in the town squares. Life in Poland resolved itself for many of the gentry into a simple round of hunting and carousing[218]." Holland and England were the only places where any intellectual activity still existed; the rest of the continent seemed frozen in a stupor.

There was no goal or direction to anything. All long-term programs or attempts of reform were abandoned by the Baroque elites. Their own financial survival became their only goal. Manufacturing, where it still survived, limped on, corrupted by the parasitism of the guilds and masters. As the economy froze, even the previous frantic search to secure a slice of the shrinking pie finally ceased. The number of Spanish university students, still growing in the 1620s, dropped sharply after 1650. This reflected the declining financial returns from holding an office—or from any other asset, for that matter. Even in the only commercial countries, Holland and England, technological innovation was moving at a snail's pace: the practical inventions of the Renaissance and the Baroque were a telescope and a microscope, a thermometer and a watch.

Between the end of the Middle Ages and the onset of the Industrial Revolution, Renaissance and Baroque have come up with very few inventions of practical use. Hundreds of years after the Middle Ages waned, Baroque machines continued to be virtual copies of their medieval models.

Outside the glitzy tax capitals, in a striking reversal of medieval trends, Europe de-urbanized. The percentage of Europe's urban populations dropped from 16 percent at the end of Middle Ages to 13 percent by 1700, and began to go up only slightly after 1800. De-urbanization of once-richest regions, like Italy, was the most dramatic. Urban populations in the Veneto region fell from 24 percent in the 1550s down to 17 percent by the 1690s and to below 15 percent by the 1790s[219]. Where medieval industries collapsed, hundreds of towns faded. Entire countries, like Poland or Germany, de-urbanized and became rural backwaters, by year 1700 producing little more than potatoes.

Life went on slowly in these new, smaller towns. Barns, horse stables, gardens, farms, and even cattle pastures occasionally appeared where medieval houses and factories had once stood. The sole *raison d'etre* for these towns in the new, overwhelmingly rural universe was to serve a handful of local *rentier* families, who lived there themselves for a single reason—to squeeze every penny possible, first-hand, from the ravaged countryside, siphon off their part, and remit the rest to the tax capital. There was no choice: Only the king and his artillery could hold this fragile reality together. In Germany, life centered around princely courts. The royal tax-and-rent regimes, their new glitzy palaces like Versailles set amid dirt-poor countryside, were all that kept total collapse at bay, and this only through their sheer capacity to coerce: Army spending rarely consumed less than 50 percent of state revenue.

*

WHILE RESEARCHING THIS book, I came across a stunning passage in Fernand Braudel's book about the Mediterranean in the times of Philip II. There, chilling in its lucidity and compassion, among hundreds of pages of dry facts and brilliant analysis, a single page stood out. It stood out, shockingly emotional in its summary of the time of absolute despair that was the Baroque. It is a haunting epitaph for all Baroque eras, past, present, and future, and must be read in full:

"A slow, powerful, and deep seated movement seems gradually to have twisted and transformed the societies of the Mediterranean between 1550 and 1600. It was a lengthy and painful metamorphosis. The general and growing malaise was not translated into open insurrection; but it nevertheless modified the entire social landscape . . . The society was tending to polarize into, on the one hand, a rich and vigorous nobility reconstituted into powerful dynasties owning vast properties and, on the other, the great and growing mass of poor and disinherited, 'caterpillars and grubs', human insects, alas too many. A deep fissure split open traditional society, opening gulfs that nothing could ever bridge . . . In England, France, Italy, Spain, and Islam, society was undermined by this dramatic upheaval, the full horror of which was to be revealed in the seventeenth century. The creeping evil reached states as well as societies, societies as well as civilizations. This crisis coloured the lives of men. If the rich stooped to debauchery, mingling with the crowd they despised, it was because society stood on two banks facing each other: on one side the houses of the nobles, over-populated with servants; on the other 'picardia', the world of the black market, theft, debauchery, adventure, but above all poverty, just as the purest, the most exalted religious passions coexisted with the most incredible baseness and brutality. Here, some will say, are the astonishing and marvelous contradictions of the Baroque. Not so: these were the contradictions, not of the Baroque but of the society which produced it and which it only imperfectly conceals. And at the heart of this society lay bitter despair."[220]

PART THREE

NOW

POTHOLES IN MANHATTAN

"Innovation has slowed down since the 1970s"
—Michael Greenstone, Chief Economist,
MIT (2011 TV interview)

*"After the worst economic downturn in 80 years, which
continues to cause immense hardship, the prospects for
the U.S. economy are the most complex and uncertain in
my adult lifetime"*
—ex U.S. Treasury Secretary Robert Rubin, 2010[221]

D RIVING NORTH THROUGH Manhattan on a pot-holed road leading toward Columbia University campus in late 2006 I could not help but to notice an enormous advertising sign hanging over a rather decrepit neighborhood. "Luxury apartments", it read, "2-4 bedrooms, $4 million to $8 million". It didn't take a math genius to figure out that the developer was asking for $2 million *per bedroom* to live in this rather unsavory, but presumably gentrifying, neighborhood—a place I would associate with high likelihood of being mugged rather than any type of luxury. I drove on, wondering who could afford to buy these apartments. Definitely not the neighborhood folk—looking at these small shopkeepers, trinket peddlers and youngsters from the 'hood, hanging around, I could not imagine them making enough money during an entire working life to afford even a smallest apartment there—unless they dealt in drugs or became celebrity rappers or ball players. These, increasingly, were the only 'career avenues' for many poor kids, in a reality where increasingly life's success depended on chance and lucky break, rather than hard work and following society's rules. Education, even if it could be afforded, did not guarantee not only success, but even a job.

While this glaring sign of a fully polarized society of our new Baroque was there for all to see, one would be hard pressed to find in this Manhattan a street with the 'normal', middle class people that still, reportedly, used to live there in the 1960s, when an Upper East Side co-op apartment would cost just $60,000, or 11 years of average wages. Today, when it costs 50 or even 100 years of average wages, these people have all been squeezed out into the suburbs, or simply turned into paupers, living in slums.

One of the key similarities between the last Baroque and the one we are entering now is the decline of the middle class, a decline driven by stagnant or falling real incomes, loss of benefits, longer and harder work and increasingly frequent underemployment or even unemployment, all in face of massive inflation of daily living costs. In October 2012, reported CNN, the lowest fifth of Americans earned only $10,000 a year on the average; yet they were spending double that, generally on daily necessities. How was this possible? These new *miserables* lived off savings, borrowing, help from family and friends, tips or perhaps undeclared labor.

Across the post-industrial world, caught between these forgotten *miserables* and the rich who were getting richer by the hour, the middle class was in a uniquely vulnerable position. Since middle class people typically did not have significant financial assets, they had to rely on jobs in order to survive. "Most people continue to rely on wage and salary income to live," stated *Business Week* in 1996, "and wage and salary income is stagnant and growing more unequal. All this suggests an epic shift in bargaining power from labor to capital. That is hardly surprising, given America's slow growth, high immigration, higher-than-acknowledged unemployment, and a shift to part-time, contract, and temporary labor."[222]

The U.S. were not alone in its decline of the ordinary working people: by 2011, British families were falling ever further behind, crippled by inflation. Mervyn King, Governor of the Bank of England "painted a picture of the nightmare facing millions of workers because of the toxic combination of soaring inflation and pay freezes or paltry pay rises" stated *Daily Mail*. "It is hardly surprising that unhappiness describes the reaction of many" said Mr. King. "One has to go back to the 1920s to find a time when real wages fell over the period of six years".[223] In fact, in most developed economies, real wages of the majority stopped growing in the 1970s, four decades ago. In 2012 USA, reported *MSN Money*, median annual wage per employee was only $26,364, meaning half of all Americans made less than this poverty-level wage[224]. In 2012 France, half of the population earned less than E19,000 a year, also effectively a poverty-level wage.

The gap between earnings and basic living costs was reaching crisis proportions. In Italy, where most young people who could find a job were only making around E1000 a month, in big cities like Rome or Milan, average apartment rent reached E1200 a month, effectively preventing them from being able to have a home of their own. For those that managed to rent, many fell behind in payments, with hundreds being thrown out onto the street every week across the country in a growing trend of misery. In Spain, since the crisis started in 2007, 400,000 families—over a million people—have been kicked out of their homes because they couldn't pay their bills.

Since the Baroque Syndrome set in, the middle class was being hit by a double whammy of elusive and insecure jobs and rapidly rising costs of daily basics. In terms of job loss and job insecurity, the middle class seemed to be the primary victim of globalization. By 2006, argued *The Economist*, "The headwinds of the global economy are being felt less by Americans at the bottom than by those in the middle. The jobs threatened by outsourcing—data processing, accounting and so on—are white-collar jobs; the jobs done by the poor—cleaning and table waiting, for example—could never be done from Bangalore."

Or couldn't they? Torrent of low-wage immigrants into countries like the U.S. and the UK solved this problem and kept steady downward pressure on most service-sector wages. "In sentencing Cao, U.S. District Judge Ericson said the scheme [to use several thousand Mexican illegals in Chinese restaurants across the American Midwest, paying them around $2/hour] was an especially 'destructive conspiracy' that amounted to modern-day 'slave labor' and treated the illegal immigrants like animals[225]." A virtual slave-trade using illegals was also operating in Britain, warned British police. Low-cost outsourcing, it seemed, could be complemented by low-cost in-sourcing of quasi-slave labour. [226]

Across all developed countries—outside of the bloated and so far sheltered government sector—almost all middle class jobs seemed to be at risk. By 2011, even the German specialized hi-tech industries were no longer immune to cheap Asian competition. After overtaking Germany in 2009 as the world's largest exporter—China was ready for an all-out assault on Germany in the country's key industrial strength areas, like precision machinery. At the onset of the second decade of the new century—starting virtually from zero just two decades ago—Chinese technology in key areas such as power generation, transmission, solar and wind technology, telecommunication equipment, and high-speed trains was already world-class. Now the battle was moving into areas such as cars, construction machinery, computers, home electronics, electrical engineering and machine tools. In mechanical engineering—an area employing almost a million people in Germany, China has already taken a lead. In mere two years after exceeding German turnover in this area, China's turnover was double that of Germany's.[227] In 2012 Chinese firm Lenovo took the lead as the biggest manufacturer of laptops in the world.

The risk to post-industrial countries was not only the prospective loss of jobs, but also of critical skills. In the acclaimed 'green technology' area, Silicon Valley companies—many with most of their manufacturing already in Asia—were considering moving their R&D to Asia as well. U.S. universities were still leading in research, but most of the jobs resulting from their various innovations were being created in Asia, with places like India and China transitioning to hi-tech manufacturing. Silicon Valley, while still better off than most of the U.S., was creating jobs only at a very sluggish pace. According to Russell Hancock, president of Silicon Valley association of businesses, "high costs are likely to prevent even the top tech companies from hiring many more people locally". Michael Moritz, a partner in large venture capital company, Sequoia Capital, agreed. "High value products are still going to emanate from the US—but these companies are not going to employ of lot of people here" said Mr. Moritz.[228]

The bottom line? During the last two or three decades the driving idea of 'post-industrial' economies was that high-margin jobs of inventing, designing, financing or insuring goods could still be kept in the post-industrial countries, while low-margin jobs of producing these goods could be pushed to China and India. By 2011 it was clear that this idea was no longer viable. Every year, more and more high-margin activities were being outsourced to where the labor was cheaper and growth more buoyant. This was really bad news for the middle class, as its safe zone of higher-value jobs was continuously being eroded. As outsourcing took more and more white-collar occupations—financial and legal research, accounting, R&D, chip design, programming—to low-wage locales, Linda Levine of the Congressional Research Service anticipated that perhaps additional three and a half million American jobs would be lost by 2015 to low-wage outsourcing[229].

Is there some miraculous solution to this problem? "We really have to get back to building things. We can't just design things" says John S. Brown, ex-head of Xerox Silicon Valley research center,[230] as the post-industrial unraveling began to truly bite. But it is doubtful that building things again in America is really a long-term solution, unless American wages, benefits, working conditions and the regulatory regime immediately converge down to the levels prevalent in China and India.

Thousands of top-educated Westerners are now looking for jobs in the emerging markets and unemployed college grads in Italy, Portugal or Ireland are talking about immigration—sometimes to fast-growing places like Mozambique—as the only solution. Global jobs market is already here.

In the meantime—short of robotic advances that would fully offset the edge of cheap Asian labor not only in manufacturing but also in services that can be operated remotely—American and German skills, technology and know-how have been percolating outside. It was a process very similar to the one that began in Italy during the Renaissance and led to the total de-industrialization of the country during the Baroque. Today, total de-industrialization of America and other post-industrial countries—perhaps other than for luxury branded goods with the cachet of being manufactured in a specific location—is becoming a distinct possibility. If this was to be the future, what were the family prospects of the middle class parents that failed to secure expensive elite education and secure for their children the eternal Baroque careers as doctors, bankers, lawyers and the like, leading eventually—same as before—to the charmed *rentier* life?

*

"Long term joblessness is especially sinister . . . it is unprecedented to have [44 percent of all unemployed in the US] without a job for more than a year. Meanwhile, a quiet cultural crisis brews as one out of five American men stop collecting paychecks—getting by instead on unemployment or disability checks, the incomes of friends and family, and in some cases illicit activity."

—Nina Easton, Fortune magazine, 2011 [231]

WHEN DECLINING OR flat incomes of the last few decades combined with soaring costs for education, medical care, and real estate—and, for the poorer of them, also transport and food—the middle classes were increasingly unable to save. Consequently, they needed the Social Security net more than ever. However, this net was failing just as middle-income jobs were growing scarcer, and unemployment spells more frequent. Free education, Medicare, and old-age security—the gains of the Industrial Era—were fast becoming luxuries that our society (now increasingly translated as "the market") could seemingly no longer afford. The hyped objective of self-financed retirement seemed totally unrealistic. Since the average American family had only $1,000 in net financial assets, household consumption would have to be cut dramatically, and the savings rate rise from the current level—zero—to over 30 percent, in order to even approach the objective. [232]

Same as during the last Baroque, ours was—and is—the era of asset bubbles. By 2005, a credit bubble had followed the InfoTech bubble. America's artificially low interest rates and resulting soaring house prices compelled those who could barely afford it to buy real estate *defensively*—the prospect of continuous property appreciation drove people to buying homes almost at any price since owning property seemed the only hope for future financial survival. In 2005, 43 percent of all first-time homebuyers took out a 100-percent mortgage; equity extraction by U.S. homeowners topped $600 billion in 2004 alone.[233] By 2007, reliance on equity extraction to support consumer spending (instead of rising salary income) produced predictable results with the subprime crisis that cost the U.S. financial institutions—read U.S. taxpayers—hundreds of billions, if not trillions of dollars in losses.

By fall of 2008, the credit and property bubble unraveled in a truly Baroque fashion, reminiscent of the South Sea Bubble of 18th century France. Banks were faltering, stock markets were crashing, inflation and unemployment were rising, as the mountains of debt that powered the growth of the preceding two decades began to rapidly unravel. In the U.S., wildly accelerating inflation swung within a few short months into a massive deflation. Sixty percent of Americans interviewed during these months believed that a depression, with accompanying mass unemployment, hunger and homelessness, was a real possibility. A mere nine percent, the lowest percentage ever, was happy with their reality.

As in other Baroque periods, combination of growing populations and static energy system produced high inflation. General inflation, very high in the 70s and early 80s, has since decreased in the 1990s, partly due to 'policy recessions' that kept wages in check, partly because increasingly, industrial goods (and Green Revolution-based food) were produced in low-wage countries, keeping prices down. However, costs of other necessities—those that could not be cheaply manufactured offshore, things like housing, health care, and education—kept soaring. Since around 2005, food and energy prices began to again dramatically rise. This was due to many factors: sky-rocketing petroleum costs, increasing costs of production across the globe and dollar devaluation. Inflation—running well ahead of wages and artificially low interest rates—became again one of key concerns of average Americans and Europeans.

We got used to inflation, but when looked at from a perspective of even a few decades—again, you might have guessed, the last 40 years or so!—inflation we've seen during that short time is stunning, significantly in excess of what Renaissance and Baroque experienced over a couple of centuries. In 1967, one could spend a night at the New York's Plaza Hotel for $30 a night and rent a Manhattan loft for $125 a month, while average U.S. monthly wage was $434[234] and average household income $7300 per year. How about daily consumables? Gas was 33 U.S. cents a gallon, a burger cost 18 cents, a dozen eggs 49 cents. A cheap paperback book might cost 25 cents, a pack of cigarettes 30 cents. A barrel of oil was $2. An ounce of gold cost $35. An average new car would cost $2,750 and an average new house $14,250. Dow Jones Industrial Average was 905.

By 2010, average U.S. monthly wage was $3472,[235] and average annual household income $46,200, an increase of 8 and 6 times respectively. But almost all prices on our list inflated by much higher factors: 20 and 28 times respectively for the New York hotel and loft; 12, 16, 6, 30, 15 respectively for basic goods from gasoline to eggs to cigarettes. This means that measured against our wages and incomes, only eggs cost the same as in 1967, all other basic goods are much pricier. Oil and gold underwent a massive rise: 45 and 48 times respectively. Average car prices increased by a factor of 11 and average U.S. house prices by a factor of 19, roughly triple their cost in 1967, compared to average income. Massive inflation in all the basic yardsticks—not only in housing, energy, food and gold but even in prices of manufactured goods like cars—suggest that average real household incomes are in all likelihood already significantly lower today than they were in the 1960s. Direct comparisons like this belie official inflation figures, full of arbitrary downward adjustments for trivial improvements and reliant on arbitrarily chosen 'baskets'.

Importantly, the incredible inflation over a relatively short period of less than 50 years—a drama of declining real incomes and skyrocketing prices—paints a dramatic picture of an economic system in trouble, unable to deliver 'more bang for the buck'. A system unable to deliver more goods relative to the effort and the labor being put into it, a system that seems essentially less and less productive, if the comparison of income from labor to prices was to be relied on.

As in the last Baroque, costs increased fastest in real estate, energy and food, but also in professional services. Between 1980 and 2000 alone, real per-person cost of healthcare in the U.S. more than doubled.[236] The number of people working in the medical field tripled since the 1970s, to about 10 percent of all Americans employed. In the early '90s, the growth of health-care costs was so spectacular, it was estimated that if these growth rates were sustained, they would eventually consume *all* of America's GDP. According to many studies, soaring health costs were one of the biggest factors that made U.S. firms push their workers into temp or contingent jobs, to avoid paying the outrageous health care prices. By 2006, according to Fidelity Investments, a 65-year-old couple retiring without a company-sponsored health plan had to set aside an average $200,000 just to pay for health-care costs in retirement.[237]

Yet skyrocketing costs of medical care and soaring incomes of medical professionals (and malpractice lawyers feeding on them) did not translate into equally dramatic gains in health of the population at large. On the contrary, the solid gains brought by the Industrial Era began to tail off. Even as expenditures for health care grew, in constant dollars, by 2100 percent between the 1950s and 1990s, life expectancy at birth (which soared by 58 percent between 1900 and 1985) only grew by 3.5 percent in total between 1985 and 2002—at an annual rate three or four times slower than before[238]. As poverty and inequality in healthcare access increased, the U.S. infant mortality rate began to go back up—an unprecedented development. Between 2000 and 2005, it had risen to the level of some developing Asian countries.[239] Life expectancy for U.S. whites without a high school diploma, once the backbone of the middle class, has dropped faster than for other groups, in large part because they could not afford health care. It declined from the average of 70.5 years to 67.5 years.

This was unsurprising, considering the impoverishment of most people during the recent decades, in an eerie mirror of the Baroque records. Same as during the Renaissance, the trend to push down wages went across all industries. Privatization fuelled a search for profits in privatized public companies, but—same as during the Renaissance and the Baroque eras—this wasn't good for workers. The Chicago Institute on Urban Poverty, comparing the wages and benefits of Chicago city employees against those of contract employees for low-skill jobs, found that privatization led to 25–to 46-percent compensation losses for entry level workers.

*

FOR THE FIRST time in the country's history, the American middle class began to shrink. In 1990, the U.S. Census Bureau showed that the number of Americans classified as middle-class had dropped from 71 percent of the population in 1969 to less than 63 percent.[240] By 2007, as decline accelerated, it has dropped to 44 percent.[241] Very few of these ex-middle-class people (statistically, virtually none) joined the ranks of the rich. Despite all the New Economy hype, even though the rich were now more numerous and much richer, their numbers—in percentage terms—have hardly grown. Instead—same as during the Renaissance—the shrinkage of the middle class was closely balanced by simultaneous growth in the numbers of the new poor and near-poor. They grew from around 15 percent of the population in the 1970s[242] to around half of all Americans in 2011.

In a process reminiscent of all historical declines, the middle class, it seemed, was slowly reverting back into paupers.

ROSA LEE AND THE IMMERSIVE BRAND TEMPLES

"Floating 50 metres off shore, the "island" designed by Peter Marino, can be entered via a 33-metre underwater tunnel lined with fine art and has its own jetty. There is a terrace in the style of a yacht's deck, sweeping floor-to-ceiling windows, and a dramatic hub with an 11-metre high pointed ceiling. Sailing ships' masts hang in the air. Marina Bay Sands [new LV shop in Singapore] is the latest of what Louis Vuitton calls its Maison concept, a select breed of giant "immersive brand temples". It is also an example of the recent explosion in the retail spending of luxury brands."

—Lucie Greene, Financial Times, 2011[243]

A S THE SUMMER of 2005 arrived, many well-heeled New Yorkers began to think about heading to the Hamptons, the luxury beach area a couple of hours drive from the city. "This year, however, some will need diamond-encrusted heels," reported one newspaper. "Fat Wall Street bonuses, roaring property prices, and a few foreigners taking advantage of the sick-looking U.S. dollar mean that summer beachfront rentals at the hyper-luxury end of the market show signs of heading into the stratosphere.[244]" *Forbes Magazine* provided the context of the roaring real estate market: "The rich had a good year" in 2004, the magazine said, with a certain understatement. Within that single year, the number of U.S. billionaires climbed from 587 to 691; their collective wealth increased by $300 billion, to a grand total of $2.2 trillion[245].

And this trend was not limited to the U.S.: In Australia, the number of billionaires rose by more than half in 2004 alone. On the back of the commodities boom, the fortunes of people like Ken Talbot, CEO of Macarthur Coal, went up by 500 percent, and the net worth of Lakshmi Mittal, owner of world's largest steel company, shot up by almost $19 billion to a new high of $25 billion.[246]

By March 2006, the number of world's billionaires had hit 793, their total net worth $2.6 trillion. Very few of the new arrivals made their billions by inventing anything new. Three people turned into billionaires overnight when their online gambling site, PartyGaming, went public in London in June 2005; Canadian playboy Calvin Ayre also become a billionaire from his Costa Rica-based Internet gambling site, even as most of his revenue came from the U.S., where online gambling was illegal. Others included people like Bernard Arnault, head of the luxury brands company LVMH (Louis Vuitton and Dom Perignon, among others); and Roman Abramovich, a Russian oil baron.[247]

The millionaires were following close behind. Again, as with all the other trends, this trend also started in the 1970s: In 1988, 1.3 million people in the U.S. had incomes of over $1million a year, up from a mere 180,000 in 1972.[248] Between 1998 and 2005—in just seven years—the number of the world's millionaires soared by 60 percent, to 8.3 million individuals, who together owned over $30 trillion in investable assets. But what stunned the analysts was that as the gap between the haves and the have-nots was widening fast, so was the gap between the merely affluent (those with assets between $1 million and $5 million) and the truly rich (those with assets over $5 million per household). The latter, while numbering less than 800,000 of American households, owned a staggering $21 trillion, an average $28 million per family[249]. In Manhattan, hotels promoted slumber parties aimed at the burgeoning market of rich teenagers: $1500 a night would get a room, facials and massages—the works—to unwind after a hard week at school. In this radically new cultural landscape, even the relatively well off could feel that they were being left way behind: "An acquaintance who earns $100,000 a year feels he's treated like dirt by many around him [in his posh suburb]," reported a New York-based Chinese journalist[250].

Within a mere quarter century, America's cultural landscape had changed beyond recognition. On the one end, the growth of the richest family fortunes was stunning. The concentration of wealth in the U.S. was flat from 1963 to 1983, when it began to widen dramatically. Between 1986 and 2004, less than 20 years, the number of billionaires soared, from 26 families[251] to 691, an increase of 2600 percent—a growth statistic beyond anything remotely comparable in the world economy. By the mid-1990s, the share of society's wealth held by the top one percent had doubled compared to 1975.[252] By 1996, the top five percent of U.S. households owned 77 percent of all equity holdings, and the top 10 percent owned *90 percent* of them[253]. The wealth concentration statistics were stunning, reminiscent of the deep Baroque. Equally Baroque was the social landscape that began to emerge to fit the evolving socioeconomic picture.

On the bottom end of the social scale, in Washington, D.C.—where by 1995 a full one-quarter of the population was comprised of lawyers, lobbyists, and government officials—most of the other three fourths of citizens had already been transformed into the eerily timeless urban underclass of paupers. One such American was Rosa Lee, a woman who had eight children through five different men. She had first gotten pregnant at the age of 14. In 1994, she was receiving around $400 a month in welfare, giving much of it to her kids so they could buy crack. When the dealers came around demanding money, Rosa Lee would go shopping. She ended up in jail a dozen times on shoplifting charges.[254]

There were many Rosa Lees in America now, and a sense of total bewilderment would have greeted any Information-Society citizen who inadvertently detoured into the vast slums of America where the Rosa Lees lived—especially those in the nation's capital. Full of potholes and rusted-out cars, it was a parallel universe in which

42 percent of young black males were either in prison or wanted by police, and the leading cause of death was murder.[255] Entering that part of Washington was like entering a different dimension, one untouched by education and the polite society of the government and banking institutions a few streets away.

This was a world where millions of poor Americans were incarcerated and millions of others were homeless. By 2004, it was estimated 3.5 million Americans, one third of them children—just like the vagabonds of the Baroque—were likely to be homeless in any given year.[256] Congressman Henry Gonzalez stated: "we have made American nomads in their own land . . . [there are] families roaming this land, some of them living in cars and under bridges" [257] As the society polarized, the old cohesion of goals, mindsets, and lifestyles that had characterized American society from its inception well into the 1960s, just vanished. It gave way to self-focused goals, mindsets, and lifestyles, which were mirrored—equally significantly—in an increasingly shorter and narrower sense of vision. On the parts of both individuals and governments, long-range thinking gave way to a quarter-by-quarter forecast. Gradually, as in previous Baroques, the ever-narrower, ever-shorter, ever-more-fragmented, ever-more-self-centered vision became the norm, at every level. In Kalaska, Michigan, a retirement haven, elderly voters voted to cut school budgets to divert funds to activities that they deemed more important, such as snow plowing. They refused to approve funds allowing local schools to stay open until the end of the school year. As the result, schools closed months early, and some children missed as much as a full year of schooling. Analysts believed that this had happened because these retirees lived away from their own grandchildren and did not much care about the grandchildren of others or, indeed, about the future of their own society. [258]

As documented in previous similar decline periods, diminishing rewards from ordinary work and widening wealth gaps were increasingly eroding traditional middle-class values. "There's a fraying of moral responsibility in this country," said Mark Bernstein, professor at Purdue University, in the aftermath of hurricane Katrina in 2005. "I've had students telling me that looting TVs is permissible because these people see others a few blocks away who are more affluent and it is understandable they want the same things."[259]

And as the society fragmented, it seemed that a radically new time had dawned, leading us into an uncharted landscape.

Just like during the last Baroque, in our post-industrial Information Era, the urban decay and corruption seemed entrenched everywhere. In Philadelphia during the "Roaring Nineties" information technology boom, the "Wall Street Journal" painted a truly Baroque picture of the city, full of human detritus, corruption and decay: "apathetic residents in ethnic and blue collar neighborhoods tolerate corrupt judges, police and politicians. As is true in many decaying cities, litter and potholes are everywhere. People sleep on sidewalks. The stench of urine and human feces often permeates downtown streets, subway tunnels, and even City Hall . . . . Philadelphia is already teetering on the brink of bankruptcy. Its entrenched municipal bureaucracy consumes an enormous percentage of general funds . . . ." Washington, D.C. suffered one of the most "corrupt and incompetent governments outside of the Third World . . . It costs eleven thousand dollars in administrative expenses for each welfare case to be processed[260]. The "Economist" echoed the gloom: in 2010 New Jersey, "corruption is rampant at [all] levels . . . Public-sector projects are notoriously wasteful. Patronage pads the payroll. Public-sector unions have won billions in outlandish benefits and wages . . ." [261]

From New York to Munich, from Brussels to Osaka, a 2010 traveler visiting the once-rich countries of our new Baroque would only have to look into the faces of the people, low-wage locals and immigrants alike, in the local train station's McDonald to see creeping impoverishment, constant financial worry, and privation. Beggars and homeless seemed to populate every street corner, but their numbers were dwarfed by the millions of the much less visible near-poor. In 2006 Orange County, California, reported one newspaper, "on small streets behind strip malls and fast-food restaurants, families, sometimes two of them, cram into small, aging bungalows. What look like tourist motels along Beach Boulevard are mostly filled by working families and single people who stay for months or years, paying high weekly fees but unable to muster upfront [deposit] money for an apartment rental." The previous year, in Orange County alone, close to a quarter million of the poor and near-poor received food donations from local charities.[262]

By the dawn of the 21st century, America had emerged as a Baroque-like landscape virtually unrecognizable to someone from Kennedy's era. It was now a society firmly polarized: two ends of a stick, Louis Vuitton shoppers on the one end, Rosa Lees on the other. On the one extreme there were the new destitute and half-literate, accounting for up to 30 percent of the population, without any assets whatsoever. On the other extreme was the super-rich one percent of the population.

In a development unseen since the last Baroque, the growing inequality *itself* became a driver of change, as profits realized from the lower wages and reduced benefits of many, plus outsourcing of jobs to the Third World, allowed top executives to amass spectacular fortunes that much faster and indulge in conspicuous luxury spending. Over the last few decades, Citibank's 'plutonomy' world has indeed become our reality. Demand for mansions, yachts, supercars, art, private jets, designer goods began driving spectacular growth of few select industries. Today's luxury spending trend mirrored exactly the societal and spending evolution experienced during the Renaissance and the Baroque, eras of conspicuous luxury consumption by the new financial aristocracy.

Spectacular growth of private fortunes and explosion of luxury industries were not the only similarities between the original Renaissance and our own. Similar to the investors of Renaissance and the Baroque, most of today's cost-cutting and investment-aggregating CEOs invented little new—their 'added value' was to cut labor and tax costs, outsource production to cheaper locales, expand operations overseas where growth was high and labor cheap, optimize returns on investments by introducing latest IT technologies or management techniques into inefficient subsidiaries, merge investments for volume cost-savings, correctly anticipate market trends, and tax-optimize (read: tax-exempt) their business. Spectacular growth of the private equity industry—an industry that institutionalized this cost-cutting, merging, and optimizing activity—and its growing importance in our business reality, seemed to again point to how similar our era was to the late Renaissance—the era that was so deeply reliant on investment, financial wizardry and efficiency.

Between the two extremes of wealth was the middle-class. Even though it was rapidly shrinking, with more and more of its members drifting into poverty, it still accounted for a large percentage—now 44 percent, instead of 71 percent a generation earlier—of America's population. It was no longer the leading force of the society. It was now the ever-shrinking, ever-scared of a financial downfall, hapless mass of individuals, terrorized by downsizing rumors, mortgage rates, home values, dropping incomes, "war-on-terror" alarms, bleak retirement prospects and even bleaker future for their kids. Typically, they had no financial assets. Their only possession was their family home.

While their only dream was to join the ranks of "the working rich"—the lawyers, doctors, bankers, corporate executives, or—the ultimate dream—sports and entertainment 'celebs' whose orgiastic lifestyles and over-the-top consumption were daily portrayed on TV, the middle class was now also terrorized by another, once-inconceivable, threat. This ominous warning was articulated by the journalist who brought Rosa Lee's story to light. "Rosa Lee's desperate existence" he wrote, "is the sort of fate that might befall anyone born outside of the narrow sphere of privilege".[263]

When social historians Bennett Harrison and Barry Bluestone ventured to describe the internal divisions of our new Service Economy, it was stunning how simple the relationship between the 'information elite' and those that served them has become and how it could just as easily apply to the previous Baroque: "The upper tier of the labor market includes the managers, lawyers, accountants, bankers, business consultants, and other technically trained people whose daily duties lie at the heart of the control and co-ordination of the global corporation and the corporate services that are clearly linked to them . . . At the bottom of the labor market is the other, less fortunate, pool of urban residents whose collective function is to provide services to the workers in the upper tier . . . They are the ones who wait tables, cook meals, sell everything from office supplies to clothing, change bed and bath linen in the dozens of new hotels, provide custodial service and child care and find lower-level employment in the city's hospitals, health clinics, schools, and municipal government itself."[264]

For the first time in centuries, maybe millennia, the physical reality itself began to diverge. Even outside of urban slums, two radically different landscapes were shaping up. Never seen before, private fortresses reminiscent of the declining Roman Empire began to appear in "Information Era" America. Many mansions or walled enclaves came to resemble regular castles, complete with 12-inch windows, 12-foot fences, security cameras, and motion detectors.[265] In some places, automatic gate defenses were programmed to shoot projectiles into the undercarriage of vehicles forcing the gates. By 1995, already three to four million people across the U.S. lived in walled towns[266] and the numbers were rapidly growing. In California, expenditure for private security forces outspent public law enforcement by 73 percent, and employed two and a half times as many people; private security ranked among the top ten fastest-growing industries in America.[267]

The people who could afford such security, the new information nobles—or, as ex-Secretary of Labor Robert Reich called them, the "symbolic analysts"—would, in Reich's words, "withdraw into ever more isolated enclaves, within which they will pool their resources rather than share them with other Americans or invest them in ways that improve other Americans' productivity. An even smaller proportion of their income will be taxed and thence redistributed or invested on behalf of the rest of the public. Distinguished from the rest of the population by their global linkages, good schools, comfortable lifestyles, excellent health care, and abundance of security guards, symbolic analysts will complete their secession from the union. The townships and urban enclaves where they reside, and the symbolic-analytical zones where they work, will bear no resemblance to the rest of America."[268]

Why should we worry about all this? One might argue—and many do—that this is how the society should be, that the welfare system and equality of the past century was an irrational period that disincentivized creativity and business acumen. However, there is no historical proof to this argument. On the contrary, both GDP and productivity growth were higher before the New Renaissance has set in around 1970; the underlying economies were unquestionably healthier. The key reason we need to worry about the trends that we call the Baroque Syndrome is that—without exception—these trends that we witness today bear such uncanny resemblance to the trends that always accompanied every collapse of every civilization.

Across all the ages of mankind and all of its civilizations, from Egypt to Greece to Rome to China and the Maya country, the hallmarks of decline were always the same.

AGE OF THE WIZARD

"Germany is increasingly getting a lower class, which it has not had for many decades, a growing class of people who do not expect to work—ever,"
—Dieter Wermuth, German economist, 2005[269]

"The current UK depression will be the longest since at least the first world war. Without a dramatic surge in output, it is also quite likely to generate a bigger cumulative loss of output than the [1930s] "great depression". All this is disturbing enough. What is even more disturbing is the near universal view that almost nothing can be done to change the prognosis."
—Martin Wolf, Financial Times, 2011 [270]

MUNICH IS ONE of the richest cities in Europe, yet as I walk from my hotel close to the city's central train station toward the old town square along the Prielmayerstrasse, I'd be really hard pressed to find much evidence of it. Beggars sleep on air-conditioning vents; crowds of tough-looking immigrant youths mill around; shabbily-dressed couples with prams and children in tow drag by, misery and worry written in their faces. Meal prices in the nearby KFC seem unaffordably high. Across all of Europe, high costs, exorbitant taxes, and high unemployment combine to create a depressing malaise sometimes referred to as "euro-sclerosis"—a condition marked by virtually no growth, cynicism, feeling of being at a dead end, and growing black market in which both the unemployed and illegal immigrants do odd jobs for cash. Unemployment in

Europe is still rising, and is now at record level. The economic sentiment is the worst since recession began, with growing apathy and disillusionment. Chances to find a job are abysmal.

Over the past two decades, only around two thirds of working-age people in Europe were officially employed, including the part-timers[271]; the rest were collecting some sort of state subsidy, whether it was called unemployment, welfare, early pension, or some other form of support. In Holland, fifteen percent of all working-age people were receiving government disability payments, even though very few were really disabled.[272] France's official jobless rate in early 2005 was ten percent—with the giant public sector dominating employment—but jobless rate among those below 25 was around 70 percent. For those aged above 55, it was around 60 percent.[273] The cost of supporting these people and providing various state subsidies to almost a third of Europe's population was enormous: Europe's welfare net, including social security, unemployment compensation, pensions, and medical insurance amounted to around 40 percent of the GDP of the European countries.[274] To this burden add the huge and growing number of civil servants: In Spain, the number of public employees has risen by a third in the decade to 2010.

All these costs were increasingly financed by debt. It was just a question of when either the governments would go bust or benefits were cut and the unemployed and the disabled left to fend off for themselves.

Even though my Munich trip was in 2010, one of Germany's best years in decades, the country's recent recovery from its long malaise was still tenuous. It had nothing to do with information era, or any new technologies. Instead, it came to depend almost exclusively on exporting to the fast-growing and newly-affluent Asia and other BRIC economies the traditional German high-quality mechanical products: luxury BMW, Mercedes and Audi cars, Siemens turbines, precision tools. Domestic consumers in Germany would hardly buy anything. Europe's old hopes—socialism, equality, safety net, and most importantly—the old democratic idea that their votes still count and that changing the government can somehow make a difference—were all in the dustbin and wages were constantly under pressure. The faces I looked into seem to say that the world has changed and there is no longer any hope for them or their children. And that they—the impoverished members of what once used to be the middle class—with their opinions, their democracy and their prams—no longer matter. Their era—the era of western middle class—is now past. Now is the age of China and India and Brazil, places supplying cheap goods and commodities to the world, and to their inhabitants a catch-up process to perhaps slightly discounted local versions of the old American 'consumer dream' of the previous century. What lies beyond this, nobody even wants to venture. This is clearly as far away from any "Third Wave" as one could possibly be.

The mantra of the magical New Economy that took hold in the 1990s was that success was no longer likely to be achieved by hard work, saving, and playing by the rules—all those boring precepts that the middle classes had had drilled into them for generations. Instead, in the Age of Wizard wealth came much faster, and in much greater quantity, but only to a select few. It came with some special knowledge, unique talent, a secret, an Ivy League diploma, or perhaps just a lucky break in Hollywood or in the arena. The quick fortunes and glamorous lifestyles of the InfoTech wizards, financial gurus, and entertainment celebs became the icons of the new era, deeply embedded in the popular psyche and, increasingly, in life objectives and behaviors.

The typical feature of all Baroques was translating of inflating elite incomes into positional goods—Ivy League diplomas, luxury real estate in top locales, membership of guild-like professional associations setting their own fees, decision-maker positions in government or large corporations giving access to power and bribe money. The soaring compensations of the elite members were enough to enable many to get such positional goods, from which all lower and middle

classes were becoming clearly excluded. In order to acquire such
assets and create vast fortunes fast, the elites needed not just huge
incomes, ideally tax-free—which the New Economy mantras and its
ethics enabled them to get—but also to invest in assets that would
appreciate well ahead of general inflation. They needed tax-free
realities and a reality of massive asset inflation, and an environment
highly conducive to financial speculation. And this is exactly what
they got.

In a clear reversal of the 50s and 60s trends, all the requirements
for allowing the rich to leave the rest behind appeared. Taxes for high
income earners were cut heavily and repeatedly, and increasingly
shifted to 'poor taxes': sales and social security taxes. Many top
income earners positioned themselves to pay little or no taxes;
progressive taxation effectively disappeared in the last three
decades. Assets skyrocketed in value, by virtue of scarcity in the
overcrowded world, by virtue of income from them being increasingly
tax-exempt, but also by virtue of leveraging. In real estate—except
for crisis periods—one could realize maybe 50 or even 100 percent
per year capital gains, if the asset was highly leveraged, at relatively
low risk. For those that were not afraid of risk, as economies grew
highly erratic, there was plenty of room for financial speculation in
risky stocks, derivatives, or commodities. While the tax exemptions
that facilitated quick buildup of fortunes were the result of deliberate
political actions of neo-conservative governments, the rollercoaster
economies, speculation, and asset inflation seemed just the part of a
classic late stage of a typical decline cycle of complex societies.

As with the soaring professional incomes and numbers of
millionaires and billionaires, the 70s seemed the key takeoff point.
In the 50s and the 60s, price increases, wages, interest rates, and
returns on assets moved generally in line. Returns on assets—whether
stock market, bonds, or real estate—were unspectacular. Yet as
inflation began to build up—and fell hard on most people—it benefited
the rich, who spent proportionately less on daily consumption, but

whose assets: real estate, money funds, or oil stocks, now were worth much more. This again mirrored exactly the Baroque trends, when the rich could and would typically invest as much as 70 percent of their annual income to grow their assets.

Real estate inflation, while squeezing millions of new entrants through skyrocketing property prices and mortgage costs—and burdening the society with heavy debts for the future—was a builder of many a fortune. The landmark example was Hong Kong (sometimes described as a 'real estate-driven economy'), where 7 million population, squeezed by property prices which increased by 70 percent between 2009 and 2012, was boiling with anger. The fury was directed at the cozy relationship between property developers and the government which drove property prices sky-high, while lining both the developers and the government's pockets. Average wages remained flat, yet ordinary people now had to spend half of their incomes on housing, up from a third just a few years earlier. Perhaps 60 percent of the population lived in what could only be described as state-subsidized slums, and stunning levels of inequality were generating anger, as the collusion of a small elite of property developers and civil servants were 'sucking up people's income'.[275]

Never forecasted in the "Third Wave", by 2000, property prices in some top cities like New York, London, Paris, Tokyo, Sydney, Vancouver, Bombay, or Hong Kong, rose by up to 50 times from their 1970 level. Between 1997 and 2005 alone, U.S. median home prices have gone up by more than 69 percent, buoyed by tax-free status and record low interest rates.[276] By September 2005, when abandoned paupers of New Orleans were dying in the wake of hurricane Katrina, prices of San Francisco properties located in the Golden Gate Bridge area reached an average of US$2.7 million[277], price of an average Manhattan apartment hit $1.4 million[278] and apartments in fancy tower planned for 80, South Street were priced starting at $29 million[279]. On the outskirts of Beijing, developers were offering fancy Baroque-style mansions, starting at 100 million yuan (around $12 million).

Stock market growth mirrored rises in property assets. Freed from social contracts to their workers, making them work harder, longer and for less, removing benefits and laying off frequently to push productivity up and wages down, dazzling investors with improving profits or merger stories, companies composing NYSE pushed the index to 11,000 by 1999—eleven times its 1968 level, and with re-invested dividends and in best selected stocks, much higher.

The rampant inflation in cost and yield of all positional assets—from top real estate to top academic titles to top jobs—typical for all decline cycles but mostly absent from macroeconomic formulas or inflation statistics, became one of the keys to understanding the last three decades. As forex and other markets deregulated, speculative money could be made (or lost) on rollercoaster of metals, commodities, and currency prices. Oil, gold, silver, coffee, dollar, pound and yen—and by 2008-2011 even basic commodities like rice or sugar—all experienced phenomenal volatility. They made a fortune for many, even as rising costs of basics and flat incomes made the misery of everybody else.

The paradigm shift became clearly visible in how corporations—and increasingly, the economies—began to be run. Before the 80s, said *Business Week* magazine, "many CEOs genuinely bought into the idea that a corporate chief executive was responsible to stakeholders, or people with a stake in the company's success; this included, besides actual shareholders, employees, customers, and the community itself. In the '80s the balance tilted radically toward the shareholders, but before all others, to the top executives themselves. 'Today," said Peter D. Capelli, professor at the University of Pennsylvania Wharton School, in 1996, "a CEO would be embarrassed to admit that he sacrificed [shareholder] profits to protect employees or a community'."[280] The shortening of corporate vision and the exclusive focus on short-term gain, legal or illegal, became increasingly well evidenced, running parallel with the polarization in society. As America's wealth, lifestyle, and education gaps grew steadily wider, the ever-richer corporate and government elites began to look down on those who served them.

The results included ruthless reductions in staff, wages, and benefits, and radically extended working hours. Driving people harder produced jumps in profits, a large portion of which could be claimed by top executives. "Indeed the CEOs of the nation's most downsized companies last year displayed a near in-your-face defiance of the notion that they should make even the smallest symbolic offering to share the pain," said *Business Week* in 1996.[281]

Same as during the original Renaissance, new wealthy, aristocratic dynasties of asset owners were emerging out of what during the Industrial Era was simply the corporate management of enterprises. "Thirty years ago the CEO of a major company was a bureaucrat—well paid, but not truly wealthy. He couldn't give either his position or a large fortune to his heirs," writes economist Paul Krugman. "Today's imperial CEOs, by contrast, will leave large estates behind—and they are often able to give their children lucrative jobs, too." [282] as hundreds of companies across the world were being privatized and increasingly owned by senior managers. The recent explosion of CEO compensations illustrated the Baroque-like transition from bureaucracy to financial aristocracy. In 1970, the average CEO earned 35 times average wages. In 1980, the ratio reached 45 times, and by 1995 had jumped to 160 times average wages. By 1997 the ratio had reached 305 times, and by 2000, CEOs were paid 458 times as much as ordinary workers.[283] These increases continued apace in the past decade: in 2004, CEO compensations increased 30 percent over 2003, and an average CEO of an S&P 500 index company was paid around $12 million per year. In 2005, CEO pay rose a further 27 percent over 2004[284], even as employee compensation had dropped to 63 percent of the U.S. GDP, the lowest percentage in almost 40 years[285].

The trend toward maximizing (and tax-exempting) soaring elite incomes seemed almost the key feature and key driver of the New Economy, the least likely to change in the future. Tellingly, these executive compensations were growing much faster than the revenue of the corporations and government organizations they purportedly served. "During the nineties overall pay of American CEOs began to bear no relationship to economic forces, [soaring] to unheard of levels, defying all laws of economics," writes economist Joseph Stiglitz.[286] While in 1953 U.S. executive compensation was the equivalent of 22 percent of corporate profits, by 1987 it had already tripled and was equivalent to 61 percent.

Privatization of any profitable areas of the economy and rise of wealthy dynasties of asset owners was one of the key features of all Baroques and one of the drivers of decay. It shifted wealth from society at large to a small elite; it pre-empted social mobility; it prevented talented people from moving up the income ladder and using their talents to society's benefit; it fostered permanent divide between haves and have-nots. It also fostered hatred and hopelessness, giving rise to "Occupy Wall Street" movements and growing sense of desperation. Contrary to stories being peddled by some media today, there is not a single historical example when growing wealth divide and polarization of society ended well.

In the world of the wizard, the wizard was the only possible winner, and everybody else was set to be the loser. Since much of the profitability increases and rises in executive compensation were generated in the first place by cutting staff, benefits, and wages, a good part of the New Economy came to resemble a zero-sum game, in which somebody's gain was increasingly somebody else's loss. "Some executives who slash workers' pensions are keeping or even padding their own fat retirement packages," commented Michael Brush of *MSN Money*. "When IBM froze its pension plan in early January 2006, thousands of its employees suddenly felt a lot less certain about their retirement security." But IBM CEO Samuel Palmisano had no such worries—after he retired, he was to receive $4 million a year in pension. This divergence was becoming a familiar theme, as benefits were not only kept but often padded for top managers, while being slashed for the rank and file. "By cutting pensions, they make their companies more profitable, thus boosting their own bonuses [and retirement packages]," concluded Brush[287].

One of the reasons why incomes of most Americans kept dropping could be clearly seen from how corporate earnings were distributed. Labor was the clear loser. In the 2001-2 recovery, the bulk of the gains "were used to boost profits, lower prices, or increase CEO compensation," said columnist Bob Herbert of *The New York Times* [288]. In previous recoveries, labor's share would typically be around 65 percent, corporate profits' share about 15 to 18 percent. But this time 41 percent went to corporate profits and 38 percent to all types of labor compensation. "This is the first time we've ever had a case where two years into a recovery, corporate profits got a larger share of the growth of national income than labor did," writes Andrew Sum of the Center for Labor Market Studies at Northeastern University. "In no other recovery from a post-World War II recession did corporate profits ever account for as much as 20 percent of the growth in national income. And at no time did corporate profits ever increase by a greater amount than labor compensation." And, as we have seen earlier, more and more of these corporate profits, growing at the expense of labor costs, were allocated to the miniscule corporate elite.

Summarizing the trend, Sylvia Allegretto of the Economic Policy Institute concluded that the success of the American economy has been decisively decoupled from improvements in the living standards of workers. The idea that increases in productivity would automatically lead to wage increases and living standard improvements—the old idea underlying the world of Keynesian economics and of dreams of futurists like Alvin Toffler, that the rising tide lifts all boats—has finally been shattered.[289]

*

IN THE AGE of the Wizard, entire industries began to grow spectacularly on zero-sum games—cutting savings, wages, and benefits of the many to reward the few. In the burgeoning mergers & acquisitions industry, the facilitating of corporate mergers—mostly helping companies realize savings by cutting out overlapping staff—might pay first-year managing directors at top investment banks $2 million annually in 2005, up 15 percent from the year before[290]. Another fast-growing industry was tort litigation. Since 1990, a lawsuit was launched in the U.S. every two seconds. Tort lawyers collected hundreds of millions of dollars in "contingency fees" for asbestos tort suits, launched in the name of victims, who lost their health but typically got peanuts compared to the legal "knowledge professionals" who helped them. In the medical sector, escalating fees—with the simplest surgery now costing tens of thousands of dollars—fattened the pockets of medical professionals, malpractice insurance companies, bill collection agencies and malpractice lawyers. However, it impoverished the sick, with savings of the whole working life often disappearing due to a single sickness or accident. Most of the million plus personal bankruptcies in America every year were related to astronomical medical bills. This massive shift of cash drained the pockets of the productive sector, but had only one class of beneficiaries: the aptly named knowledge professionals—the wizards.

Government bureaucracies were not far behind the private ones. During the last forty years, governments grew more complex, creating mushrooming divisions, hiring ever more people and paying them more. They were staffed with thousands of top talent, elite-school diploma holders, cream of the crop. And just like during the Baroque, they now paid themselves more than the productive sector—much more. In the U.S. in 2009, average compensation package—salary and benefits—of a federal civilian worker was double private sector average salary and benefits, according to Dennis Cauchon of USA

Today[291]. In Canada, a controversial study showed that, on the average, salaries in public sector already by 1991 were twice as high as in the private sector, for corresponding positions. That was a complete reversal of the norm of the 1950s and 1960s, in which the public servants (or even some professional association members) were well known to be paid less than salaries in private industry, where working hours were longer and stress and job insecurity higher.

All the elites of the new era—whether elected officials or corporate executives—were rapidly converging in their outlooks, lifestyles and wealth levels. Describing 2005 China, "what do high-ranking Chinese Communist Party cadre and an executive working for a foreign multinational in China have in common?" asked a Beijing-based analyst. "Both live in guarded, walled compounds, send their children to foreign [private] schools, drive about in imported luxury cars".[292]

As governments privatized their business, lobbyists, lawyers, and insiders secured a growing, rent-like claim on existing and future profits. By 1990, there were 50,000 lawyers in Washington, D.C. specializing in buying political influence, and more than 33,000 lobbyists—up from merely a few hundred in the 1960s. Securing a verdict or bill that could cripple a competitor or remove undesirable regulation could bring better profits than years of production. No matter what administrations did, the numbers of lobbyists only kept growing. By 2005 on one Washington street alone (K Street), you could find well over 30,000 lobbyists and the industry was taking in more than $2 billion a year in fees.[293] In response to their efforts, legislation—and especially tax laws—were growing more complex, opaque and convoluted every year, requiring specialists to guide taxpayers through the maze.

How lobbying paid could be seen from a case of a coalition of 60 corporations (such as Pfizer, Hewlett-Packard and Altria) that spent a mere $1.6 million in lobbying fees to persuade Congress to create a special low tax rate for the earnings from their foreign operations. Their investment got spectacular return when just such a law—reducing the rate to 5 percent from 35 percent—got signed in late 2004. The tax saving to the companies was around $100 billion in 2005 alone.[294]

Increasingly, lobbyists began taking on a growing role in raising funds for politicians. By 2005, 273 former members of Congress or federal agency heads were lobbyists[295] and lobbying seemed to be the expected future for elected 'people's representatives'. These shadowy wheeler-dealers were epitomized in the figure of "Casino Jack" Abramoff, who wined, dined, and treated U.S. politicians to extravagant favors. These favors were rewarded—as Abramoff testified in early 2006 when faced with up to 11 years in prison—with legislations favorable to his clients.

Same as during the last Renaissance, in the Age of the Wizard gradual privatization of many government offices and functions went hand in hand with unprecedented wave of corruption and sleaze. Few countries were immune. In Europe since the 1980s, evidence showed that fraud has risen significantly. There were thousands of reported cases of abuse of EU programs and fixing grants. In the seven years to 1995, in Frankfurt alone, anti-corruption squads have uncovered 1500 cases of public officials on the take. A driving license could be obtained for $2000, and $3500 was a going rate for a residence permit allowing a foreigner to work in Germany. Licenses for bars, restaurants, and nightclubs could be all arranged at a price and one could quite easily buy one's way into a subsidized council flat. "We have convicted mayors of towns of taking bribes. That is a development that would have been unthinkable in Germany a few years ago . . . Corruption now goes right through the hierarchy", commented one observer.[296] In Canada, kickbacks and a money laundering scandal toppled the Liberal government of Prime Minister Paul Martin. In Germany, as soon as Chancellor Gerhard Schroeder was out of political office, he got a plum private job as chairman of a Russian gas pipeline company, the business he had promoted as a politician. The rise of business-government collusion and worldwide corruption during the last three decades was so massive that the term "feeding frenzy" seemed an understatement. By 2005, said *Financial Times*, corruption in Russia had increased by a factor of 10 times in a mere four years, with the amount of money changing hands through bribery equivalent to double the government revenues.[297]

Everywhere, the new wizard ethics of money-first seemed to gradually trickle down to a street-level mentality, increasingly taken for granted and treated as a 'new normal', but contributing to an atmosphere of hopelessness and cynicism not seen for decades. In some of the worst cases, like in Russia, "people want to leave because they feel there is nothing more for them in Russia" said *The Economist* in 2011. "The sense of future has been amputated . . . the degradation of infrastructure, institutions and, most important, human capital, creates a desire to tune out of it all . . . Today, Russian society as a whole is much more cynical and distrustful than it was in Soviet times. Aggression, hatred and nationalism have risen to levels not seen even after the Soviet collapse in the 1990s . . . the middle class is much less cohesive and idealistic." Corruption, cynicism and sense of hopelessness envelop the Russian society like a blanket, stated the newspaper.[298]

The growth, and scale, of fraud, theft, deception, bribery, collusion, and false accounting during the last few decades is simply stunning. The world's biggest corporate frauds and scandals ever *all* happened within the last 15 years. Enron was the world's biggest fraud-based corporate bankruptcy, until WorldCom topped the record. The $1 billion theft of Iraqi defense funds by U.S.-installed occupation officials was billed in 2005 as "the biggest theft in history."[299] Altogether, a total of $12 billion went missing in U.S.-controlled Iraq, as stories of corruption and theft by military officials became daily fare. A Department of Defense enquiry in 2010 found that incredible 96 percent of the funds advanced since 2003 by the U.S. taxpayer toward the reconstruction of Iraq, money administered by the U.S. Army, some $9 billion, could not be accounted for and was most likely stolen.

In the U.S., gray-area profits from crony connections, "tailored" deregulation, and accounting fraud all flowed smoothly into quaint, old-fashioned bribery: Richard Scrushy, ex-CEO of Health South, accused of masterminding a $2.8 billion accounting fraud at his company, was also charged with bribing ex-Alabama Governor Don Siegelman; the ex-governor was indicted for "widespread racketeering conspiracy." [300]

Republican ex-Congressman Randy "Duke" Cunningham, who collected millions in homes, yachts, antiques, and other bribes from defense contractors and others, was sentenced in 2006 to eight years in prison.[301] In Illinois, as soon as Barack Obama vacated his senatorial seat after winning the presidential election in 2008, Illinois Governor proceeded to semi-openly sell it to the highest bidder, an incredible abuse of office that would have been considered inconceivable a generation earlier, but now got only a few minutes of attention with the jaded public. While the Iraq adventure clearly brought huge benefits to well-connected firms like Halliburton, the 9/11 terrorist attack was followed by allegations of ineptitude, corruption, and cronyism in allocation of funds on a scale previously unimaginable by American taxpayers.

Examples of the dominant "get-rich-while-you-can" ethos showed up in the borderline between the illegal and the merely distasteful. Richard Grasso, New York Stock Exchange chairman at the time of the 9/11 terrorist attacks, resigned in disgrace two years later amid outcry about his outrageous $140m payout package.[302] Smoothly joining public and private interests, Peter W. Galbraith, former U.S. ambassador, acting in 2004 Iraq as advisor to the local Kurdish government on getting them an oil deal with Baghdad, received an enormous stake in one of the oil fields, worth at least $100 million or more.[303] The incredible scale of the $50 billion Bernie Madoff pyramid scheme fraud revealed in late 2008 was a fitting symbol of the new Age of the Wizard, so similar to the Baroque era of wheeler-dealers and scamsters.

As the new century opened, then, the peculiar process of privatizing the government by selling influence and privilege began to resemble the first stages of the Baroque. It was in the early '90s that analysts noticed with amazement a dramatic shift in American attitudes. The focus shifted from producing value to securing, one way or another, a claim on the largest slice possible of the existing money pie. Assorted information wizards: divorce, tort and malpractice lawyers, corporate raiders, Wall Street sharks and investment gurus replaced captains of industry as role models in the New America.

In the decade of the 1990s, ten lawyers graduated from North American universities for every engineer. The Age of the Wizard, if one dug a bit deeper, was distinctly non-magical in terms of creation of anything new; it was mostly smoke and mirrors hiding a reality where the engine of growth has slowed down, while populations and demand for energy and raw resources were rapidly growing and—just like during the last Renaissance—information and claims on positional assets, including increasingly outrageous or even openly fraudulent claims, replaced any true innovation.

TWO ENDS OF THE STICK

"[During Spain's] century of artificial prosperity . . . schools had multiplied, but they had served mostly to produce a half-educated intellectual proletariat who scorned productive industry and manual labor and found positions in the bloated . . . state bureaucracy, which served above all to disguise unemployment."
    —Carlo M. Cipolla, *Before the Industrial Revolution* [304]

A S I STAND in the empty, cavernous production hall of Solar, a swimwear manufacturer based on the outskirts of Bayreuth, Germany, the story of what some describe as the 'Flat World'—a world of globalized manufacturing and global competition for jobs and business—can be read in the company's history. In the 1970s, it employed hundreds of workers. Now it has less than ten, with all actual production moved completely offshore. It went through management buyout, then bankruptcy. Finally, it was bought by a Hong Kong swimwear company interested in Solar's brand name and intellectual property—hundreds of patents protecting proprietary design that allows people to tan right through the fabric.

Over the last four decades, the massive explosion of global trade, hailed as a sign of progress, was almost entirely driven by Renaissance-style crude, old-fashioned outsourcing, labor cost cutting and search for faraway resources. This trend completely belies the hyped technology and progress mantras. Unlike in the ascending cycles of leading civilizations, characterized by rising general technology, labor saving devices and rising average income, now cheap labor was triumphant and mechanical progress stagnated.

There was no middle ground, and effects were immediate. Removal of U.S. and European quotas on Chinese textile exports in 2005 caused an immediate depression in the Mexican textile industry, reducing the number of jobs by 25 percent in one year alone.[305]

If one looked at the world as a truly global system—not composed of nations or races, but simply of groups of people of different skills, family wealth, and educational backgrounds—the true outlines of the new 21st century reality, our New Renaissance bordering on New Baroque, would become immediately clear. With outsourcing (or, if you want, globalization), the once-localized wealth, education and income divisions were now spread across the globe. The vast labor market of China has become part of America's (or, more correctly, global investors') new internal economic setup—a sort of hidden, polluted, unfuturistic offshore factory, with $200 a month wages, well hidden from TV cameras and human rights and or environmental or labor regulations enforcers. In many developed countries, push down on labor costs resulted in creating a two-tiered labor market: a 'legacy' one, for those that got their jobs during the better times, and the 'competitive' one for unfortunate newcomers—typically youngsters or immigrants. In Europe—where regulations used to make it nearly impossible to fire workers or cut their wages—corporate costs were cut by losing workers through attrition and not hiring any new "official" labor. As in the U.S., an explosion in temporary and part-time work has led job growth, while full-time, regular jobs have led the decline. By 2006 in the Netherlands, 36 percent of workers were part-timers[306]. In Spain, 33 percent of workers were part-time; in Norway, more than 20 percent; in the UK, nearly 40 percent[307]. This trend was unlikely to change, as European companies desperately wanted to cut costs in face of global low-wage competition.

It was globalization and shifting jobs to lower-labor cost countries rather than automation, argued Michael Spence, a Nobel-winning economist, that was the main reason for rising unemployment and underemployment in the rich countries. Tellingly, almost all of the 27 million net new jobs created in America in the last two decades—1990 to 2008—were in 'non-tradable sector of the economy'—mostly government and health care, jobs that could hardly be outsourced offshore. Outside of this charmed sector, the world was increasingly moving toward a single market for labor. One example of how this was being accomplished were Internet platforms like oDesk, which farmed out white-collar jobs—computer programmers, copywriters, back office staff—to places like India or Philippines, often cutting the employer's costs by as much as 90 percent.[308]

The desperate search to cut cost and lower price of labor was not just international. I also operated domestically. In search of cheaper labor to offset rising raw material costs, Tak Shun Technology Group, a Chinese contract maker of watches, phones, and other consumer electronics, announced in 2005 that it was moving its factories from the coastal Fujian province to the interior Henan province. "Labor costs in Henan are about half those in Fujian," said executive director, Henry Law. Instead of paying about 800 yuan a month (around $100 at the time) to the workers, Tak Shun could pay the Henan going rate of about 400 yuan.[309]

In theory, globalization was simplicity itself. As it took advantage of low labor wages in China, resulting fat profits, additionally boosted by lower taxes and lower regulation, (whether health, safety or environmental) could be passed onto functions like design, marketing, branding, insurance, finance and other high-margin roles, for the moment still kept in the post-industrial countries.

Just like in previous Renaissance and Baroque periods, these flows of money skimmed from the bleak hinterlands of India or China, from locales where labor costs were low and architectural marvels non-existent, were being spent in iconic centres—the new 'global cities'—grouping high-income professionals, this new "working aristocracy". One could easily name these new 'global cities' serving—and draining cash from—their regional hinterlands: London covering Eurasia and Africa, New York the Americas. Singapore, Hong Kong and Tokyo covered East Asia, Dubai the Middle East. Regional sub-capitals—let's call them 'regional cities', were taking shape in places like Johannesburg, Sydney, Moscow, Shanghai and Sao Paolo. Same as during the last Renaissance and Baroque, these centers of elite spending sprouted new architectural marvels and cleaned up antique monuments free of industrial grime, witness to new prosperity.

Globalization's underbelly, seldom mentioned by today's apologists of the brave new globalized 'flat world', was sordid, lawless and desperately poor, standing as the witness of the true face of our new Baroque. Far away from the 'global cities', deep in the countryside not only of the 'emerging countries' but often places like America, infrastructure was decrepit, mafia-like cliques of strongmen and corrupt officials controlled towns, villages, mines and plantations. In most backward places, effective slavery was growing.

The cross-border integration of both top—and low-income functions across the globe, plus global "flexibility" that universally pushed the wages of the paupers worldwide down to subsistence, sometimes near-slavery level, plus massive borrowing from the future—*that* was the real engine of the change we all witnessed over the past few decades, the root of the transformation of our reality into the new Baroque. Technology, while much acclaimed, played a much lower role, mostly as a facilitator of this process and of the ascent of global elites relying on faster, global exchange of information.

*

WHILE MANUFACTURING—AND increasingly, higher value added activities—were moving to China and India, post-industrial America was now based in the acclaimed Service Economy, whose relentless growth had been once hailed by futurists as one of the "signs of the future." Sure enough, by 2005, more than 85 percent of all Americans worked "in services," while only 10 percent still worked in manufacturing. Rosa Lee's world was part of this futuristic reality—in its most literal sense. Her children worked the service economy MacJobs that had been created in their millions during the de-industrialization of America. One of her sons cleaned the ovens at night at KFC. Others might have been waiting tables, shining shoes, pumping gas, tossing boxes. Born into servants' lives, in a post-industrial society, half-literate and utterly disposable—able to be fired on a whim—they served.

While the nature of the Service Economy has been much debated, every new economic mini-cycle has revealed a bit more. The vaunted "information sector" of the Service Economy has not created jobs in any significant numbers. Generally, very few middle-class, mid-income jobs were being created. Instead, most of the new jobs are in the low-income sector of services.

In the 2003-2004 recovery, low-wage service industries like temp-dominated administrative support, waste management, health care and social assistance, residential construction, and restaurants collectively accounted for 60 percent of total job growth.[310] Job market realities consistently contradicted the official spin about technology as godsend provider of jobs and higher incomes: the overwhelming majority of jobs that the U.S. economy has created in the last 30 years were not hi-tech, but in the low-end of the services market: restaurants, hotels, medical care, retail, security, and office admin sectors. Even for the hyped hi-tech workers, wages remained low: in 2002, reported hi-tech workers association of Washington State, 90 percent of them earned less than average wage.[311] Indeed, low-end services allowed more bang for the buck: in 2006 Britain, analysts estimated that a large part of the economic growth—around 2.5 percent of GDP—was due to the low wages of hundreds of thousands of East European immigrants who had flocked to the country since EU expansion, producing more GDP for less money. 21st century productivity gains had increasingly unfuturistic flavor.

In the current slow recovery from the 2007-2009 recession, again hardly any middle-class levels jobs were being created. Bureau of Labor Statistics expected these ten occupations to provide the greatest number of new jobs over the next decade: registered nurses, home health aides, customer service reps, cooks and waiters, personal and home care aides; salespeople; office clerks; accountants; nursing aides and orderlies and teachers. Six out of top seven fastest-growing occupations were low-skill and/or low-wage jobs; none could be described as hi-tech.

Most of these jobs, interestingly, shared one common Baroque flavor: they provided personal services to the rich. Salesmen, waiters, cooks, hotel staff all served the affluent shoppers, travelers or diners. Nurses and nursing aides, orderlies, personal and home health aides were serving ailing pensioners—those who could afford care. Virtually all focused on servicing and maintaining our reality rather than inventing or producing something. Ours was becoming a static universe.

Many full-blown features of the Baroque reality were already here. In its 2011 special report 'The Future of Jobs', *The Economist* so painted the future for those without the celeb talents or elite school diplomas: "What about the people who do not command any kind of premium in the marketplace?" asked the newspaper, and answered: "The new rich are generating demand for household staff, and this sort of work can be very well paid. A private secretary and general factotum can earn up to $150,000 a year nowadays. Salaries for standard butlers range from $60,000 to $125,000 and a head butler can make as much as $250,000 . . . As more and more people live to a ripe old age, demand for home-care workers is likely to soar. America will need 2 million more of them in the next decade alone . . . But there are winners and losers even among domestic workers. Many of them are badly paid, get little or no time off and are vulnerable to injury . . . a high proportion of them are illegal immigrants who have no come-back against ill-treatment."[312]

So where was the insurance against not 'commanding a premium in the marketplace'? What were the alternatives to looking for a career as a servant, whether a high-paid 'factotum' or a near-slave domestic?

*

PIAZZA SAN MARCO, the salon of Venice, is full to the rim with people during the summer months, especially in August. Sitting in the Florian Café, where a cup of coffee costs a fortune, as it includes not only the mandatory cover charge but also the salaries of an entire orchestra playing music nearby, you and I might be inclined to believe that Italy is booming and money is no object.

But nothing could be further from the truth. The crowds filling the piazza are almost exclusively tourists, increasingly from places like China or Russia. Population of Venice, a mere 27,000 and declining, is a fraction of what it used to be 500 years ago and is employed almost exclusively in the tourist business. Italy's economy has stopped growing two decades ago, and is kept alive mostly due to export of luxury products and specialized machinery, plus living off government debt. The population of the country is now rapidly shrinking: Italian families, contrary to expectations, are now some of the smallest in the world, with an average of only 1.2 kids per woman. By 2050, demographics experts predict a population collapse. That is, unless the numbers are made up by continued wave of low-wage immigrants, most likely from Muslim North Africa.

What on earth is going on? Why are people in the rich countries having fewer and fewer kids, while people in the poor countries are having more? The answer, so critical for our future, as always, has to do with money.

A generation or two ago, again roughly until the pivotal 1970s, there was an incentive for people from Italy to Russia to Singapore to have many kids. As economies were expanding, and incomes were rising, kids tended to make more money than their parents and traditionally acted as an informal old age insurance policy, supporting their parents if needed during their old age. Public education was generally of good quality and was free. So, in many cases, was healthcare. Living spaces were both bigger and cheaper than today. Middle class jobs were plentiful. All in all, raising extra kids did not cost that much, and rewards to parents could be substantial if even one of the kids landed a good job. In many cases, most of them would—but this world is now gone.

Even with some twists, my own experience was not that different from most of the people of my generation, the baby boomers. Born in Poland, I went through high-quality, free public school system, followed by free university. I hardly saw a tutor. Healthcare was free. My education cost my mother next to nothing. When I began working, my income was substantially higher than that of my mother and I helped to support her in her old age.

The answer why people in rich countries have fewer kids is simple. As my friend, a former Wall Street banker, would say, nowadays kids are the worst investment in the world—providing a "guaranteed negative return" as he put it. He wondered why people bothered having children at all. Private education costs were staggering, yet private education was increasingly a must in face of declining quality of public schools, international mobility of parents, and expectations of top employers. Educating a kid in a private primary and secondary school would cost, in tuition alone, easily $25,000 a year. With college costs at least as much, and potentially—for U.S. institutions—around $50,000 per year, not counting accommodation and out-of-pocket expenses, it would cost at least $500,000 to privately educate a single kid. Some kids educated at such cost would become doctors, lawyers or bankers to secure their claim on the shrinking money pie, but even their comfortable incomes would no longer be sufficient to cover not only their own expenses and education for their own kids but to still leave room to support their parents or in any way repay them such massive investment in their education.

Often, the kids that would cost half a million dollars to educate would start their productive lives with $1000-2000/month jobs and continue to rely on their parents for financial assistance for years, rather than the other way around.

Recent surveys showed that nearly a quarter of so-called 'millennials'—people between ages 18 and 34—were unable to make ends meet and afford even the basics. The generation faced lackluster job prospects and mounds of student loan debt. A December 2011 survey by Pew Research Center showed that:

- 49 percent have taken a job they don't want just to pay the bills.
- 24 percent have taken an unpaid job (you need to put something on the résumé).
- 35 percent have gone back to school because of the economy.
- 24 percent had their own place but then moved back to their parents' home. [313]

So this was the explanation of why people—especially educated middle class people, were having fewer kids. The numbers spoke for themselves: a 2012 study in one of the EU countries showed that while only 1% of childless couples could be classified as poor, as many as 44% of families with 4 or more children poverty lived in poverty.

Obviously, not everybody could pay for elite education or be smart enough to get a Harvard scholarship. For those—and they were the vast majority—that could not go to elite schools, the seemingly oddest yet of 'Information Era' trends—the steady devaluation of college degrees—began to take shape. By 2011, almost half of all minimum-wage workers in the US—a poverty-level $15,000/year income—had some or full college education.

The long-repeated official 'Information Era' mantra—the fantasy that hails college education as cure for all ills—now seems outlandishly naïve. We simply do not live in a reality where all of us can be managers or white collar professionals; the stagnant technological reality makes sure of that. Same as during the last Baroque, as the supply of college graduates rapidly grew—by 2000 as many as 60 percent of all college-age kids in the U.S. (and similar percentages in other rich countries) went to college—there were simply not enough white collar jobs (let alone high paying jobs in top professions) to absorb them. Supply of college-educated graduates clearly exceeds demand. Consequently, many quite menial jobs today ask for college graduates simply because they can, in face of overwhelming supply. This creates another fantasy, namely that today's menial jobs (or any jobs) require more education than before.

As the slower economic growth and economic responses to it—offshoring, delayering, automation—eliminated millions of middle class jobs and replaced them instead with mostly low-wage, menial jobs, demand for academic careers began to drop. By 2006 in Australia, universities' IT departments witnessed collapse of up to 60 percent in student numbers as dearth of IT jobs caused two thirds of graduates to still be unemployed, months after leaving university.[313] As Edward N. Luttwak, senior fellow at the Center for Strategic and International Studies put it this way: "[for all economic ills] the ruling orthodoxy has a remedy—to educate all and sundry to the levels that will induce the Microsofts to employ them. Unfortunately, Microsoft and all its companions have no use for many employees, not matter how educated."

Directly contradicting the 'college education as remedy for economic ills' mantra, in the last three decades, a steady dwindling of career jobs and an oversupply of young college graduates resulted in increasingly bleak prospects for most educated young people. They received lower starting salaries and fewer chances for career advancement compared to college graduates in the past. Wage decline did not spare them: Between 1987 and 1991 alone, real wages of U.S. college graduates fell 3.1 percent. By 1995, more than 35 percent of these people who had worked so hard to better themselves had been forced to take jobs that did not require a college degree—up from 15 percent in 1990.[314] By 2006, half the workers in restaurants, grocery stores and department-store chains—all low-wage service occupations—were young people under 24, many of them college students or graduates.

Soaring costs of schooling and housing, declining government help, and low pay for entry jobs caught masses of college grads in a debt trap. "You go in believing that a BA (Bachelor of Arts degree) is your ticket to the American dream," said college graduate Lorena Bravo. "But for most of us, college just didn't pan out the way we expected." Bravo emerged from college in 2003 with $18,000 in student-loan debt. "That's nothing," she said, "I know people who graduated with $100,000 in debt. I was one of the lucky ones." Still, she wasn't able to find a job that paid more than $20,000 a year, even with the degree and plenty of college work experience.[313]

"After 2000"–reported *The Economist* in 2006–"most people lost ground, but those in the middle of the skills-and-education ladder have been hit relatively harder than those at the bottom . . . some statistics suggest that the annual income of Americans with a college degree has fallen relative to that of high-school graduates for the first time in decades." [315]

The steady devaluation of university education and increasing lack of market demand for college graduates seemed the oddest yet and most contradictory of Information Era trends, flying right against the accepted mantras that college education will fix everything. This trend afflicts all post-industrial countries. In Japan, as the country's vaunted hi-tech economy began stagnating in the '90s, graduates of respected four-year universities were competing for jobs as sales clerks, secretaries, construction workers, and entry-level bookkeepers. "I am looking for a job as a receptionist, a sales clerk, it doesn't matter," said college graduate Takako Nakahara at the Japanese Ministry of Labor 1995 job fair. "I got an interview with one company, a maker of bathtubs, and told them I really wanted to be a receptionist. But the prospects for me to get that job are low because many other people wanted it." [316] By 2006, the country expected to have more than a million households on welfare, or two percent of all households–a 60-percent jump from ten years before.[317] In Europe, unemployment for young college graduates ran over 60 percent in some countries.

*

SO WHAT KIND of education can get one away from such problems? Degree from top, brand-name, elite university does.

In China, to publish a book with the word "Harvard" on the title page would guarantee instant sales success, no matter what the book content. When the new Baroque dawned, brand-name, elite education seemed the only solution, to get ahead of the pack virtually at any cost. As competition for jobs was getting extreme, and supply of college graduates overwhelming, parents got forced to enroll kids into exclusive, brand-name schools and iconic universities with global name recognition—Harvard, Oxford, Stanford, Yale, Columbia, MIT, LSE and the like. This was, apparently, the only remaining way to secure a stable career and stay away from the specter of poverty. Some of these brand-name institutions began opening branches in Asia or Middle East, in order to cope with demand. The explosion of the elite education paralleled—and was related to—the rapid decline of the public education sector, under-funded by semi-bankrupt states and robbed of its best teachers and students by the elite private sector. In all countries of the globe public schools were being privatized, with immediate massive jumps in fees.

In Japan as in most other countries, as prospects deteriorated, competition to get kids into exclusive private kindergartens, which led to top private schools, which in turn facilitated entry into top-name elite universities, became an almost grotesque obsession. This was at the same time that Japanese education became a decadent, Baroque version of what it had been in the ascending cycle. By 1995, more than 60 percent of all children were taking heavy tutoring courses focused exclusively on memorization, training them how to pass exams and to recognize clues that would help them pass. Passing an exam to secure a "brand-name" college degree to secure a lucrative career became the only object of schooling. From Seoul to San Francisco, from Moscow to Mexico City, parents who could barely afford it were sending their children into elite kindergartens and schools with an eye toward family economic survival. In Korea, parents were willing to go deep into debt, spending more than half their incomes to send kids to top private U.S. schools. The alternative was for their families to stay stuck forever at the bottom of the new global society's ladder—the new global society that, it was clear to all people, will be increasingly divided between the rich and the poor. A Baroque nightmare from which there will be no escape.

As I left the Florian Café to wander in the semi-deserted, narrow streets off the beaten tourist path, I kept thinking about the words of the clergyman from the Toledo Cathedral, Sancho de Moncado, when he noticed the dramatic drop in birthrates at the beginning of the last Baroque. People were having less children, wrote Sancho, not because of epidemics or migration, but because they could not support themselves and raise families.

Obsession with elite schooling that grew over the last few decades had a solid economic base, as most obsessions do. Unlike regular graduates from a no-name college, who were often forced into unemployment or menial work, delivering pizza or moonlighting as waiters, graduates of the Ivy League or similar top schools usually had their pick of jobs. In fact, they fully shared in the global tendency toward surging salaries for the top-educated elite, a living proof of how flat our world has already become. During the spring 2006 recruitment drive at Indian Institute of Management in Ahmedabad, the top salary offer to a fresh grad was $185,000/year; in the Bangalore branch of the school, the top offer was $193,000; the top salary package for a fresh grad of the Indian School of Business in Hyderabad was $223,000. In the U.S., 2005 annual packages for fresh Harvard grads averaged $175,000; Stanford and Dartmouth MBA graduates averaged $150,000[318], all a far cry from the $18,000-$25,000 annual salary ordinary college grads would get—if they got a job at all.

In their decline cycle, all complex societies, from Rome to China to Spain, shared the same obsession with exclusive academic education, one that opened doors to ruling elites, to the life of money and power, to family future of investor dynasties. In turn, such top schools, including the ones of our Baroque, insisted both on tough schooling standards—within the accepted norms of their era—and skills that would visibly and immediately differentiate their graduates from others. Today, excellent articulation—aimed at executive level public speaking and business writing—rules US-style education; in 1920s England, it was all about the accents, manners and literature; in dynastic China, it was memorization of thousands of Confucian poems and proverbs.

In Baroque Spain, schools taught kids Greek and Latin, Roman law, plus ability to speak and write in a convoluted, florid, hard-to-imitate Baroque style, which instantly differentiated them as elite members. The standards were high, as befitting the future information elites. "At an age when other children played in the streets, or trailed their mothers in the kitchen, the boys from the best families were swallowed each morning at 6 o'clock behind the sinister oak doors of the *collegium* . . . Even after the bell has sounded, there was homework awaiting them. After several years of this regime they were linked to their classmates and to their teachers in a solidarity which excluded the children of ordinary people from whom they were separated by their newly learned habits of thought and even by the language they used . . . they learned to speak disparagingly of merchants . . . . [Eventually] the leading families of many cities tended to divorce their own interest from those of bourgeois communes which they had served and led in the past" wrote historian Huppert about the eternal impact of elite schooling.[319]

Our new Baroque is now being born somewhere between the empty production halls in Bayreuth and the mushrooming enrolments in pricey elite universities. On the one hand, there is a drive to cut every penny and push the new *miserables* into underemployment and destitution; on the other, a push to spend almost irrespective of cost to get the brand name diploma. Yet they are just two ends of the same stick, both desperate obsessions with finding an edge—lower production costs, more prestigious degree—that would put the investor an inch ahead in a reality that has run out of technological options to grow.

In the decline cycle, both the obsession to save and to spend, are simply the two ends of the same stick. They both invest in economic survival.

THE BEAUTY, THE LIBRARY, AND LORD SANDWICH

"One of the core puzzles in economics is the productivity slowdown that began in the early 1970s . . . Even after accounting for factors such as the oil price shocks, changes in labor quality and potential measurement errors, most researchers still find an unexplained residual drop [of about 75%] compared to the first half of the post-war period. The sharp drop in productivity roughly coincided with the rapid increase in the use of information technology."
                    –Erik Brynjolfsson, Shinkyu Yang, MIT, 1996[320]

F YOU EVER watched "Beauty and the Beast" Disney animated movie–where action takes place in a vaguely Baroque France–you may remember the gigantic, churchlike, fantastic domed library, full of thousands upon thousands of books, the library that sweeps Belle off her feet when she visits the Beast's castle. Displaying books, reading them, quoting them, writing them, discussing them were all the hallmarks and the very essence of the Baroque culture as much as burning witches, waging war and collecting taxes. Incidentally, many books of the Baroque were, in fact, written about hunting and disposing of witches.

Books and information contained in them were as much a cultural and business part of Baroque life as computers and Internet are today. Books were everywhere–on the shelves, in Belle's hands, when she was reading while walking the old medieval streets of her town. Lord Sandwich invented the sandwich–slice of meat between two slices of bread–because he could not be bothered to interrupt reading books for his meals. In paintings of the era, we see hundreds of books cascading from tables, or strewn on the floor. During the Renaissance and Baroque, incessant reading and writing–activities that gradually disappear in today's age of half-line tidbits, YouTube videos and pictures circulated online–both blossomed, part of flood of information as overwhelming as today, even if delivered through a different medium. Yet this obsessive Baroque infomania–just like today, mostly full of trivia–did not, as we have seen, rescue the people of the Baroque from their economic horrors. Recessions, wars and epidemics ruled the Baroque, whether people were awash with information or not.

Interestingly, when computers first began being introduced into American offices in 1966–an event then hailed as "the biggest technological revolution men have known"[321]–they were initially not looked at as mere information or communication devices. Instead, futurists looked at computers as the first step toward artificial intelligence, seeds of artificial brains that would spark another industrial revolution, free us from toil and want, perhaps guide us to the stars. What people hoped for was a technological "quantum leap", where–thanks to computers–productivity, profitability, and wages would not merely continue growing at the comfortable '50s and '60s rates, but that they would all explode the way they did in the 1850-1950 era, when powered machines and fossil fuels replaced horses and human muscle and productivity increases going into thousand of percent were common.

There were good reasons for optimism. In U.S. factories, introduction of numerical steering–this precursor of computerization–in the late '50s brought immediate and measurable productivity improvements. In large part based on such technology improvements, just between 1957 and 1964 manufacturing output of the U.S. doubled, even though the number of blue-collar workers fell by three percent[322]–a jump in manufacturing productivity unmatched ever since, despite the subsequent arrival of computers.

Yet this awaited 'quantum leap' failed to happen. Despite all expectations and despite much higher levels of investment than ever before, there was no quantum leap in productivity or general technological progress due to introduction of computers. Instead, amazingly, overall productivity growth began to slip. After having invested, during the 1980s alone, over $1 trillion in IT—with nearly 90 percent of this investment in the service sector[323]—corporate America found the nation's productivity from 1992 to 1996 growing at a dismal 0.3 percent per year.[324] Productivity in services actually *dropped*.

For a machine ostensibly invented to revolutionize the office, the place where most of the IT investment was concentrated, decline in service sector productivity came as a special shock. In the '50s and '60s, productivity in services was growing at the same rate as productivity in manufacturing. However, between the mid-70s and 1986, while manufacturing productivity grew by solid if unspectacular 17 percent, output per "information worker" decreased by almost seven percent during the same time. "We have in essence isolated America's productivity shortfall," wrote Morgan Stanley's Stephen Roach, "and shown it to be concentrated in that portion of the economy that is the largest employer of white-collar workers and the most heavily endowed with high-tech capital."[325] He concluded that introduction of information technology efficiently supported continued automation of factories, but failed to affect the bloated ranks of white-collar services, especially finance, that were less exposed to international competition.

*

THIS FUTURISTIC NEW Economy—the "Service Economy" of the post-industrial countries—increasingly relied on debt to grow, and debt was dependent on cheap credit. As with *all* the other trend reversals, the explosion of debt took place in the 1970s.

In the 1950s and 1960s, the U.S. was still the world's biggest lender. Its own debt was growing, but very modestly, at a rate close to that of the national income—despite paying off war debt for the Second World War, and wars in Korea and Vietnam. But since the pivotal mid-'70s the rate of growth of debt soared well ahead of any other economic statistics.[326] Not just in America—all post-industrial economies went into debt since the 1970s at rates far exceeding any GDP or productivity growth, or any other conceivable measure of economic performance. All of them opened the new millennium with enormous levels of debt.

By early 2005, America's total debt (federal, state, and local governments' debt, plus all household and corporate debt) stood at $40 trillion—$31 trillion private debt plus a $9 trillion all-time record public debt. This was more than $136,000 for every man, woman, and child, and was well over 300 percent of the GDP.[327] By April 2010 this total debt increased to $57 trillion, or $744,000 for a family of four, and equivalent to around 5 years of the nation's total output.

Three quarters of this debt were created after 1990. Commented one analyst: "since 1990 it is clear the economy was 'driven' almost entirely by the biggest injection of new debt in history, which produced a much diminished lower return in national income per dollar. Just as one hooked on drugs needs ever increasing amounts of drugs to 'survive', it appears America needs ever increasing amounts of new debt to eke out diminishing amounts of growth—even with 2 wage earners per family."[328] Huge amounts of the government debt went to pay the swollen civil service, thus creating unsustainable spending pattern, with debt—both private and public acting as the main engine driving the post-industrial economies during the last two decades.

Just like the first king of the Baroque, Philip II of Spain, U.S. President George W. Bush borrowed more in a few years than all his predecessors combined. It seemed that his successor, Barack Obama, was well on his way to topple this record.

The global financial crisis that hit in the fall of 2008 worsened the already massive debt overhang. It was estimated that the final cost of various stimulus packages—to bail out the finance industry, rescue the housing industry and bail out the auto industry, plus generally prevent the job losses and economic situation from becoming even worse, would burden the U.S. government with maybe 2 trillion dollars in additional borrowing, on top of its already crippling debt load. The only other alternative seemed to print money—an approach that was attempted through the so-called 'quantitative easings', but one that, if continued, would eventually result in roaring inflation.

The biggest problem with government debt was that, short of sudden and massive increase in government revenues, it was very difficult to cut it without damaging the economy. By 2010, around 60 percent of all Americans receiving income relied on a government check—whether paycheck, welfare check, unemployment check or else—for most of this income. In turn, U.S. economy depended on their spending. Oddly, large part of today's acclaimed Service Economy was actually government service. It was massive, and it was inefficient, hanging on the society like a gigantic, costly, unproductive burden. Many civil service jobs were completely useless, as witnessed by many casual testimonies. In France, a new graduate having joined the civil service described in her blog that she could easily finish in 5 to 6 hours all her monthly tasks. Public sector kept people off unemployment roll, but at a prohibitive financial cost.

The growing pile of government debt was matched by the growing pile of personal debt. During the last few decades, as real wages were falling and housing, healthcare, transport, food and education costs kept skyrocketing, American consumers were getting deeper into debt. Between 1981 and 2005, the savings rate fell from 11 percent to below zero; credit card service went up from four to 12 percent of income; half of retiring baby boomers had no retirement accounts.[329] By late 2008, just as the first massive wave of job losses began to roll, the American consumers owed around $900 billion dollars on credit cards alone, around $3000 per every man, woman and child in America. In Britain, where more and more people were putting essential spending, like food, on credit cards, average personal debt per British adult was almost GBP30,000, or 122 percent of average individual earnings.[330]

The last two decades showed growing reliance of low–and middle-income families on borrowing–whether on personal credit or house equity. U.S. consumer debt, growing dramatically since the 1960s, by 1995 virtually exploded and amounted to over $4 trillion; 1994 Federal Reserve report said over a quarter of family income went to pay debt[331]. It was this kind of spending, unsustainable in the long term, fuelled by exhausting savings and pension money, and borrowing against house equity, that provided essential fuel for U.S. economic growth over the last fifteen years, as it was gradually bankrupting its middle class and making millions into paupers.

With the massive growth of debt at all levels, the interest rates gradually acquired a disproportionate, critical importance. The fate of "Information Era" America, supposedly the world's most innovative economy, appeared to stand not on innovation but instead on a precarious foundation of foreign debt–increasingly contracted in places like China–and lending-rate management wizardry. Since the 1970s, interest rates were used to engineer "the policy recessions": drastic increases in interest rates designed to repeatedly cool down rising inflation–at the cost of massive increases in unemployment and business bankruptcies. Ultimately, says brilliant historian David Hackett Fisher, "the principal victims [of policy recessions] were not a class but a generation–young people who had no hope for the future and no memory of better times in the past."[332]

*

AS THE LANDSCAPES of the new America polarized, so did the mindsets. There seemed to be a major cultural change underway. Its surface signs were a baffling rise in corruption, cynicism, hypocrisy, and pursuit of self-enrichment at any cost. "Economic analysis," said Irwin Stelzer of the Hudson Institute, commenting on the massive wave of corporate scandals in the first decade of the new century, "[has] little use for such concepts as honor, trustworthiness, or duty . . . . We live in an age in which members of the business community—as well as others throughout society—place less value on these virtues than in times past . . . . The behavior of corporate executives in a number of instances suggests that we are faced with a collapse of the constraints on behavior that were once imposed by conventional morality.[333] The unashamed display of wealth and luxury consumption, fuelled by combination of debt and obscenely high compensations for some; growing privation and borderline poverty for as many as a third to half of all population; the sea of red ink combined with fraud and loose ethics—all these features were fast becoming hallmarks of the new Baroque-like reality. And just like in the late Renaissance and early Baroque, the middle class was shrinking and withering, slowly turning back into the eternal poor.

Unforeseen by Toffler, his Third Wave future saw majority of British families having to ration heating to be able to cope with heating bills. In the winter of 2010, already "half of all households went without heating at some point to keep their energy costs down, risking health and well-being" reported *The Independent* newspaper. In the winter of 2011, "89 percent of families will ration their energy use to save on bills . . . people are being forced into making potentially dangerous choices" reported the newspaper, due to further 21 percent increase in electric bills during the preceding 12 months.[334]

This was the Third Wave, 2011 style.

At street level, acceptance of gaping societal divides and growing selfishness went hand in hand with coarser mores and daily brutality. Reflected in the media, there seemed to be a hardening of hearts unseen for centuries, a darkening of vision, a steady lowering of ethics. In the 1940s America, General Patton was almost court-martialed for slapping an Army private, and had to publicly apologize in front of all the troops; as the new century opened, military brutality and abuse began to seem normal, and—incredibly—long-forgotten questioning under torture had officially returned, its "evidence" even admitted in American courts during the George W. Bush presidency.

Significantly, incidents of abuse took place not only between the detainees and U.S. forces overseas. They were increasingly common within the U.S. military itself, between petty officers and privates, and even within the officer corps. They included beatings, rape, sexual, verbal, and other forms of abuse, racial and other discrimination, and a general lowering of ethics—all freely depicted in today's media showing the brutal army training camps and daily abuse of recruits. While this no longer shocked most people, it was because most had forgotten the high level of ethics in the U.S. or British military during the Second World War. Incidents of prisoner torture or abuse were unheard of, even if they existed, since—unlike today—they were simply unacceptable in the context of the mores of the time. It is today's social acceptance of the lower ethics that is the most terrifying feature.

America, the futuristic land of the Information Economy, shared with China, Iran, and Vietnam the distinction of massive and rising prison populations and a growing number of people on death row. Just like a banana republic, the U.S. began—according to a 2005 Amnesty International report—running "an archipelago of prisons" around the world, secret camps into which people were disappearing.[335] Prison camps like infamous Guantanamo openly bypassed the country's justice system, with torture or near-torture 'enhanced interrogation techniques' being widely practiced.

Where once the draft-based Vietnam War raised massive protests from middle-class parents galvanized into action by the prospects of body bags for their kids, and spawned a generation of conscientious objectors, now the brutal Iraq and Afghanistan wars seemed carved out of the common psyche. There was relatively little concern for low-income enlistees and anyway, by 2010 more than half of all the troops were already mercenary 'contractors'. In German army, the new enlistees did not even have to be German. As during the last Renaissance, which moved from medieval-style popular militia to paid mercenaries, a similar move today seemed to complete the picture. This kind of transition was seen virtually in every historical decline process before, all the way back to the evolution of the Roman military from citizen-soldiers to mercenaries, whose loyalty could be bought by anyone.

Why is this important? Simply, democracy and mercenaries, as history has proven, never went together. For some strange reason, arrival of mercenaries always heralded the end of the republics.

As the 21st century opened, old, obscure threats that were thought to have been eradicated for generations suddenly reappeared, and it was hard not to see them as outbreaking symptoms of a greater malaise. Incidences of viral diseases—thought virtually conquered in the 1960s—rose by 58 percent between 1980 and 1992, and the trend continued. Among these diseases were the rejuvenated old scourges: TB, E coli, cholera, drug-resistant pneumonia, hepatitis, but also newer pandemics like AIDS, SARS, and the swine flu. Smallpox, thought eliminated in 1977, came back with a vengeance. Malaria, decades after it was believed to be eradicated, infected half a billion people in 2004, with a million deaths a year from the disease—50 percent more cases than WHO had forecast, with infections outside Africa 200 percent higher than official predictions.[336]

Market-driven policies made the situation worse. "Given that tuberculosis kills more people than any other infection, one must ask why there has been such inaction on new tuberculosis drug development," wrote Lee Reichman of the National Tuberculosis Institute at New Jersey Medical School. He blamed TB's spread on drug companies, whose shareholders believed tuberculosis R&D to be unprofitable—"despite the high prevalence of tuberculosis, the population that get the disease are often poor and lack insurance"—but also on cuts in federal health care funding since the 1970s. Poor funding has meant that patients with incomplete courses of treatment were not monitored, and so were allowed to spread the disease. By 2005, in China, tuberculosis had become the number one viral killer, with dramatic increases in fatalities almost every year.[337]

As in previous Baroque Syndrome cycles, the return of killer diseases seemed to originate in growing poverty, political mismanagement, elite corruption, declining sense of social responsibility, decaying infrastructure, and increasing apathy toward the dead-end existence of the masses—all socio-economic drivers against which medicine alone seemed helpless.

Incredibly, piracy, eradicated at the onset of the Industrial Era, now almost 200 years ago, reappeared in the midst of our Information Era. It began to make front-page news from around the mid 1990s, with ever-bolder attacks in the Straits of Malacca, but virtually exploded by 2008, with Somali pirates having attacked over 90 ships in the Gulf of Aden in the preceding 12 months[338] and collecting over $150 million in ransoms. For the first time since Suez Canal opened, many shippers began to consider again going around Africa. By 2012, piracy began to reappear in West African waters.

In another throwback to the past, as the 21st century opened, slave trafficking grew so quickly that it began to rival the drugs and arms trades, raking in an estimated US$10 billion in revenue a year.[339] According to author Kevin Bales, there were 27 million slaves in the world in 2002, more than at any other previous time in human history.[340] Yet even this number was a massive underestimate, as it only included the trafficked illegals, but not the tens of millions of legal laborers and domestic servants, living in effective slavery to their sponsors across richer countries of Asia and the Middle East. These domestic servants and laborers, contracted at subsistence-level wage—had their passports taken away and were forbidden to leave their quarters without permission. They were frequently unpaid and abused. Under local laws in a number of host countries, police were required to hunt them down as criminals if they ever ran away from their abusive sponsors. It is possible their fate was worse than the slaves of the Antique, whose owners tended to be careful with their investment.

At the bottom of the new slavery system were the 'illegals'—the illegal immigrants. In Paris, residents joked that the outsourcing of the local textile industry to China had already happened, except that the cheap Chinese factories were not located in China, but in Paris.

By early 2005, some 600,000 Chinese laborers were working in underground sweatshops in the Paris region alone, earning maybe E400 or E500 a month, for a 14-hour, seven-day week; naturally, they received no social security or benefits. These laborers were indentured quasi-slaves who paid to be smuggled into France in order to work and support their families back in China. The ultimate objective, of course, was to allow their children or grandchildren to get an education in order to climb the society's ladder. Once in Paris, they could never leave their dormitories, since they had no papers[341]. Even in places like Sweden, Chinese crime syndicates reportedly controlled asylum-seekers: out of 135 Chinese who applied for asylum there in 2005, only two or three remained accounted for; the rest had disappeared into the economic underground of slavery and sexual abuse.[342]

Privatization was another common feature linking the past Baroque with the present one, but it was in China where it began to most closely resemble the past. Increasingly, said Shao Daosheng, a researcher at the China Academy of Social Sciences, junior government posts were being sold to the highest bidder. In Shanxi province, party secretary Wu Baoan sold 253 junior posts in less than a year for a total price of about 5 million yuan; Yin Liming, appointed deputy governor in a Yunnan county in 2003, bought the post from local congress members; Suihua county party secretary Ma De accepted six million yuan for the sale of 12 posts—including that of the city's deputy party secretary, which alone fetched half a million yuan[343]. And it was not just officialdoms that were on sale—so were academic careers. A 2006 survey of 180 Chinese Ph.D. holders revealed that 60 percent had paid to have papers published; a similar percentage had plagiarized others' work or falsified research[344].

The key here was, in both decline eras, that anything that provided a claim on rent-generating positions became a tradable asset.

In 2010, the wave of suicides at China's 'factory town' of Shenzhen, starting at Foxconn—a Chinese company that was the world's largest electronics contract manufacturer with a headcount of almost a million, a maker of iPhones and Playstations—and other Chinese companies, combined with a wave of massive strikes, all signs of desperation of the poverty-stricken working class, brought forth large salary increases. They more than doubled, in a single year, the basic pay of top assembly line workers and supervisors to around US$290/month, possibly heralding a gradual end of an era of cheap Chinese "stuff" to the American consumer. China was gradually moving to a mid-income country status, duplicating the move made earlier by places like Taiwan or South Korea.

What was missing in China—this biggest economy of tomorrow—was any sign that the country was ready to lead the world as America or Britain once did, through technological innovation, democracy, equality, corporate governance, or rule of law. Despite its phenomenal growth replicating the goodies of American consumer society—its cars, TVs, highways, plentiful consumer goods, shopping malls, over-the-top lifestyles of the elite—the essence of what once made America truly great was completely lost, and there was nothing new and original to replace it. Instead, if you stripped away the superficial modernity, China seemed to be just another replica of its former dynastic self.

*

AS THE NATIONAL People's Congress opened in Beijing in March 2005, there were thousands of petitioners who had flocked to the capital. Every year, they were growing in numbers. They were farmers squeezed by officials enforcing illegal taxes, laid-off workers, those forced off their land or illegally evicted from their homes by strong-armed officials working in collusion with property developers. Just like the poor once flocking to the imperial capital, Madrid, these people had traveled for days from their destitute hinterlands hoping to have their grievances heard. They were petitioning for justice, praying that the National People's Congress would settle their fate[345]. Those who, despite tight security, managed to get close to the Great Hall of the People were arrested and taken away in police vans.

And yet they kept coming—even though dozens, sometimes hundreds of them were being preventively arrested to avoid embarrassing protests in front of TV cameras. In the frigid Beijing winter, hundreds of paupers in thick winter coats gathered outside an unmarked, obscure building in Beijing's south, where the state petition office was. Standing for hours behind yellow police tape, they hoped to gain access inside, even though it was unclear how such a thing could be done. Thugs sent by provincial governments kept an eye on people from their regions, with almost as many policemen as petitioners in the crowd. Some petitioners, such as Wang Yuemei, an unemployed woman from impoverished Gansu province, had ended up moving to the capital to seek redress. She lived in a tiny room in a single-storey brick building, and had come to Beijing every year since 1993. "Ten years have passed and I have had no response," she said—but added, hopefully, that she just had been advised that her case had been received.[346]

As the new century opened, billions of ordinary people across the world felt growing fear as they began to suspect that the future was failing them. Except for a small elite, cocooned in its world of privilege and focused on getting richer every day, visions for mankind's better future and broad-based progress darkened and began to slip away. For thousands of petitioners flocking to Beijing—and for billions of people across the globe—the clock of progress slowly began turning back. The new Baroque, it seemed, was on our doorstep.

PART FOUR

BEYOND

STORY OF THE FEATHERED SERPENT AND THE ROMAN SUNBELT

E VEN THOUGH I don't remember the date, otherwise the memory is crystal clear. I must be around 6 years old, in my childhood home in Cracow, listening to news on the radio when the newscaster announces that our planet's population has just reached 3 billion people. I still remember wondering about this number and how enormous the world must be to accommodate all these people.

The second memory is quite recent. In early November 2011, one out of about half a million babies that are born every day on Earth, a newborn baby in the Philippines was declared to bring the number of our planet's human inhabitants to 7 billion. This more than doubled the number of humans compared to 1960. By 2050, a generation from now, the planet's population was expected to grow to 9 billion. In under a hundred years, then, the number of humans was set to triple, an explosion exceeding anything that history has ever seen. One population expert said that the world population needed to be lowered by nearly two-thirds if climate change was to be prevented and comfortable lifestyles for all mankind made possible. Pointing out that humans were now exploiting about 20 percent more resources that could be replaced each year, Professor John Guillebaud of the Worldwatch Institute in Washington said, "We urgently need to stabilize and reduce human numbers. There is no way that a population of nine billion can meet its energy needs without unacceptable damage to the planet and a great deal of human misery." [347]

Compared to the environment—with global warming issues daily in the media—overpopulation seemed almost a forgotten topic, despite clearly being one of the major drivers of carbon emissions, environmental change and massive demand for resources driving prices up. By any historical standards, population increases of the late industrial era were simply stunning. We can only realize how dramatically human numbers rose during recorded history when we find out, for example, that only around 2 million people lived in Egypt when the incredible works of engineering—the pyramids—were being built around 2500BC, and there were only around 10 million humans in the whole world at that time.

Just like during the last Baroque, by 2011 it was clear that the combination of massive population growth, an increasing pressure on commodities and food and resulting dramatic price increases were threatening world growth. It is unlikely to be a coincidence that most of these trends seem to have originated in the pivotal decade of the 1970s, when the price of oil went up dramatically. Equally dramatic price rises of non-oil commodities have followed more recently, thanks to industrialization of places like China and India: tripling in price of these commodities in just one recent decade has reversed an 80 percent price drop during the course of the entire Industrial Century, ending around 1950. As in previous decline eras, in a static energy regime, growing demand for energy and commodities from the swelling populations now was meeting with increasingly sluggish supply. "Optimists bet on human ingenuity to spring the Malthusian trap, as it has done so often before" said the Financial Times[348] reporting the dilemma.

The question is: will this be the case this time? Or perhaps, we will have to wait for some new miracle technology that will deal with this problem, like we did four hundred years ago—for centuries?

*

THE GREAT MAYA pyramid of Kukulkan, or the "Feathered Serpent", at Chichen Itza on Mexico's Yucatan peninsula, is relatively easy to climb. As I look down from one of the steps perhaps halfway to the top, all around the pyramid complex, the deep-green jungle stretches in every direction. It once fooled historians, who pictured the Mayan pyramids as isolated worship centers in the jungle, worship centers of a sparsely-inhabited, peaceful civilization.

They were proven completely wrong. In the last few decades, it was discovered that Maya homeland was once one of the most densely populated and heavily urbanized places on Earth. There was not much jungle: the region was then covered with irrigated fields and dotted with some of the biggest cities on the globe. It was also the stage of a continuous, bloody warfare, a place where even fields were fortified with defensive stone walls, and pyramids like the one I am standing on were witness to bloody human sacrifices of war prisoners. Mayas were far from peaceful. Their world was a place where massive population growth, increasing shortage of resources, unbearable burden of supporting the escalating costs of the elites with their wealth and its ostentatious display, plus damages from incessant warfare could no longer be sustained past a certain point. When decline arrived, it first manifested itself as poverty, then increasing malnutrition among the masses. Skeletons of lower class Maya of the decline era bear unmistakable signs of starvation and disease, even as monumental construction by the elites was just reaching its peak. And then, within mere decades, the Maya civilization unraveled and utterly collapsed. Once the overhead of civilization disappeared, with its irrigation works and government structures, the remnants of the population dispersed. Jungle overgrew the fields, the cities, the pyramids and the irrigation works. The Maya civilization vanished into the jungle, as if it never existed.

The Classic Maya Collapse continues to be considered one of the biggest mysteries in archaeology. Many are mystified by the suddenness of the Maya collapse 'despite the high level of sophistication attained by their civilization' as says the relevant article in the Wikipedia. They should not be. High level of sophistication and speedy collapse go well together. They are not an exception; they are the rule.

The last Baroque was not the only one. It was one of many. Some of these periods, like the collapse of the Maya, still have gaping holes and have to be largely reconstructed from archeological finds. Among the better-documented, if still misunderstood Baroques that mankind has experienced, the decline era of the Late Roman Empire exhibits all the classic malaise symptoms: mushrooming costs of the elite, rapidly increasing inequality, huge income gaps, ostentatious display of wealth, massive inflation, frantic monumental construction, fading of ancient democratic institutions into farcical rituals, race to education as the key vehicle of social advancement and profit, massive corruption, stagnant innovation and growth, and finally creeping privatization of the public domain. The teachings of the decline of Rome may not be more interesting than the teachings of the collapse of the civilization of the Feathered Serpent, but we certainly know more about them.

The story of the decline of Rome reads like a thriller. Around 200AD, the Roman Empire has reached its economic limits. Within its niche, within the limits of its technology, and within the confines of its social setup, no more energy or new wealth could be produced. The initial benefits of expansion, long-term peace, population increase, removal of piracy, new crops and new lands under cultivation, of welding disparate regions into a single economic market through safe sea routes and impressive roads: All have been fully digested. Technological innovation was non-existent; slaves worked the fields, urban populations consumed the produce. Parasitism, long dominant, now became the only way of life, once commerce faded and merchant class declined. One of this late period's hallmarks was the steady growth of large estates, similar to the gigantic *latifundia* of the Baroque, growth that made analysts talk about the 'agrarian capitalism'. Same as during the later Baroque, most trading cities entered a period of slow, undignified lull, and then decline. In Lyon, once the richest and the largest city in Gaul, whole city sectors started to be abandoned as early as 197AD. The decay of the city was reminiscent of the decay of Manchester or Detroit, or before that, Regensburg or Toledo. After 230AD, visible signs of a rapid deterioration of the socioeconomic system began to appear everywhere. Pirates, not seen for centuries, re-emerged again and began to prey on trade. One by one, remote areas started to disappear into darkness.

How this happened can be traced in the story of Brittany, a remote corner of Gaul. It is a bit like a story that could make a Michael Moore movie. Written records stop there around 240AD. Archeological digs show that forests gradually overgrew abandoned farmland, and that the level of technology began to recede. Along the coasts, pirates overcame Roman troops stationed in maritime forts. After 300AD, weeds and wild growth advanced across the fields and squatters took over abandoned patrician villas—a sign that the soldiers were pulled back and the Empire effectively withdrew from the province. There was a significant population drop; use of money disappeared around 360AD and Brittany reverted to barter. Gradually, the region began to be considered bandit, or 'enemy' territory. Similar quiet, unpublicized withdrawals from remote regions that cost Rome money to protect, but did not generate positive returns, occurred in places like Africa, Britain, the German borderlands, in the mountainous regions of the Balkans and Turkey. In the mountains of Isauria (modern Turkey), robbers and bandits established their own republic, terrorizing most of Anatolia in their looting raids. Pirates, not seen in the Aegean for centuries, captured and plundered Greek and Anatolian shores, including Athens itself. As imperial armies seemed paralyzed, powerful landlords began to fortify their farms with walls and lookout towers. Some of these soon came to resemble regular castles. Such castles gradually became common in the vast plains of Hungary and Spain as the late Roman Empire continued to decay.[349]

While public authority and security eroded daily and as funding for the protection of remote provinces was cut, other areas enjoyed a Renaissance of prosperity and ritzy construction. Huge gaps in funding and wealth opened, not only between social groups, but between cities and regions, gaps hard to explain by agricultural base or trade alone. In some places, money budgeted to govern and defend provinces was evaporating and people lived in cave shelters; in others, especially sheltered cities in Asia and Africa, prosperity, unseen for centuries, suddenly blossomed. A peculiar Roman Sunbelt appeared under the Late Empire. It was nothing short of a parallel universe: archaeologists were amazed to discover, dating from this era of supposed decay, plenty of new construction and spending. Excavated houses of the new bureaucratic elite, sheltered in the East, where since the 320s the center of the Empire was shifting, were among some of the largest and most splendid ever built, with lavish decorations, mosaics, and gilding. In Antioch, there was a sharp increase in costly mosaic floors installed in houses built after 300AD. Diggings in Sardes and Ephesus confirm that the rich in the decline cycle spent more lavishly than ever before.

Massive increase in elite consumption, in an otherwise stagnant or shrinking economy, had to show up as inflation or government debt. Since Rome had no China to borrow from, it could only produce new cash by spoiling coin: its inflation was staggering. As always, the primary producers were not getting rich. As might be guessed, they were the victims of the worthless money system. Arable lands everywhere were being abandoned because of crushing taxes and other squeeze screws applied to farmers. Just like during the Baroque, only the best lands were still profitable.

Under emperor Valens, studies show that up to half of all the arable land has been abandoned in some provinces; and yet wealth, concentrated in a few cities of leisure—the quasi-'financial centers' of the Roman world—was displayed more than ever. While thousands of people were leaving their lands to turn into serfs, squatters, bandits, or beggars, the exploding new elites were no longer satisfied with simple Roman togas, used for centuries. Fancy fashions appeared: mosaics from Ravenna to Antioch show officials dressed in long, heavy robes of silk, stiff with pearls and precious stones: the equivalents of Gucci bags, Ferraris and other status symbols of the elites of the time of decline. Even in the depressed West, there were few outstanding centers of prosperity, new boom cities like Trier, Aquileia and Ravenna. Where did their wealth come from? They were all, for a time, temporary centers of power and bureaucracy, the places to spend wealth scooped from vast, ravaged, bleak and increasingly empty countryside. Their ruins still testify to a dazzling time of display and construction, in a reality that was utterly broke.

Tellingly, under the Late Empire, education suddenly became *the* big business. Bureaucracy, almost unknown before, now first appeared under the Late Empire and quickly grew in size and importance. It now provided the key avenue for social advancement, the only way for people with modest means to enter the establishment. It was done just like in China, by years of persistent memorizing the classics. As in all decline cycles, formal education soon acquired an absurdly exaggerated importance, once it became recognized as the only entry ticket into the universe of quick profits. And as in all such decline cycles, it had nothing to do with acquiring knowledge: Its only purpose was a diploma securing entry into the civil service and access to the trough of tax, bribe and extortion money.

Late Empire records quote fathers encouraging their children to study zealously: "Look at that poor fellow, born of lowly parents, who [studied and gained] great positions in government, great wealth, won a rich wife, built a splendid house . . . [350]" In a society without any other option of economic advancement, to join the officialdom and get corrupt was the only way for an individual to get out of the bleak anonymity of poverty and clientship, to get rich quick, to make a name for himself and for his family. When parents of Saint

Augustine, small-town people of modest means, noticed in the 360s that the boy was exceptionally smart, they pooled all their family funds to secure him an academic career that would eventually make him an official. Not just education: every step, every promotion of an official's career was an investment financed by family, relatives, friends, or loan sharks, an investment that later had to be repaid in patronage, money, and favors. Corruption was an inevitable, implicit, built-in factor.

Growth of the legalized oppression system paralleled the rise of bureaucracy. Just as in other Baroques, under late Empire, growth of the 'business' of courts, lawyers, court clerks, and judges created a parallel officialdom, a source of money bonanza, and another employment outlet for graduates of elite schools. Number of courts and lawyers more than doubled between 250AD and 300AD. Just as Brittany was falling off the map, law became the preferred tool of financial extortion.

The rise in litigation was nothing short of phenomenal. As regular business opportunities were shrinking, and returns of any productive activity, from landowning to commerce, dramatically declined with abandoned lands, banditry, and inflation, lawsuits became the way to get rich quick. The judicial ferocity—always the telltale sign—rose rapidly, and capital punishment began to be freely administered for even minor or administrative offenses. In every major city, basilicas, usually located right next to the forum, started to resemble regular torture chambers. The more regulation grew, the more 'paper progress': advances in law, bureaucratic complexity, institutions, regulations, and prohibitions, were rammed in, the less human life and suffering seemed to be worth. The more there were lawyers, the less immune people were from legalized terror. A society that once used to pride itself on being tolerant, liberal, and concerned about its citizens' rights, a society that—just like America not that long ago—used to congratulate itself on its civility, was now rapidly turning barbarous. Return of torture under George W. Bush had its Late Empire precedents. Roman courts now recommended, as a routine, impalement, gouging out eyes, cutting off noses, pouring molten lead into the mouths. Beheading was recommended not only for corruption, but even for small misdemeanors. The most common sentence of the Late Empire judges (routinely described as 'ferocious' by their contemporaries) was: 'cut his head off!' The Late Roman world has turned, just like the later totalitarian 'peoples' kingdoms', ruled by bureaucratic cliques, into a full-fledged house of horror.

The more reality was crumbling, the more paperwork was produced. And the more paperwork was produced, the more an obsession to rule by decree possessed the officials. It was this time of decline that produced the most elaborate, rational, and detailed pieces of legislation ever invented until modern times: the Theodosian and Justinian Codes. As problems mounted, dealing with them by multiplying decrees became an obsession. By 300AD, the bureaucracy, so far growing by leaps and bounds, virtually exploded. A sudden addition to the trough of tens of thousands of officials, all with power at their fingertips and all under pressure to make money quickly, all manipulating tools of escalating regulation and extortion into personal money machines, in order to build fortunes overnight, increased parasitism to an unprecedented and destructive level. Every new law, every new regulation, was a chance to squeeze money. As laws got more repressive, obstructive, and vague, ever higher and higher bribes could be extracted. Money was demanded at every level: to submit a petition, to talk to court clerks, to actually see the judge. Extravagant bribes were asked to see the almighty household servants of the emperor—the ultimate decision-makers. Random "protection money" was being extracted by soldiers stationed in the cities or by the legionaries living off the lesser landlords in the unprotected countryside. They continued the original loot activity that gave rise to Roman Empire—except they now preyed on Roman citizens, rather than barbarians. Immunity from random prosecutions had to be bought, time and time again, by the most innocent of citizens. Professional witnesses and professional 'victims' of imaginary wrongdoings offered their services for sale in front of the basilicas. While some degree of greasing the wheels was always present in the Roman system, the degree of corruption after 300AD was completely unprecedented. Every piece of power and influence was sold and re-sold, time and time again. Litigation for fabricated offenses made things especially profitable. Elsewhere, diggings unearthed semi-official 'price lists' for chunks of power offered for sale by civil servants.

Commercial activity, already in deep decline, was being shown unconcealed, mandarinian contempt by haughty officialdom. A decree of Constantine said: "Let no one enjoy any standing or rank who is of the lowest merchants, the money-changers, lowly offices . . ."[351] The bureaucracy was talking.

Curiously, even in the midst of a crumbling reality, faced with obvious evidence of decay, people of the 4th century Empire still expected their world to continue forever. Self-congratulatory speeches abounded as much as the servile rituals of prostration and praise. Like countless times before and after, the contemporaries failed to notice the utter transformation of their reality, and even when they did, they failed to believe it might signal the end.

This decoupling of imperial delusion from reality, the loss of common sense became a hallmark of the cycle itself. Late Rome's delusions were unreal, grotesque. In the reality of decayed provincial cities, full of burnt-out buildings, rebellions and civil wars, barbarian raids, depopulated provinces, growing poverty and returning killer diseases, an absurd and myopic world of bureaucratic pettiness, political correctness, 'patriotic' oratory, ritualized nonsense, intrigue, and infighting, was growing by leaps and bounds in the few sheltered tax-fed cities, to overshadow all productive action. In a society that shed away all productive pursuits, all higher goals, all pretence of fairness, some sort of mental threshold seems to have been crossed, beyond which reality started to resemble a tabloid, or a soap opera script, spiced with, and focused on, intrigue, sex, backstabbing, treasons, executions: the full theater of officialdom. Administrative or clerical functions became family fiefdoms, entire clans of ancestral bureaucrats, eventually morphing into manorial barbarity. Rituals of bureaucracy and ranking permeated any social interaction. Breaking rank in table seating could lead to bloody revenge. Strict rituals of greeting were devised, teaching people how to address each rank. They were observed with dead seriousness.

As power was privatized and became the main source of business and career, the late Roman society acquired surprising dynamics. Now vast fortunes could be built, virtually overnight, from the proceeds of bribery, extortion, and litigation. Massive amounts of money found its way into the hands of a brand new class: the bureaucrats. Piles of cash could be made, just by buying those who could whisper into the emperor's ears. As power was artificially escalated to prey upon rich and poor alike, and then re-sold for profit, it both distorted and impoverished the society by making the struggle for life the main activity. By that time, all the props and lip service to democracy and the republican system, still maintained in the 2nd and sometimes even the 3rd century, had been long forgotten. Now power was exercised behind closed doors, by cliques of civil servants, corrupt judges and court clerks, and the emperor's domestics. Declining Roman statecraft acquired a surprisingly oriental character. Embassies from cities complaining about official abuse, once valued as a direct contact between the emperor and the provinces, stopped being received in Rome. Contemporaries now compared power to meat: it could be bought and sold in chunks in the market every day.

Unlike before, in more civil times, where the illusions of equality were still maintained, now open contempt, typical for all bureaucratic societies, was being shown to the poor. For the first time in many centuries, the very term 'poor' (a term that begins to be increasingly used today) started to be used openly in court proceedings to describe the previously 'humbler' citizens, and the judges began to profess for the rich and influential a law very different from that for the poor. The O.J. Simpson trials were not our own invention. In the Late Roman era, money and legal sophistry could also provide a special type of justice.

As decay progressed, the only escape from the growing horrors of officialdom, from the squeeze of lawyers, soldiers, bandits, and tax collectors, became selling oneself into serfdom to big landlords, often government officials themselves, or those intermarried with civil service families. From 300AD on, there is ample evidence of this supposedly medieval practice, as the rich began to slowly privatize actual power in their hands. Not only were the poor selling themselves into serfdom: even affluent property owners were forced to accept bonds of allegiance to, and protection from, the super-rich, the '*potentiores*'. Even the affluent were not immune from fraudulent taxes, extortion by Roman soldiers or barbarian bands, or from legal terror: whimsical lawsuits that could force them to forfeit their fortunes to the lawyers or their lives to the judges. What could be considered a stand-alone 'middle class' of affluent property owners, well-off professionals, and merchants, was disappearing fast. Unless they were rich enough to control judges and bribe the officialdom, or even richer, able to field private armies that would gradually put them beyond the reach of the whole extortion system, they had to put themselves and their fortunes under protection of the super-rich, the owners of the huge *latifundia*, defended by castles.

In a process typical of every decline, combining both wealth and power in the hands of one group, the *potentiores* arrived in the wake of economic stagnation that gradually eliminated the middle classes, those of mid-sized landowners. The *potentiores* eliminated, subjugated, or bought out their smaller struggling neighbors, or anybody unable to weather the crisis on their own. Only resources as vast as theirs enabled them to protect their subjects and assets, fortify villas, grain stores, or farms, and turn them into castles. Only they could equip and field private armies composed of slaves and clients/serfs. Only they could control and manipulate to their advantage the legal squeeze that was destroying the lesser people. Evidence shows that where smaller villas disappeared, fortified baronial residences of the *potentiores* were enlarged after 350AD with private bathhouses, sprawling gardens, bronze sculptures, mosaic murals, storehouses, and dormitory buildings for farm workers, slaves, clients and soldiers.[352]

The power of the *potentiores* did not come just from wealth: in order to attain complete dominion over the whole society, they needed to collude with officialdom and enter the vast networks of profiteering, collusion, corruption and squeeze that transformed the once cohesive society into feudal 'privatized fiefdoms'. Bureaucratic dynasties made their appearance. Powerful families, powerful people were now described in official documents as belonging to a "Magistrates Clan", a "Councilors Clan", "Gymnasiarchs Clan", according to some ancestral bureaucrat holding such appointment, which gave him and his descendents a quasi-dynastic access to the redistributive trough. Records tell us that the Late Roman world, shrunk and stagnated, was now ruled by "men great, powerful, vigorous, who master the largest cities by virtue of some authority". Not only cities, but entire regions became private fiefdoms of *potentes, magni, maximi viri*, the 'Big Men': the rich and the officials, blending into each other without distinction.[353]

Manorial feudalism, this most primitive of social and economic systems, was a legacy. It was a dying gift to European civilization from the Roman bureaucracy—sometimes even complete with the same families, barbarized descendants of some Roman magistrate, lawyer, or imperial household servant, surviving regimes and centuries parasiting on the same manorial estate—as the documented cases in Spain—from Roman times, through Gothic kingdoms and Arab Caliphates all the way to the 18th century Baroque.

The Roman Empire seems to effectively have collapsed on its own. The speed with which it happened was astonishing. In a single generation, between 380 and 410, the imperial government west of Greece simply disintegrated. Ability to collect and remit taxes to the capital collapsed. This indicated that provincial *latifundia* owners refused to participate in the farce of Roman officialdom any longer. They likely did so given complete ineffectiveness of Roman troops to protect their holdings. Going forward they were able to shield themselves and their serfs and vassals from imperial taxmen and their ineffective troops and capture any surplus themselves. The farce of officialdom: the decrees, the taxes, the law system, the for-profit litigation, the paper soldiers, all collapsed within a few years in an unraveling similar to the one that brought down the Soviet Union.

Under the late Empire, it does not seem that its average agricultural wealth per capita diminished in any degree to account for its collapse. But the control and distribution of this wealth became skewed and predation, corruption, and collusion, unpredictable to the extreme. It was the forcible acquisition and desperate protection of individual holdings—whether from looters, soldiers, lawyers, tribesmen, or taxmen, that became the only business of the dying decades of the Empire.

Amidst the great cash-in, this last generation's desperate race to scoop as much land, as much gold as possible into its pockets before things changed, the cost of the Empire and the feeding of its exploding predatory sector, became unbearable. If the Empire still had some value to its citizens, this value has long been eaten away. The Goth tribesmen were amazed that, when they entered the city, the citizens of Rome helped them chase away the last remaining imperial tax collectors and facilitated the enemy take over. In the provinces, the key power holders, the feudal owners of large *latifundia*, now consolidated their holdings and dispensed with further predation of the bureaucracy by shifting their allegiance to tribal kings.

The Roman Empire never really collapsed. Instead, it was simply privatized. And the privatizers were mostly the stars of the hugely successful education system that created the last civil servants, lawyers and judges in Europe before the Dark Ages set in. It was their excellent education, smarts, and information professional status that enabled them to acquire, in the last few generations before the end, whatever income-producing assets they still could. Based on these assets they founded manorial dynasties that outlasted the collapse of the Roman civilization, in some cases for more than a thousand years.

THE ACCIDENTAL ARCHITECT, OR DAWN OF THE SEMI-DWARVES

T HE MOUNTAIN ROAD is full of potholes and the jeep is shaking horribly, threatening at every turn to spill us out into the ravine. But the landscape is incredible: we are looking down at hills, mountains and valleys, as far as the eye can see, all carved by human labor into rice terraces, all covered in lush green. These are the famed terraced mountains of central Luzon Island: the food basket of the Philippines.

This is the place where one of the most important revolutions of the past century took place. In this area, almost half a century ago, in 1966, Dr. Norman E. Borlaug developed a new semi-dwarf variety of rice. He called it IR8. Dr. Borlaug was working at the time within the framework of IRRI, an agricultural research institute sponsored by Ford and Rockefeller Foundations. A cross of Indonesian and Chinese rice varieties, IR8 could grow significantly more grains of rice per plant if grown in an irrigated environment and supported by certain types of fertilizers and pesticides.

IR8 was the child of well over a decade of research. As early as 1953, Dr. Borlaug began working with a wheat strain which contained a highly unusual gene. It had the effect of shrinking the plant, but without shrinking the seed head. That meant that a smaller plant (the so-called semi-dwarf) could still produce a large amount of wheat. Since the reduced stems decreased the plant's demand for resources: matter and energy, the dwarfing process diverted resources to the grain alone and made plants more stable mechanically. When the gene was later transplanted into tropical plants and high fertilizer levels were applied, the results stunned the researchers. On the same amount of land, output could be tripled or quadrupled.

Dr. Borlaug's approach used molecular genetics to breed high-yielding varieties of key food plants: rice, wheat and maize to create new breeds that could efficiently absorb and retain nitrogen-rich nutrients. To support genetics, it used targeted fertilizers, targeted pesticides and scientific irrigation. In short, Dr. Borlaug set out to re-engineer the basic food plants of humanity to maximize food output.

The first practical test of effectiveness of his method came in India in 1961. At that time, India and many other developing countries teetered on the brink of famine. Their traditional agriculture was no longer able to cope with exploding populations. With help from the Ford Foundation, Indian government embarked on an ambitious experiment of breeding new plants, developing intensive irrigation, and massive introduction of agrochemicals.

Punjab was selected to be the first site to try the new technology. As soon as IR8 was developed in 1966, India adopted it. Already by 1968, Indian scientists reported that under optimal irrigation conditions IR8 could yield almost 10 tons of rice per hectare with fertilizer, and as much as 5 tons without fertilizer. This compared to average Indian rice yields of about 2 tons per hectare before.

What happened after has been since known as "The Green Revolution". Nicknamed the "miracle rice", IR8 was widely adopted across Asia. By 1974, India became self-sustaining in terms of cereals production. By 1990s, average Indian rice yields have risen to 6 tons per hectare, effectively tripling within a single generation. Rice, which cost around $550 a ton in the 1970s, dropped to under $200 per ton by 2001. India, a net rice importer in the 1960s, became one of the world's most successful rice exporters. Using IR8, the Philippines more than doubled its rice production over a mere two decades. It also became a rice exporter, for the first time in a century.

Mostly based on the semi-dwarf varieties, developing countries more than doubled their food production between 1961 and 1985. Dropping costs of rice helped to stem food inflation after 1980. For a while, Malthus' theories seemed to be defeated: human ingenuity once again managed to come up with solution to delay the basic crises of too many mouths and not enough food.

When awarding Dr. Borlaug a Nobel Peace Prize in 1970, the Nobel committee stated: "More than any other single person of this age, he has helped provide bread for a hungry world". He did more. Largely forgotten by now, Dr. Borlaug accidentally became, along with Margaret Thatcher and Ronald Reagan, one of the key architects of today's neo-Baroque reality: the neo-conservative, overpopulated world of declining wages and global outsourcing. The engineered crops that he developed in the 1960s enabled the massive rise in populations of the developing world, supplying cheap labor to global investors and to the emerging Chinese elites of officials and professionals. By inflating human numbers, Borlaug's inventions created demand for energy and commodities that increasingly outstrip the planet's resources.

The cheaper food provided by semi-dwarves also indirectly resulted in lower prices of Chinese manufactured goods, keeping U.S. and Europe's inflation—at least for food and cheap manufactured goods—at bay over the last three decades. While these costs were kept low, the real inflation—inflation of costs of real estate, professional services, health care, education and energy, things that did not much depend on cheap engineered rice or low labor costs in China—continued skyrocketing.

The 'Green Revolution' of the last few decades had its Baroque precedents. It was very similar to the 'potato, maize and sugar' revolution of the 18th century. By supplying these cheap and reliable foodstuffs in mass quantity, the 'potato revolution' of the 18th century put—for a while—the end to famines of the early Baroque. For a few decades—almost a century between 1660 and 1760—potato-and-sugar based energy flooded the system, enabling a precarious economic revival. In some places, potatoes replaced close to half of traditional bread consumption; sugar soon accounted for around a fifth of total energy consumed. Since at the same time Europe's populations dropped dramatically—reaching a low point of around 60 million in 1700—causing a dramatic drop in asset prices and rents, the squeeze on the poor temporarily eased. Wages increased somewhat, and living standards improved. Subsequent massive increases of the population of Ireland, recovery of the populations of Germany and Poland—were mainly based on potatoes. In England, introduction around 1700 of the seed drill—a simple device that pushed seeds into the soil, rather than relying on scattering them around—significantly increased yields. This was especially the case when the seed drill was used on new, huge agricultural estates, owned by absentee investors. Atlantic ports experienced a sugar-and-slaves based commercial revival.

Just like the engineered rice during the last few decades, potatoes and sugar created a temporary boom. The key beneficiaries were countries that combined their colonial trade with new, efficient agriculture: England and Holland. Among Baroque darkness, the phenomenal rise of England in the 18th century, same as the phenomenal rise of Holland in the 17th, and odd prosperity of both countries among surrounding depression, were based on profits coming from increased efficiency of agriculture but mostly from colonial trade. These profits came courtesy of both countries' liberal economic and political setup, combined with Atlantic location. They allowed the oases of mercantile activity to survive and prosper in the bureaucratic world, sustaining exceptional environments in which something like Industrial Revolution, just conceivably, might happen. How critical were the colonial profits? During this era, outside of rent-and-tax capitals—these equivalents of today's 'global cities'—and some smaller princely 'rent capitals' in Germany, the only commercial cities that grew and prospered were Europe's Atlantic ports: Bordeaux, Lisbon, Cadiz, Hamburg, Bristol, all ports connected to the colonial trade and focused on sugar, tea, coffee, tobacco and soon cotton.

While both countries relied on profits from their colonial trade, another source of strength was their large-volume export of inexpensive manufactured products. Especially Holland—where wages were some of the highest in Europe—became a large exporter of manufactured products. These products—just like these coming today from China—may not have been of the highest quality, but they were cheap. Relying on unmatched efficiency of its water—and wind-driven manufacturing, efficiency of its agriculture, and cutting margins to the bone in order to maximize the volume of its exports, Holland—amazingly—even exported cheap wines, mixed and distilled from various sources, undercutting vine-growers like France.

But hardly anybody in the 18th century—this late Baroque flowering—focused on the new energy sources and economic structures that underpinned the temporary improvement in their reality. Instead, the contemporaries—as always, led by the glitterati—came up with something very similar to the 'Information Era'. They called their reality the time of the 'Enlightenment'.

As the economies gradually recovered, rents and taxes collected from fast-growing, potato-fed peasant populations began to fatten again the pockets of the asset owners, enabling the gilded culture of the Rococo and the flowering of the encyclopedic 'Enlightenment'. But in the end, all the potato revolution did was to double the number of humans, roughly within the space of a century. The potato boom ended up with the general impoverishment and misery. New famines that hit in the early 19th century—the times of Malthus—were some of the worst. The infamous 'potato famine' of 1845-52 killed around a million people in Ireland when the potato harvests failed.

The Green Revolution might have been similar to the Potato Revolution of the late Baroque, but with one critical difference. It came at a much steeper price. Massive quantities of fertilizers, pesticides, and water resources had to be committed to the re-engineered semi-dwarf agriculture, making the food industry heavily dependent on petroleum. This struck home a few decades later: when crude oil prices doubled within a short time to almost $150 per barrel in mid-2008, so did the basic food prices, causing wide-spread food panics, starvation and rioting in some of the poorest countries of the globe, from Egypt to South America to Pakistan. Price of rice tripled within months.

There was a curious Baroque/Renaissance déjà-vu in these events. The stinging *Harper's* magazine July 2010 report "The food bubble: How Wall St starved millions and got away with it" pointed the accusing finger at the speculators: the global commodities investors who reportedly drove the prices up during the bubble to bank massive profits. The article pointed that the value of global investments in commodities index funds alone rose from estimated $13 billion in 2003 to $200 billion in 2008. It was certain that speculation was rife: for example, Glencore, one of the world's largest commodity traders, while publicly encouraging Russia to impose a ban on grain exports during the drought of summer 2010, made a speculative bet on rising prices of grain and corn. The company made a fortune few days later when Russia followed with a ban and grain prices rose steeply.[354] While it was difficult to really find out whether speculation or sudden rise in oil prices, or both, were the culprit of massive rise in food prices, certainly something new—or old, whichever way you look at it—was happening. The extreme volatility of food prices in the last few years, a déjà-vu of historical trends of every decline cycle, was part of a larger, sustained trend of price inflation of basic commodities. Soybean prices have risen since 2002 by almost 400 percent; corn by up to 300 percent; wheat by almost 400 percent, with unprecedented year-on-year volatility.

Baroque-style speculation in basic foodstuffs, deciding fate of millions of the poor, was back with a vengeance. Just like in the previous Baroques, instability and starvation, as they re-appeared in the struggling realities of the decline eras, were always a flipside to massive speculative profits. And just like during the decades that led to French Revolution of 1789, by 2010 the effects of the Green Revolution that supported, for a while, the massive increases in the human numbers, began to wear off.

*

WE'VE COME TO the point in our story where we need to again stop for a while and try to answer two essential questions. What drives decline? What do we mean when we talk about history's 'cycles'?

Let's start with decline. Centuries ago, the process of decline was attributed to the almost biological process of "ageing" of civilizations. Historians of antiquity saw the rise and fall of the Egyptians, then the Persians, then the Greeks and finally of the Romans as the natural laws of the world. To them, it was as 'natural' that civilizations should rise and fall as it became 'natural' to us over the last two centuries that there should be continuous, ascending, perhaps even accelerating, progress. In China, with its regular dynastic cycles, the cycles of rise and decline acquired an almost poetic aspect of 'spring and autumn'. To the ancients, the rise, flourish and finally the decline of civilizations seemed as natural as winter following the summer. Often—and not without some justification—the historians and the prophets would put the blame on the sins and the decadence of the elites of the collapsing empire. No other convincing explanation of this phenomenon was arrived at until reasonably recently.

Within the last few decades, some—seemingly more sensible—explanations began to be circulated, even if they still did not fully displace the official 'progress mantra'. Most of them try to explain societal decline as the result of three linked processes: exhaustion of available energy sources, massive growth of human numbers, and escalating costs of social complexity—a situation where more and more resources are spent on feeding the societal overhead—basically, feeding the elites. In a typical setup, decline comes when the productive system supplying food, energy, and manufactured goods can no longer support the growing size and voracious appetite of the sector not directly involved in production: government workers, defense establishment, financial engineers, asset owners and swelling masses of their servants.

Overpopulation and depletion of energy sources and raw materials are closely linked. One way of looking at human civilizations—same applies to any form of life—is to see them simply as energy-processing systems. Not unlike plants and animals, civilizations use energy and stores of pre-existing information (accumulated, transmittable knowledge in case of civilizations, DNA in case of plants and animals) to perpetuate themselves, to expand, to grow large and complex. Once established and successful in tapping some energy source, they usually tend to stop evolving. They get set in a rut, freeze in their patterns, but massively grow in size. Once adopted and proven workable, ways of operation of a successful civilization—the patterns—are seldom changed. They become enshrined in the basic programming.

As civilizations grow in size, to manage this size and complexity and make more efficient use of resources, a ruling class of professionals—the 'information professionals'—emerges to perform specialized management functions. Gradually the overhead costs of this elite—whether priests, warriors, scribes, bankers, imperial bureaucrats or, during decline times, increasingly the purely parasitic elite of noble asset owners working together to perpetuate the establishment—grow exponentially. As the civilization gets large and complex, technological innovation, which originally contributed 'growth inventions' allowing humans to harness new energy sources, now gets refocused on administering the new complexity. Eventually, 'information processing'—inventions spreading faster and more efficiently the accumulated knowledge, management expertise and so on through the system, crown this evolutionary process. Dearth of new energy and productive inventions, growing costs of complexity and growing human numbers combine to set the stage for systemic decline.

When the money pie per average human no longer grows or even starts shrinking, with declining productivity growth, the problem is further exacerbated by the continued growth of costs and appetite of the elite. As competition for resources increases, the 'information professionals'—before perhaps medieval merchants or industrial era engineers—turn into Renaissance bankers and then Baroque dynastic asset owners. The move from riding growth to squeezing basic producers—whether farmers, factory workers or other producers of food and goods—soon results in dramatically declining living standards of the majority.

Decline always starts first at the bottom, with gradual pauperization—and sometimes malnutrition—of the average people. In the end, it has typically been followed by complete collapse of the civilization.

In a static energy system, history seems to tell us, collapse can only be averted by either of the two historical solutions. The first one is a wholesale slaughter of the elites and killing of any surplus mouths, to clear the land for a new cycle. This is what I called earlier the 'Chinese solution', where surplus humans, but especially entire elites—complete with asset ownership documents and debt records which were burnt—were wiped off the face of the earth at the end of every 'dynastic' cycle. The cycle would start now with a clean slate, and with much smaller human numbers. This solution underpinned the longevity of the Chinese civilization and its ability to regenerate. It also underpinned Europe's recoveries from the overpopulation crises of the 14th and 16th centuries, in each case restarting with fewer mouths—wiped off by war and epidemics—but with the same pool of agricultural wealth and physical infrastructure.

This cyclicality was what gave rise to the notion that history repeated itself.

The second solution we saw in history was the adoption of a new energy converter or a new energy source. This solution underpinned medieval Europe's spectacular growth and—critically—it underpinned the miracles of the Industrial Era. Invention of new energy converters was what reversed the misery of the last decades of the Baroque—the decline era of late18th and early 19th century. This solution—in a more simplistic form of potatoes and sugar—also underpinned the brief boom of the Enlightenment. To some extent—in form of the semi-dwarf plants—it also underpinned our recent New Renaissance. Interestingly, both of these mini-booms also relied on increasing 'economic globalization'—sourcing resources, including cheap labor, globally—to provide additional energy boost and raw material subsidy to the ailing, static energy systems at home.

This, in a nutshell, is the simple cycle of rise and decline of civilizations.

In every cycle, as the amount of energy available to the system would grow, it would create all the usual paraphernalia of success—burgeoning cities, material abundance, artistic flourish, all the visible signs of wealth. And invariably, added per capita energy supply would allow more resources, feeding more people, growth of the overhead sector. The growing energy surplus—if coupled with mechanization or automation of manufacturing—would allow more and more people to be part of the overhead rather than having to directly produce energy or goods. It was the phenomenal productivity of Industrial Era agriculture and manufacturing sectors that eventually enabled a mere 10 or 15 percent of the population to be engaged in these productive activities and feed the rest—the incredible 70 percent or so, for example, that depend in the U.S. on government for a living or work in the health care sector—all of them, so to speak, maintaining the system rather than producing anything. But as the limits to producing energy and goods are met and innovation slows down, the costs of supporting all these people—whether rulers or priests, bureaucrats, researchers, doctors, bankers, investors or lawyers—at one point cannot be met. The system atrophies and then eventually collapses—unless saved by another breakthrough in provision of energy and goods, perhaps like the one promised by nanotechnology.

Unfotunately, we did not see any such breakthrough for many decades now.

It is still a mystery why Baroque Europe suffered a dramatic decline but did not collapse altogether, why the government structures and elites held firm, even in an utterly impoverished reality—eventually shaken by revolutions every few decades. Could this be somehow related to the fact that, since the 16th century, all civilizations of the globe became much closely interconnected than ever before and single collapses, common before, ceased taking place? Or perhaps this could be due to the improvements in military technology? These improvements allowed the ruling elites a much easier repression of the underprivilegded, not to mention elimination or subjugation of much of the unstable barbarian hinterland—like nomadic Central Asia—that contributed to collapse before.

Whatever the answer to this question, it is beyond any doubt that neither the economic system nor the 'information technology' made much difference in respect of the process of economic decline. Societies as different in terms of their 'information technology' sophistication as Stone Age society of Chaco Indians and the Roman Empire—the latter with all its lawyers, philosophers, plumbing wonders, libraries, engineers and massive information flow—both collapsed in very similar fashion. Having run out of energy to support the runaway costs of their overhead, they collapsed—read: reverted to the next lower level of complexity.

Even though cities, aqueducts, baths, lawyers and irrigation works disappeared and populations typically would drop significantly, peasants still continued to seed and harvest, and human populations, even if greatly reduced in numbers and complexity, continued to exist. They might have been more vulnerable to invasion, but they no longer paid a lion's share of their harvest to support the elite overhead.

The idea that in a static energy environment the growing cost of complexity and growing human numbers drive the decline—and eventually the collapse—of complex societies, has been getting more and more traction in the last few decades. "More complex societies are more costly to maintain than simpler ones, requiring greater support levels per capita," wrote collapse specialist Joseph A. Tainter in his notable book *Collapse of Complex Societies*.

"As societies increase in complexity, more networks are created among individuals, more information is processed, there is more centralization of information flow, there is increasing need to support specialists not directly involved in resource production, and the like . . . As the society evolves towards greater complexity, the support costs levied on each individual will also rise . . . This is an immutable fact of societal evolution, and is not mitigated by energy source." Writer Jeremy Rifkin echoes Tainter's logic: "[Eventually,] the society reaches stage three, where its institutional complex (its economic and political organization) is so centralized and enlarged that it takes more energy to maintain it than the system can afford . . . The institutional complex, which was supposed to facilitate the flow of energy through the culture, becomes a parasite, sucking up much of the remaining energy source. All along the energy line the flow slows up, and the society begins to atrophy. In the final stages, even the institutional complex cannot be maintained with the energy it needs from the environment. At that point the entire complex begins to disintegrate."[355]

If people like Rifkin or Tainter are right—and history seems to prove them right—then the rise and fall of civilizations would be largely a question of depletion of finite energy sources by rising human numbers, compounded by society's growing complexity costs.

The basic routine of events would be always the same. A civilization would go through several evolutionary stages. In the innovation stage, a specific energy source or an energy converter would be invented and implemented, greatly increasing the amount of energy per capita available to the civilization. Such an energy converter would be for example an iron plough or an internal combustion engine, while energy sources might be not just coal or petroleum, but also wheat, maize or potatoes. The energy source could be a river, like the Nile, with easily irrigable, fertile land around it. The energy converter could be an ocean-going sailship, harnessing the energy of the wind, or a watermill harnessing the gravitational energy of a river, or even various implements harnessing energy of a horse.

Entire human societies, civilizations and empires would be built, discoveries, battles and dramas would spring from these simple discoveries and inventions—an irrigable river valley, an iron plough, a sailship, or horse accessories like stirrup and saddle—all the way to coaches and eventually cars and airplanes.

And yet, in every case, these energy sources and the new energy converters would eventually prove inadequate when faced with declining pace of innovation, depletion of cheap energy sources, rising human numbers, and rising costs of elite overhead.

OK, you might say. If this is the case, and the root of our problem is that we have too many people and no new energy converters and no new cheap sources of energy, why don't we simply invent these new converters and the new energy sources?

Unfortunately, the problem—the eternal problem of all Baroques—is that, as proven by history, short bursts of invention and innovation are followed by long stagnations, periods when we invent less and less.

POWER UNDER THE ICE

"Major breakthroughs in technology come [only] on the heels of qualitative changes in the energy source"
—Rifkin, Entropy [355]

IT'S 1991 AND I am walking on the sandy floor of the Arctic Ocean, fifty miles north of the Inuit town of Tuktoyaktuk on Canada's northern shore. Eighty meters or so above me, the frozen surface of the ocean is covered with mountains of ice. There, the temperature reading is minus 63 degrees Celsius, with the howling winds coming straight from the North Pole. I've had a good chance to experience this literally first hand when—to take pictures on the ice surface a few days earlier—I took off my fur mitt. The exposed skin froze in a couple of seconds. But down here, in the floodlights of the giant oil rig Molikpaq, inside the rig's well-heated open core from which the ocean water has been pumped out after the structure was lowered to sit, half-submerged like an island, on the ocean floor, it's balmy.

I am wearing a T-shirt.

The Molikpaq—a mechanical structure custom-designed to withstand the enormous pressure of the Arctic ice and allow Arctic oil drilling almost year-round, symbolizes two things. First, mankind's stunning progress in mechanics achieved during the Industrial Era. Second, mankind's thirst for oil that powered—and continues to power—all this machinery and our whole world.

Fossil fuel—first coal, then oil and gas—was what enabled mankind to finally break free—for the first time ever—from dependence on energy contained in food consumed by humans or their domestic animals. Medieval water—and wind-powered machines made some inroads into that dependence, but these technologies were no match for steam–and oil-fired engines. The Molipaq–a machine, or perhaps an artificial island, that allows people like me to walk, wearing T-shirts, on the bottom of the Arctic Ocean, could not have been built before the Industrial Era. And what distinguished Industrial Era from others was its use and reliance on cheap, efficient, easily accessible fossil fuels.

The Industrial Era increased many fold what we could achieve. The enormous increase in the amount of cheap energy available to humans literally changed the world. It mass-produced cheap industrial goods and cheap food. It exported these things around the globe at low cost, thanks to stunning progress in transport technologies. The civilization, to make it all work and to explore the newly opened bonanzas, transformed. As it needed more and more engineers, technicians, inventors, factory workers and middle managers to administer this new industrial complexity, it created productive occupations and life-long careers–increasingly coupled with reliable incomes–for most average people. It re-created, almost from scratch, the long-forgotten 'middle class' and democracy. It created cult of work and achievement. But most importantly, it created untold wealth. Fossil fuels provided an energy subsidy like no other seen before, well ahead of the energy released before by the iron ploughs, watermills, horse trains or potatoes.

With the energy of fossil fuels and powered machines, the whole Baroque reality of *rentiers*, landlords, bankers and lawyers, their manservants and rent-and-tax cities, all fed by agriculture, dissolved and shrunk within a few decades of the 19th century, absorbed by the new industrial world. As the stagnant, impoverished Baroque Information Era of year 1800 got an energy injection and transformed into the super-charged Industrial Era of year 1900, people's mindset changed. The whole world focused on science and engineering. It was the new direction–almost the only direction–where careers could be found, where spectacular profits could be made. Unlike today–or during any previous Baroques–during the Industrial Era, public interest in technology, science, and mechanical tinkering was simply enormous. By 1922, a national survey of 6,000 high school seniors showed 31 percent of the boys choosing engineering as their profession of choice.[356] This only began to slowly change after 1946, when scientists of the University of Pennsylvania revealed ENIAC—the world's first fully electronic, programmable, general-purpose digital computer—and the interest in mechanics began to be increasingly channeled instead into enthusiasm for computers starting in earnest in the 1960s and the 1970s.

The speed of advance between 1850 and 1950 was so breathtaking that it seemed natural to the forecasters of the 1950s and 1960s to expect this advance to keep on going, even to keep on *accelerating*. It was naturally assumed that the cumulative effect of accumulated information, and the massive investments in R&D, would kick in and add further fuel to the supercharged technological advance. By year 2000, predicted the forecasters of the '50s and '60s (and even into the '70s), there would be a massive wave of technological miracles—completely robotized space worlds, or at the minimum flying cars, colonies on Mars, massive affluence as a matter of course, enclosed electronic cities with controlled weather, highways across the Bering Strait, tunnels under the Atlantic.

These things clearly failed to materialize. They failed to arrive because we don't have enough money (read: cheap energy and cheap resources) to implement them. They failed to arrive because our technology fell short.

And our technology fell short because we simply invent less and less.

Why we invent less and less, and why things already invented take forever to get implemented, is not completely clear—as you can imagine, this is not a well-researched discipline, as even the topic itself goes completely against the still-ruling, although increasingly wobbly, conventional mantra of accelerating progress. One reason could be that many existing inventions and machines—like the *Concorde*—are too expensive to operate in today's reality of shrunken growth, increasing regulation and high energy prices. Consequently, incentives to invent machines and technologies that cannot bring immediate, high profits, essentially disappeared.

On top of this, a hurdle to innovation may be the fact that our science has been heavily compartmentalized. Each discipline has been broken into dozens of narrow, specialized fields. Instead of leading groundbreaking research, universities have become—just like during the last Baroque—mere copy machines to produce narrowly-focused specialists that fill positions in government and corporate bureaucracies. With fewer and fewer educated 'non-specialists', we increasingly seem to have lost the ability to come up with new ideas that transcend the established routines and paradigms; to see, as the saying goes, the forest for the trees.

Another reason is the growing complexity of prospective new inventions. As simpler inventions have already been invented, the difficulty level increases. The problem has been noticed by famous physicist Max Planck who said "with every advance [in science] the difficulty of task is increased." Today's prospective new inventions are too expensive and complex to be tackled by barnyard or garage inventors, the likes of Tesla or the Wright brothers. Today's research needs large funds. It has consequently become the business of large government or corporate bureaucracies, not always a recipe for success. On top of this, it has been permeated by geriatric concerns about lawsuits, patents, liabilities, and short-term financial return calculations. In government-funded research—once the leader of innovation—many now say it takes an Act of Congress to make an invention. Even as more and more investment into pure research is needed, cash-strapped governments are cutting research budgets. Nuclear energy of the 1940s and trips to the Moon of the 1960s were funded by massive amounts of U.S. government money, with teams of thousands—tens of thousands—of scientists mobilized to the task. But later—again in the 1970s, as the economy got tougher—governments stopped putting huge sums of money into pure scientific research, thus reducing chances of 'unintended discoveries'. Unlike the governments, private corporations, struggling with profits, are unlikely to invest in anything other than relatively shorter-term and targeted research, aiming for specific profitable products. This kind of approach resulted in a wave of improvements to older inventions, such as combining the old inventions like the TV, the microchip-driven computer, the radio and the telephone into various communication and information devices that crowd electronics stores today—the iPhones and the iPads—but failed to deliver the hoped-for major technological breakthroughs.

Statistics can give us the taste of what's actually been happening, squarely contradicting the wishful mantra of accelerating progress. Since 1920 the global investment in research and development has risen about 2800 percent and the numbers of scientists and engineers have likely risen even more. But the actual number of inventions and patents per capita has been dropping for the whole 20th century. Globally, it has begun declining since as early as 1873. In the USA it has been declining since 1915.[357] Indexed growth of new patents compared to growth of the numbers of scientists and engineers declined between 1870 and 1950 from 10 to 1.2. In the U.S. health-care system, the productivity index has dropped from 15.5 in 1954, its peak year, to 7 in 1982.[358] In most areas, there is clear evidence to show steady decline of innovation—compared to investment in it—throughout the entire 20th century.[359]

Fantastic amounts of money have been allocated since 1950 to fund research, but what has increased instead is just *quantity* of information—quantity of scientific and research papers, numbers of books, magazines and articles. Yet the massive ballooning of quantity of information cannot substitute for quality: real results like practical inventions and patents and quantum leaps in technology. It cannot replace the real breakthroughs that futurists and common people expected from the 21st century: higher incomes, dramatically increased lifespans, more affordable and better living environments, declining pollution and disease, eradication of poverty. These were the signs of most basic of progress taken for granted decades ago, but which have all failed to materialize.

If we measured technological progress by the number of scientists, or research dollars, or scientific publications, we should be in the midst of the greatest breakthrough in every single science and technology field—all happening right now. Yet a walk in the streets of any American city today proves that the apex of change has passed. Increasingly, just like the people of the Renaissance and the Baroque, we live off not only old science, old inventions and old technologies, but even off the old physical substance of our cities. Outside of electronics stores, there is a very Baroque feel to our reality—decaying slums in one neighborhood, luxury fashion stores in another—one that should give every thinking person a pause.

The global tendency to derive rent, rather than innovate, did not spare the IT sector. When in 2011 Google paid billions to buy Motorola's 17,000 patents, and Apple soon followed in its footsteps, analysts clearly saw this as a move to strangle innovation. "You'd much rather see Apple spend some of that $4 billion on new inventions, and Google invest that $14 billion to generate new knowledge" said Josh Lerner, an economist at Harvard Business School. "[Instead, buying old patents] is a transfer of wealth from innovators to bondholders and stockholders who have no motivation to innovate. It's disturbing." The journalist who brought the story to light, commented: "It now pays to sue over patents as a routine business practice."[360]

As the wider technological progress slowed down since the 1970s, what the last quarter-century could show instead of new miracles was an endless recital of blunders, cost overruns, delays, and cancellations of continued applications of existing technologies. There has been no landing on the Moon since 1973; the U.S. space program is basically grounded after repeated space shuttle disasters, the shuttle itself being almost a generation-old technology; the Space Station program is moving at a snail's pace and its practical application remains uncertain. The Stealth bomber program turned into a financial and technical embarrassment. The Desertron in Texas—America's flagship of technological expertise, set to be the largest superconducting supercollider in the world—enthusiastically approved in 1987 against a budget of $4.4 billion, ended in a fiasco in 1993, when construction stopped after spending $2 billion, with estimates to complete the project then running at $12 billion. Relatively simple engineering projects such as the Chunnel—the short railway tunnel linking the UK and France, using century-old technology—often turned into enormously expensive technical and financial fiascos, plagued by cost overruns, inefficiency, and delay. The Denver airport, hailed in the 1990s as "The 21st-century era of air travel," was delivered 18 months behind schedule and at three times the estimated cost. Many such examples abound.

Outside the newly industrializing countries in Asia, there has been a visible slowdown in major engineering construction projects worldwide. We can see broad technological slowdown in virtually every field. Household appliances, cars, buildings, urban and long-distance transport, generation of electricity (still in many cases with the same belching coal smokestacks), mining (still done by grimy miners, with daily deaths), packaging, logistics, shipping, aerospace, even space exploration—all are areas operated by a generation-old technology, with the basic science behind it at least half a century old. If we watch a half a century old 1960s movie, except for computers, we can see in it our world with hardly any technological change.

All these patterns of arrested progress and slow growth are utterly without precedent within the context of the Industrial Era. Supersonic passenger travel, introduced in the 1960s with the *Concorde*, has been abandoned. The 1960s hypersonic spaceplane technology—the scramjet—that was supposed to take passengers from New York to Tokyo in two hours, seems to be going nowhere. For the first time in hundreds of years—maybe ever—there was a step back in terms of how fast an average man can travel.

The world of today—the crude 'plutonomy' resembling all the previous Baroques—is increasingly old-fashioned in its trends and income sources, and less and less futuristic. Computers and plasma TVs are the only futuristic thing about our present. But even they are a generation-old invention.

AN UTTER HOLE

"In the days when its glory has passed away, Greece seemed to officials sent there from Constantinople 'an utter hole'"
    −Gordon East, The Geography behind History[361]

"Most ironic, in the age of the New Economy, we also underinvested in research, especially the basic sciences . . . we were, in part, living off past ideas, breakthroughs of an earlier day, such as transistors and lasers. We were counting on the foreign students . . . to sustain much of our research capabilities, while our best students were putting together the financial deals."
    −Joseph Stiglitz, The Roaring Nineties[362]

AS FUTURISTIC FORECASTS got discredited, how does the future look to the—usually more sober—business forecasters in their shorter-term visions? Even before the recession of 2008, there was no more talk of short work hours, electronic cottages, leisure eras, or affluent masses. Instead, Goldman Sachs analysts saw centers of growth shifting toward countries with either cheap and productive labor or cheap raw resources. Goldman expected Brazil, Russia, India, and China (the so-called "BRICs") overtaking all of today's leading industrial countries well before 2050: The 'BRICs' would have China and India at their centre with Russia prospering through export of oil to fuel their growth. Brazil would be exporting natural resources, mostly iron ore, and soya beans (key ingredient of animal feed). In a world desperately seeking cheap labor and cheap raw materials, post-industrial Europe—unless it were to undergo a major change—would become "little more than a tourist destination . . . for the wealthy from the BRICs." [363]

By 2012, much faster than anticipated, this picture of the world was already becoming a reality.

From any old futurist's point of view, the BRIC-dominated planet of cheap-labor Indian and Chinese factories turning out cars, TVs, and sneakers, fuelled by Russian oil and fed on Brazilian soya beans, looks rather pedestrian for what was once expected to be the super-wealthy, futuristic 21st century full of technological marvels. Yet even this slightly repellent—and quite unfuturistic—picture may be too rosy. Many analysts doubt China's sustainability; Russia is vulnerable to social problems, halted reforms, massive corruption, and terrorism; Brazil and India, poor and corrupt, with huge semi-literate and near-destitute masses, appear to be unlikely leaders for the coming future. Notably, few of these new leading BRIC countries are truly democratic, despite the hype of democracy's global triumph. If the BRIC is truly to dominate the world, where does this leave global democracy, equality, and old ideals of progress?

How about the post-industrial model that until very recently seemed to be leading us to the future, outsourcing dirty and mundane tasks to low-wage locales? There have been examples of post-industrial societies in the past, and none have been too pretty. In 1750, the leading industrial powers of the world were China and India: China had a third of the world's industrial output, India had a quarter. Late Baroque England had a mere two percent. Even on a per capita basis, industrialization levels of China and India in 1750 were comparable to England, with England only slightly in the lead.

By 1880, the picture has changed dramatically. In 1880 Britain had almost a quarter of the world's industrial output, USA had 15 percent, China 13 percent and India—forcibly de-industrialized by British policy—dropped to three percent. As England and USA raced ahead thanks to new machines and new energy converters, per capita industrialization level of India and China dropped to a staggering level *at least 40 times* lower than England. Compensations and wealth levels adjusted accordingly.[364] 'Post-industrial' China's and India's living standards underwent a catastrophic collapse, as they could not compete against cheaper, machine-mass produced, imported goods. As workshops closed, and peasants flocked back to overpopulated farms, towns shrunk, wages and nutrition levels dropped, skills disappeared. 19th century wipeout of both their manufacturing wealth and their artisans and traders (what could be described as commercial or middle class) happened at the time of massive population increases—also based to some extent on new crops like potatoes and maize—and resulted in the stunning pauperization of both China and India. China, from one of the richest countries in the world per capita still around 1760, became, a mere century later, one of the poorest. By 1900, both India and China looked like Malthusian horror. Just like Baroque Italy, they turned into depressed, backward, neo-conservative, rural backwaters, with living standards possibly the lowest in recorded history, possibly lower than in Africa.

Flood of exports of British factory-made textiles de-industrialized India completely, both in relative and in absolute terms. From an exporter of industrial goods, India became an importer within a mere couple of generations. In 1820 it imported 11 million yards of English textiles, in 1840 this rose to 145 million yards. The collapse of political power in both India and China during England's Industrial Revolution can be linked not only to the regular dynastic upheavals, but also to the growing economic imbalance with the West and de-skilling and pauperization of populations.

Why do countries completely de-industrialize, as we have seen in the examples of Baroque Italy or China in the 19th century? It seems that once the size of a certain domestic industry drops below a certain critical-mass level, loss of competitive edge entails a general societal de-skilling. General 'manual' skills—those of mechanics, tailors, carpenters, electricians, plumbers, machinists, print-setters, call center operators—tend to disappear first. Some became technologically obsolete, some become 'outsourced', for the remainder, at a certain stage, the talent pool would shrink below critical mass required to sustain it.

History shows that de-industrialization tends to gradually percolate through the entire society, with de-skilling slowly creating higher illiteracy levels and eventually impacting the intellectual elite. Societies with very high wealth polarization levels show that as the middle class disappears and literacy levels drop, intellectual activity slowly atrophies and eventually dies. The process may take many generations, but seems irreversible within a given energy system. This is what happened, as just one of the examples, in post-Classical, Hellenistic Athens of around 280BC, ravaged by wealth polarization and disappearance of the middle class of artisans and craftsmen. Athenian middle class, the backbone of society during the Classical Era peak was destroyed by cheaper mass-production of replicas of Athenian craftsmanship in places like Alexandria or Antioch, places that Alexander the Great's conquests integrated into the Hellenistic 'global economy' in a way somewhat similar to the way BRIC integrated itself into the Western, post-industrial world.

As decay—and frequently, famines—set in, Athens shrunk and turned into a depressed, backward hinterland—a little university town, eventually a dirty village. The process took centuries but ended up with the total destruction of what was once Greece. Once the decline cycle set in, great artists, inventors or philosophers were never born in Athens—or indeed, in Greece—again. By Byzantine times, the unfortunate officials sent there from Constantinople described the place as "an utter hole".

In Baroque Italy, during the Middle Ages and early Renaissance an industrial and intellectual superpower, one could hardly find literate artisans, or mechanics. The country that once used to flood Europe with its manufactured exports came now to import all of its manufactured goods and export only agricultural products: wine, cheese, olives. The decline of basic skills was absolute. Baroque Venice had to send her best gun-founder, Alberghetti, to London, to learn modern techniques of working metals[365]. In Baroque Italy, not many craftsmen could be found with skills to make simple wall-clocks. Those that could, copied slavishly the styles, even the mechanisms of those imported from England.

*

DE-INDUSTRIALIZATION IS A process that has been largely edited from the official history books. Yet it is the one of much more critical importance than the Templars or Jesus dynasties. If you are looking for an ancient mystery, here's one: it literally shaped our world.

De-industrialization and related de-skilling tend to have a devastating impact. In many American cities researchers might already find today, as they did in 1937 Carnegie Trust inquiry in Glasgow, during Britain's first industrial decline—before it adopted the American consumer and credit model in the 1960s—that more than a third of 18 to 25 year olds were so 'deficient in physical and mental qualities' as to be unfit for training for basic-skill jobs. Yet it is precisely acquisition of such skills—and not necessarily those of dotcom wizards, investment bankers, and corporate CEOs—that, in the ascending cycles, normally provided to many the means of advancement, career, and good pay. The irony of every decline cycle is that as such opportunities disappear, so does the middle class and with it the societal structure allowing both democracy and even the modicum of social advance to exist.

Every historical decline saw massive waste of human capital resulting from shrinking and pauperization of middle class and loss of skills. Compared to periods of growth and expansion, which invariably produce large and growing middle classes and explosion of talent and creativity, every period of decline is characterized not only by dramatic polarization of incomes, erosion of the middle class, of growing numbers of the destitute. The polarization and fragmentation of society is accompanied by a massive drop in creativity and innovation, as the human capital of the society, increasingly locked away in illiterate underclass, or dead-end middle class—or simply in prison—is simply wasted. No technological toys, no monumental architecture, no Baroque elite displays can alter this situation.

EMPIRES OF DREAMS

"In 1595 in Callao, Peru, Don Alvaro de Mendana and his formidable wife were recruiting in the streets while their ships made ready in the harbor. They were planning the colonization of the Solomon Islands, which had been discovered twenty-seven years before, and unvisited since, ninety days' sail away on the far side of the Pacific Ocean. Peru was already, as far as the inhabitants knew, on the furthest rim of their world; its settlers were mostly first-generation pioneers . . . and yet the Mendanas were able to raise a following of three hundred people prepared to venture across another ocean, to a land so far away that even the promoters of the enterprise had only a vague idea of how to find it."

—Felipe Fernandez-Armesto, *Millennium* [366]

I N THE HOT SUMMER of 1911, Sankt-Petersburg was booming. Apartment rents were the highest in Europe. Factory workers slept five to a room, in damp basement suites, inundated each spring by the flood of the Neva River, on dirty mattresses thrown on the floor. Six thousand people crammed together in Prince Vyazemski's tenements. Entire families lived in a corner of a room, such corners separated by hanging laundry. The city's population shot to two million souls, some 600,000 of them peasants who had arrived from the countryside just in the preceding five years. Fortunes were made overnight on land speculation. Industrial land in Spasskaya Ward, where most of the new factories were being built, was selling for four times the price of residential lots. Bars were full every night and fortunes were lost in gambling, vodka, and women. [367]

The boom of a century ago was a strange déjà-vu, a mirror image of today's boom of places like China or India, based on simple industrial expansion and cheap labor.

In six years government revenue doubled; personal savings on deposit in Russian banks tripled in value. Industrial output doubled or tripled within ten years and millions of dollars in foreign investment poured into Russia. Domestic capital and valuations of Russian companies grew at fantastic rates. Just like in Japan and Germany of the '60s, or China of the last decade, the domestic sector of Russian industrialization was largely an experiment in "state capitalism." As in today's developing countries, labor-intensive textile industries predominated. And as in today's China or India, the state controlled and regulated all sectors of the economy, providing loans and subsidies where it wanted, directing investments to meet its own goals. For Russia, the most important goal was to build a powerful military machine. The fantastic speed of growth in Russian armaments production frightened the Germans of 1911. It was that fear that pushed Germany to start the war on the flimsiest of excuses, in the summer of 1914. Following the new pseudo-Darwinian principles of survival of the strongest, Germany was desperate to defeat Russia and control her before she grew too strong.

Ten years later, the summer of 1921 was again hot and dry. The crops were disastrous. Russia was experiencing a widespread famine, the first in history to be substantially created by a country's own government, through a unique combination of bureaucratic delusion, ineptitude, and deliberate genocide. According to reports, as many as 27 million people were starving. As many as three million would die during the coming winter, the horrible winter of 1921-22. In desperation, the Russian government turned for help to the enemy: It appealed to the American Relief Administration. The city of Saint-Petersburg, later to be renamed Leningrad, was now half-empty. Hundreds of thousands of people escaped the horrors of the new reality.[368]

What happened in between, within the intervening decade, was an event usually called the Communist Revolution. The Communist regime in Russia lasted almost a century.

You may be wondering how does an event like this fit into our story? The fact is, history is replete with such phenomena—major events usually based on religion or 'secular religion' such as Communism, often sparked by wars, economic distress or other periods of instability—that cannot be explained just by simple reference to energy converters, or population increases, or resource exhaustion. These revolutions, or religious outbursts, all aim for redemption for the downtrodden, for opportunity, equality, fairness, participation of the poor and the meek in creation of their world. They may happen—as they did in Russia a hundred years ago—in a situation when a newly industrializing economy brings rapid change and hope into a society, yet it benefits mostly small elites, where improvement for the underprivileged is far too slow. We may find similar powder kegs in many developing countries of the globe today. Often, the new movements proclaiming justice and change—such as Christianity or Communism—succeed for a while to have a major impact on reality, even if sooner or later the reality invariably returns to its usual rut, the world divided between the rich and the poor.

These events open up a window into what makes us human, into what drives our hopes, even if they are eventually dashed. They belong to the emotional dreamworld of the human race.

*

BORN IN WHAT was during my childhood the Communist Poland, I experienced the Communist experiment with humanity first hand.

Why did Communism, despite its repression, its very doubtful quasi-Darwinian 'science', manage to claim at some point millions of ardent believers and was able to exercise enormous power—able to bring the world to the brink of a nuclear catastrophe? Very little, as it happens, of its attraction was related to the knowledge or understanding of its Marxist theories or its evolutionary interpretation of history. Despite its obvious shortcomings—shoddy goods, lack of democracy, repressive police state—the system's strength essentially rested on its program of social and income equality, full employment, free education, free medical care, cheap housing. It was a society that—for a while—fulfilled the hopes of many of the downtrodden. The system was continuously reinforced by skillful propaganda, 'patriotic' exhortations, deception and stories of 'enemy threats', similar to these that served so well George W. Bush administration.

Yet even for the vast number of people that did not subscribe to Communism, the enforced equality: equal sharing of common problems and successes, both joys and miseries of daily life, had an effect of fostering a unique sense of social unity. It fostered the feeling of belonging to something that exceeded the individual—belonging to a community of equals, people with shared problems, hopes and concerns. It was a phenomenon similar to that experienced during the Second World War in America. This was the time, contemporaries reported, when rationing and price controls had the strange and unexpected result of creating a sense of fairness and justice and thus sustaining the collective war effort.[369] The society felt unified and able to produce results that escape today's administrations, beset by divisions and unyielding, often hateful partisanship.

Societies are more than just a number of robot-like individuals competing to win in a quasi-Darwinian, ruthless world. This image is a gross over-simplification and to a large extent, a misrepresentation of what our societies are about and who we really are as the human race. Our dreams, our aspirations, overlaid over the simple mathematics of population numbers and available energy, acquire their own life. These dreams create various political and economic experiments. They fuel religions, spark revolutions, launch explorations and migrations. They underlie the most noble of dreams and the most horrible of crimes, as these extremes often go hand in hand. What happened in Russia was an example of such forces at work.

Humankind might be, at some level, just a biological superorganism eating the planet's resources as it grows in numbers and appetite. But it is also much more than that. To its members—to us—it is, just like a family, a critical mutual-support organization. It is a give-and-take system. The lesson of Communism—both its triumph in 1917 and its demise in 1989/1991 is that society's functioning and ultimate survival depends on cooperation and willing participation of the majority of its members in the game. And this cooperation is ultimately tied to the perception of whether or not the particular system of give-and-take is fair—or at least gives people a fair chance to fulfill their dreams. Ideologies and religions of change and social justice will rise, rebellions and civil wars will erupt when inequality and unfairness exceed what the common man can bear. Because, ultimately, as in the story of the Solomon Islands explorers, it is the common man—and woman—who creates reality.

*

CAN WE CHANGE the Baroque future? Any attempt at change must begin with re-igniting broad innovation. The objective of this innovation would be to increase wealth of society at large, raising productivity of our stagnating system and raising average incomes, in order to rebuild the middle class, this eternal anchor of every society. Broad investment in innovation must be accompanied by policies aimed at reducing inequality, narrowing wealth, income and education gaps, and elimination of political corruption.

Fighting inequality and re-igniting innovation are the two critical issues facing us today. Growing inequality destroys this key mainstay of a progressive and democratic society, the middle class. Without the middle class, progress cannot be sustained, society atrophies. This is the key lesson of history and of this book. But in order to sustain the middle class, society needs to create plentiful, well-paid jobs accessible to average-educated, regular people, not elite-school wizards and 'celebs'. And in order to create such jobs, the society needs growth, which—as we have seen before—can be provided by various drivers, but most assuredly can be provided by broad technological growth and innovation, both in very short supply today.

The smoke and mirrors of new iPads, iPhones and other electronic communication devices cannot conceal the fact that in the critical area of our reality—energy—we still operate with 1940s technologies. Lack of innovation in this area and massive growth in demand for energy made it very expensive over the course of our new Renaissance—from $3 per barrel of oil in 1967 to over $100 per barrel today, increase of about 30 times in nominal terms and perhaps 5 times in real terms. Possibly an effort on the scale of another Manhattan program or the Space Race—the money spent during the race to the Moon in the 1960s—is required to find solution to our problem. The only solution will be the introduction of new, cheap and clean energy sources.

But new cheap energy source is just the start of re-igniting the stalled progress. We need new, better means of transport to move beyond the generations-old ground transport—cars, trains and railways—and old-fashioned fixed-wing airplanes that still completely dominate our reality. We will need new construction technologies to produce cheap, quality housing at affordable prices and new cheaper materials outside of expensive metals and plastics. We will need new agriculture technologies to lower the escalating costs of food; the list is almost unending. We need so much more than mobile phones and tablets and social networks, it is stunning that the whole world of technology got reduced to discussions about a few computerized gadgets and most people seem to be taking for granted that this means we live in an era of accelerating progress.

If history is any guide—and I firmly believe it is—only a broad technological advance—and especially dramatic breakthroughs in energy sources—can decisively stop and reverse the current Baroque trends of decline.

How about fighting inequality? Inequality is more than a simple moral issue—beyond the non-resolvable question whether high or low incomes are "fair" or "deserved"—in historical context there can be no doubt that very high levels of inequality and polarized society are and always have been, absolutely destructive. It is historically proven beyond any doubt that, unless reversed by a sudden breakthrough in new cheap energy sources, growing inequality always heralded an incoming societal and economic decline. While it might have initially been just a symptom of the deeper societal malaise, by the time the society reached a 'plutonomy' stage, inequality would also become a catalyst of further deterioration of the system. This is what the ancient historians labeled as 'decadence'—the excessive wealth, conspicuous display and corruption of the elites breeding apathy, discontent, drop in ethical standards, hate—and justly labeled it as the perennial mark of the incoming era of economic and political problems.

As such—just as with climate change—we need to combat excessive inequality not so much on moral grounds, but simply for our own survival. And as with climate change, awareness of the problem is the first step to action.

Excessive inequality, widening income gaps, illiteracy, unequal education, quick buildups of massive private fortunes related in part to regressive taxation, tax-exemption and speculation, political corruption and dynastic politics, buying political influence, erosion of civil society, legalized violence—all these trends, so firmly entrenched by now, must first be recognized as intolerable and as destructive to the society at large. And they must all be countered in tandem, through a concerted political action and everyday education. This can be done by administrative measures—taxing spectacular income "chimneys," re-introducing wealth and estate taxes; by removing poll taxes, excessive sales taxes, and other measures and laws squeezing the poor or even criminalizing poverty; by reintroducing basic safety nets; eliminating growing inequality in education by improving quality of free education and controlling growth and eventually phasing out elite schooling; scrapping laws legalizing torture; firmly outlawing any form of political dynasties and nepotism; separation of business and politics and ban on the easy flow of people between the two sectors; enforcing total transparency of decisions and personal finances of all politicians and bureaucrats; by public funding of political campaigns, and so on. Finally, by investing money in people through different means than employing them in absurdly oversized government bureaucracy. If only encouraged and allowed, the creativity of the average people could do wonders and sweep over the jealously guarded little fiefdoms—today fiercely defended by various 'experts'—into which our reality has been compartmentalized.

The list of what can be done through administrative measures to clean out the rot is almost unending and could be in itself a topic of a separate book. The most important of these is the realization—seemingly forgotten over the last few decades—that democracy means that people must actively engage into directing the affairs of their country, rather than just passively listen to various leaders, gurus and politicians, perhaps elected by the people but frequently paid by special interests. People need to actively re-engage into the decision making process, rather than just vote every few years for some talking heads on TV peddling fake promises.

How to enact these changes when often the culprits are in charge? The failure of older civilizations that took purely administrative measures to reform should be our warning. Why did they fail? Obviously, Count-Duke Olivares (and so many others) tried to solve the problem by enlisting the governing elites to enforce elimination of the social rot that benefited those very elites—a sure recipe for failure.

One of the possible solutions that may bring us success in system reform might be a systematic reduction and maybe even elimination of the representative system. Instead we could manage the system through direct democracy—basically putting all key issues for instant electronic referendum. After all, if we have Information Age and Internet, let's put it to some use. But direct democracy is something that has not been attempted on a vast scale in modern times. It may or may not work and certainly needs a lot of thought and preparation before it is introduced, even on a limited scale. Despite the naïve illusions and mantra of the 'Information Era', average voters have very limited understanding of the economic or political issues affecting their lives and ability to vote on such issues in an informed way. Perhaps, rather than employing millions of people as civil servants in some small compartments of bureaucracy, with not much to do, money could be better spent educating them as decision-makers in their own business—the business of their society.

We need to invest, and invest on a massive scale, in not just rectifying the social imbalances of our societies, *but also in generating growth and wealth that does not rely on pushing down average incomes, a clearly regressive approach*. Labor-saving devices—their development abandoned, like in ancient Rome, in the face of cheap and abundant global labor—need to be promoted. New inventions in this area need to be encouraged and related R&D heavily invested in, so that we can counter the regressive search for cheapest human labor. The same applies to general automation, robotization, artificial intelligence, nanotechnology truly able to manipulate reality at a molecular level. If human labor is currently cheaper than that of robotic machines, we need to discover how to alter this and make machine labor cheaper again.

Despite very slow progress in robotics and continued very high costs—costs that continue to force manufacturers to opt for cheap human labor—it seems that manufacturing will eventually become largely automated, as small advances slowly percolate through the system. In Philips' new Dutch factory new generation robots can be programmed to do four functions with their arm, rather than just one, as the current generation of industrial robots already in use since the 1970s. In this factory each robot, costing around a quarter million dollars, replaces two workers making $50,000 per year. Against this cost benchmark, over its 15 year life, each robot saves around $23,000 per year in labor and productivity. [370]

While this is still quite modest, and such simple yet expensive robots cannot compete with China, where labor costs less than $4000 per year, we can expect that eventually both the robotic technology will improve—and costs of capital investment in robotics drop—and that robots take over most of the manufacturing sector. What happens then? What happens to the millions of factory workers left jobless by such development? And who will reap financial benefits of this advance?

This has happened before. When agricultural productivity improved dramatically during the Renaissance/Baroque era, farmers who had to forfeit their land to educated, cash-rich investors, went to the cities to become servants or factory workers. Exactly the same thing, on a much larger scale, happened in the 19th century—ordinary people moved from one manual activity (farming) to another manual activity (factory work). In the 20th century, as industry became more efficient and increasingly automated, surplus wealth allowed massive upgrade of these manual workers into the swelling urban middle class of office workers, clerks, mid-level managers, salesmen and the like. With massive productivity increases those that were still at the assembly line were able to force from the employers continuous wage increases. But this achievement rested on a combination of factors, unlikely to be repeated: very high increases of the overall productivity of the system, creating material abundance; unionization of millions of workers and their control over factory production; populist governments, supportive of socialist ideals. None of these factors exists today; and socialist ideas are dead.

So we can guess that gradual robotization of manufacturing, instead of distributing to the average people the benefits of cheaper manufactured goods, will not alleviate the current distress of the consumers in post-industrial countries. With current globalization and growth of BRIC markets, it is likely that robotic factories will be increasingly based in the new manufacturing powerhouses like China or India, close to the new consumer. In the post-industrial countries, where manufacturing employs only around 10 percent of the workforce, with ever-lower wages, gradual shrinking of the sector will not make much of a difference. Just like over the last 40 years, displaced factory workers will simply continue to blend into the huge existing masses of the Baroque service world: the low-paid millions delivering pizza, changing bed linens, answering calls, providing home care or selling Gucci bags, all quasi-manual activities, requiring not just the most basic of educations but often only limited literacy. The pool of industrial skills will shrink further in the post-industrial countries and wealth gap will increase further.

So here is the issue: manufactured products are just a fraction of what we use in our daily life, and costs of labor that goes into the final prices of such products is again just a fraction of their costs, dwarfed by the costs of raw materials, energy, transport, distribution and marketing. Without a drop in costs of energy, food, housing and transport, automation of the labor element in manufacturing will not by itself lower the dramatically rising costs of living. The financial squeeze is likely to continue.

Another recent manufacturing advance is development of 3-D printing—a technology allowing creation of objects by injection and binding of granules of raw materials into computer-designed forms. It is possible that advances in 3-D printing can be combined with new generations of significantly more sophisticated yet cheap robots that could assemble '3D-printed' components into finished goods. Will such development counteract the push for cheap labor and halt further moves of manufacturing to low-cost locales? It might for a while—until this technology is also adopted in places like China that already may have by that time advantage in newer infrastructure, production scale, R&D, plus faster growing consumer markets. But even if these new developments bring back some life into the manufacturing sector in the post-industrial countries, making sure that the benefits of this accrue to all people, not just asset-owning elites, is what legislators—and educators—should be striving for.

In the 1960s, the Race to the Moon succeeded because of incredible investment—in money, talent and sheer numbers of people working toward a clear, common objective—made possible by the government. Yet this investment—maybe a trillion dollars in today's money—was no bigger than the costs of the war in Iraq or of rescuing the financial system during the Great Recession of 2008-2009. It is possible that efforts on this kind of scale could result in breakthroughs in currently underfunded yet critical areas such as artificial intelligence, cheap energy and nontechnology, perhaps things like scramjets or space elevators. These are certainly more worthwhile investments by taxpayers in their own future than more trillion-dollar military adventures.

We should also beware of spending more taxpayers money and digging a deeper debt hole in order to shore up the economy for a year or two more. While taxes on very large fortunes could certainly be increased to reduce the mountain of debt, the real solution to the debt mountain lies in reducing government waste, and not focus on raising taxes. Excessive role of the government sector in the economy, huge military spending, many wasteful programs—all these are areas where savings could be found. Cutting down the size and hopefully eliminating the mountain of government debt is bound to make post-industrial economies significantly healthier.

With all this having been said, the secret of effective change is not to fight economic trends only through policy and administrative measures. They may ameliorate the situation to some extent, but are not the real solution. History shows that administrative measures rarely worked in the past. The secret is to quit deluding ourselves with the few gadgets of our "Information Era" and concentrate on truly re-igniting our inherent inventiveness, our ability to lift the general human condition, as it was done over the last couple of centuries, toward improvements in all facets of everyday life—security of income and education, better health, and higher living standards for all. In order to even tackle this issue, we need truly visionary leadership that would also have the courage to fight special interests and corruption and have an electorate supportive and intelligent enough to implement change.

*

WHENEVER WE PLAN for a new future, we need to remember that during our long history, the societies that succeeded were those where a vast number of people, not just a select few, actively invented and created their own reality. It was this inclusive mass-participation of ordinary people in society's actions that animated builders and discoverers in the growth stage of their societies. Growth stage of societies—building of pyramids, medieval cathedrals, or great engineering works of the industrial era—were accompanied by waves of popular enthusiasm. These pyramids and cathedrals were built by regular, ordinary people animated by creative fever and power we are finding difficult to explain; great works of art, towering monuments, and global discoveries were often the handiwork not of elite-educated wizards, but of ordinary men and women animated by vision and enthusiasm. Their dream was the basis of the astonishing years of America's peak.

"All the European overseas empires were to be established by the almost unaided initiatives of private enterprise, with little or no state patronage," writes Felipe Fernandez-Armesto in *Millennium*. "No royal jewels were pawned for Columbus; the Portuguese crown spent more money on junketing for royal festivities in the sixteenth century than on Africa, India, and Brazil combined; the most successful of early English emigrants were fugitives from, not agents of, home government."[371] Led by visionary adventurers—like the Mendanas in this chapter's quote—followed by mere handfuls of misfits, animated by vivid images of treasure and romance, it was the ordinary people whose energy was released. These were the enterprising dreamers who built global empires.

These masses of ordinary entrepreneurs and people seeking to better their fate would succeed time and time again where imperial bureaucrats—like Chinese admiral Cheng Ho during his global voyages in the 1420s—would always fail. Even if China discovered America in the 1420s, it hardly left a trace.

Where ordinary people were allowed to use their initiative, genius, and ability, where—unrestricted by college diplomas, wealth gaps, and privilege—these people could raise themselves up, rather than be pushed down into dead-end Baroque servitude and torpor, that's where masses of ordinary, low-educated people created the successful civilizations of the past. But when economic circumstances deprived people of jobs, self-expression, economic opportunities and ability to excel, to drive their own destinies, it seems that a reverse process occurs in every historical decline. "Men's minds quite naturally close up when new experiences cease to be a normal part of life," writes historian Thomson.[372]

*

UNLESS WE WANT to make use of what we can learn from past events, there is not much point in studying history. Without learning from the past, we're left to float on the surface of events, hostages to either the randomness of "market" forces, or to new breeds of populist, radical, or fundamentalist leaders.

A society where semi-literate poor serve the elite-educated rich, a society where middle class is shrinking and getting poorer, is a society that—no matter how brilliant its elite, or what kind of 'information era' it claims to belong to—must atrophy and decline. This is the essential lesson of history.

Deep down, we know that we are all equals, all the same, part of a chain of life that is the human society. Without this community that nurtures us, we can do little. Each of us depends on millions of others to make us who we want to be, to achieve our goals. We depend on other people contributing their energy, talent, and education to our success, and we owe the same to them. Our key goal should be to preserve this civilization on which we so depend—by learning from the successes and failures of societies now past. We need to learn the lessons of history—what worked and what failed, and what made us great—in order to be able to counter the dangerous signals of the present: the Baroque Syndrome.

We need such a goal. There is none today. Once, civic spirit was fired up by the building of cathedrals, or by great engineering projects, or by new inventions, or by the race to the stars. Common goals, visions that could be shared by entire communities, or even by all humanity, fired popular imagination and belief, stimulated our minds, and provided a sense of accomplishment.

Today, social, human, and infrastructural decay of much of our post-industrial reality, stunning inequality, growing fragmentation of the society into isolated groups, massive wealth and education gaps, are all reflected in the apathy and discouragement of the common people. Locked in dead-end, disposable underjobs, drifting through life without any understanding of or influence over their reality, the masses of today have no longer a vision of a hopeful future. This is one of the most terrifying features of our reality.

We know today, and we always did, that each of us has infinite potential, far beyond what we have achieved so far. It is up to us to break the charmed spell of the debilitating patterns of injustice, selfishness, and societal divisions. But we need to break this charmed circle together, as a society, and not as individuals racing to our own individual goals. We need to re-engage the masses of ordinary people into the direct political process, into feeling that they also own the resources of the community—but as stakeholders and decision-makers and not as dole recipients or hapless 'voters' for some deep-pocketed politicians.

As long as we grasp that we, and not some mythical laws of progress, are in charge of our future destinies, then we truly have the power to change the patterns of the past. Whatever happens during the centuries yet to come, we may need to repeat and believe just one thing—that we are all one, all equal, all children of the same God. That our wealth should principally come from our own hard work, ingenuity, and skill, not from privilege, family wealth, taxes, rents, or ownership of some other legal claim on the work of others. That no matter how rich we are, the misery, humiliation, and hunger of the dispossessed on which we tread is likely to prove to be the seed of destruction—destruction not only of the ideals of liberty, equality, and justice we once proudly proclaimed but recently all betrayed, but of the very societies into which our children and grandchildren will be born. That no matter how much we focus on ourselves, we need to serve a greater good—the survival and prosperity of all. That our first and foremost obligation is to preserve the wellbeing of others, and to help the society that has given us in abundance, so that we can all succeed in the future.

Because the future, contrary to what we used to believe, is not guaranteed. It can still fail. It is up to us to ensure that is does not, and that the new Baroque never arrives.

THE END

ENDNOTES

1   Euan Ferguson, The Observer, *South China Morning Post,* Sep. 11, 1996
2   *Census: 1 in 2 Americans is Poor or Low Income,* NPR website, Dec.15, 2011 (http://www.npr.org/2011/12/15)
3   Fisher, *The Great Wave,* p. 203
4   Drexler, *Engines of Creation,* opus
5   Toffler, *Future Shock,* opus
6   Toffler, *The Third Wave,* opus
7   Lanjouw, Jean O. and Shankerman, Mark, Patent Quality and Research Productivity Measuring Innovation with Multiple Indicators, *The Economic Journal,* 114 (April) p. 441-465, Royal Economic Society 2004, Blackwell Publ., Oxford
8   Nouriel Roubini and David Backus, Lectures in Macroeconomics, Chapter 4. Productivity and Growth (http://people.stern.nyu.edu/nroubini/NOTES/CHAP4.HTM)
9   Thurow, *The Future of Capitalism,* p. 1
10 Rick Newman: How the Government Is Swallowing the Economy, *money.usnews.com,* Nov. 9, 2009
11 *MSN Money, Financial News*: Rising poverty rate shows holes in safety net. Httpy://mny.mobile.msn.com/en-us/articles.aspx, 5:25pm EST Sep. 13, 2011
12 Dolan, Mike. Waiting for trouble, but unready, *The Times,* June 30, 2011, p. 15
13 Buttonwood, Marx, Mervyn or Mario: What is behind the decline in living standards? *The Economist*: Finance and Economics, March 26th, 2011, p. 75
14 Arianna Huffington, *Third World America,* p. 4
15 Editorial. *The Economist,* August 14, 2010, p. 56

16   Editorial. *Bahrain Tribune*, February 7, 2010, p. 1
17   Leaders: The Future of Food, *The Economist*, Feb. 26, 2011, p. 10
18   Editorial. *The Times*, December 13, 2010, p. 31
19   Editorial. *The Times*, July 5, 2011, p. 32
20   Editorial. *Gulf Insider*, January 2011, p. 22
21   *Children Advocacy Institute website*, Aug. 17/05: California Children Budget 2002-2003
22   Elizabeth Warren, chair of the Congressional Oversight Panel for TARP, quoted in Huffington, *Third World America*, p. 5/6
23   Editorial. *Time Magazine*, December 13, 2010, p. 22
24   Thurow, *The Future of Capitalism*, p. 34
25   Thurow, *The Future of Capitalism*, p. 24
26   Editorial, *The Economist*, June 17, 2006, p. 26
27   Thurow, *The Future of Capitalism*, p. 24
28   Thurow, *The Future of Capitalism*, p. 24
29   Domhoff, *Who Rules America?* p. 6
30   Thurow, *The Future of Capitalism*, p. 25
31   Feller, Stone, *Center on Budget and Policy Priorities*, 2007, p. 1-2
32   Domhoff, *Who Rules America?* p. 6
33   *http://money.msn.com/family-money/poverty-has-a-new-address-suburbia-fiscaltimes.aspx* accessed Feb. 22, 2012
34   Kapur, McLeod and Singh. 2005, Plutonomy: Buying Luxury, Explaining Global Imbalances, *Citigroup Investment Research, Citigroup Global Markets*
     www.scribd.com/doc/6674234/Citigroup-Oct-16-2005-Plutonomy-Report-Part 1
35   Editorial, *Financial Times*, October 16/17, 2010. p. 9
36   Editorial. *Gulf News*, April 1, 2010
37   Thurow, *The Future of Capitalism*, p. 23
38   Domhoff, *Who Rules America?* p. 8
39   Editorial. *The Straits Times*, March 18, 2006, p. H17
40   Domhoff, *Who Rules America?* p. 8
41   Wien, Byron. US capital productivity must be reversed. *Financial Times*, Feb. 17, 2010, p. 22

42 Editorial, *Economist*, Feb. 27, 2010, p. 45

43 Editorial, *Financial Times*, Mar. 23, 2010, p. 14

44 Rifkin, *The End of Work,* p. 191

45 Rifkin, *The End of Work,* p. 167

46 Editorial, *Financial Times*, Sep. 23, 2010, p. 2

47 Thurow, *The Future of Capitalism*, p. 165

48 Rifkin, *The End of Work,* p. 37

49 Editorial, *Sunday Telegraph*, Feb. 8, 2009, p. 12

50 Editorial, *The Phoenix Gazette*, March 14, 1993

51 V. Anderson, *Calgary Herald*, Oct. 11, 1992

52 Editorial, *South China Morning Post,* June 12, 2005

53 Editorial, *The Economist*, June 17, 2006

54 Editorial, *The New York Times*, Feb. 9, 2009, p. 4

55 Editorial, *The Straits Times*, March 30, 2007, p. 6

56 Editorial, *South China Morning Post*, Dec. 28, 2005, p. A8

57 Thurow, *The Future of Capitalism,* p. 30

58 Gibbon, *Decline & Fall of The Roman Empire,* opus.

59 Michael Brush, *MSN Money* website, April 18, 2012, 12:54 pm

60 Feather, *G-Forces.* p. 55-56, 59-60, 117, 127

61 V. Anderson, *Calgary Herald*, Oct.11, 1992

62 Donald Ratajczak, *McLeans Magazine*, Oct.12,92

63 Editorial, *The Province*, (Alberta, Canada newspaper), May 4, 1993

64 Thurow, *The Future of Capitalism,* p. 28

65 Editorial, *International Herald Tribune*, Feb. 15, 1996

66 Huffington, *Third World America*, p. 18

67 Huffington, *Third World America*, p. 13

68 Zepezauer, *Take the Rich Off Welfare,* opus.

69 Thurow, *The Future of Capitalism,* p. 25

70 *Business Week*, May 6, 1996

71 Schor, *The Overworked American,* opus

72 Schor, *The Overworked American,* opus

73 *MarketWatch e-newsletter, update: 3:44 PM ET Aug 22, 2006*

74 Associated Press, Washington, Oct. 28, 2005

75 Editorial. *South China Morning Post*, Sep. 14, 2005

[76]   Braudel, *The Mediterranean and the Mediterranean World in the Age of Philip II, Vol.II*, p. 735

[77]   Cipolla, *Before the Industrial Revolution*, p. 129

[78]   Rifkin, *The End of Work*, p. 194

[79]   Macdonald, Arthur, So what went wrong? *Gulf Daily News*, Jan. 3, 2011

[80]   Braudel, *Civilisation and Capitalism: The Structures of Everyday Life*, p. 133-143

[81]   Cole, Postgate, *Common People*, p. 307

[82]   Cole, Postgate, *Common People*, p. 315

[83]   *http://money.msn.com/investment-advice/latest.aspx?post=b0922a19-be45-45a1-8967-9055b8c94c67* accessed Jan. 8, 2012

[84]   Rifkin, *The End of Work*, p. 129

[85]   Fisher, *The Great Wave*, p. 190

[86]   Fisher, *The Great Wave*, p. 159

[87]   adaction.org/Income 2004, p. 7

[88]   Fisher, *The Great Wave*, p. 172-173

[89]   Thurow, *The Future of Capitalism*, p. 4

[90]   Newby, *Country Life*, opus

[91]   Stephen Cass, Unthinking Machines: Artificial Intelligence Needs a Reboot, May 4, 2011, *MIT Technology Review*, *www.technologyreview.com/computing*)

[92]   Cowen, *The Great Stagnation*, opus

[93]   Robert J. Samuelson, *The Great Reversal*, Washington Post, Opinions, Oct. 9, 2012

[94]   Gimpel, *Medieval Machine*, p. XI

[95]   Jack, Andrew. "Supply Running Low". *Financial Times*, February 10, 2011, p. 7

[96]   Jack, Andrew. "Supply Running Low". *Financial Times*, February 10, 2011, p. 7

[97]   Huffington, *Third World America*, p. 105

[98]   Editorial, *Financial Times*, April 2011, p. 9

[99]   Editorial, *South China Morning Post*, Feb. 7, 2006

100 Heirs of Mao's comrades rise as new capitalist nobility, Bloomberg News editorial, quoted in *"Today"*, Singapore newspaper, Dec. 29, 2012, p. 15, World section

101 Quoted in Gimpel, *Medieval Machine,* p. 145-146, NOTE: Content of pages 105 through 115 is to a large extent based on "Medieval Machine: The Industrial Revolution of the Middle Ages" by Jean Gimpel and the author wishes to recognize with thanks this key source for the material.

102 Boserup, *The Ends of Earth,* opus

103 Gimpel, *Medieval Machine,* p. 205-206

104 Cipolla, *Before the Industrial Revolution*, p. 195-197

105 Cipolla, *Before the Industrial Revolution*, p. 195-197

106 Gimpel, *Medieval Machine,* p. 27

107 Gimpel, *Medieval Machine,* p. 233-235

108 Gimpel, *Medieval Machine,* p. 142

109 Gimpel, *Medieval Machine,* p. 16-17

110 Gimpel, *Medieval Machine* p. 66

111 Gimpel, *Medieval Machine,* p. 225-227

112 Thomson, *Decline in history,* p. 45

113 Huppert, *After the Black Death,* p. 30-35

114 Pirenne, *Medieval Cities,* opus

115 Gimpel, *Medieval Machine,* p. IX

116 Fisher, *The Great Wave*, p. 41

117 Fisher, *The Great Wave*, p. 30

118 Fisher, *The Great Wave*, p. 33

119 Fisher, *The Great Wave*, p. 33

120 Fisher, *The Great Wave*, p. 34

121 Fisher, *The Great Wave*, p. 26

122 Fisher, *The Great Wave*, p. 28

123 Fisher, *The Great Wave*, p. 29

124 Gimpel, *Medieval Machine,* p. 171-172

125 "Outsourcer reaps benefits of rural India's talent". *Financial Times*, Feb. 8, 2011

126 Cipolla, *Before the Industrial Revolution,* p. 198

127 Aston, *The Fifteenth Century,* opus

[128] Thomson, *Decline in history,* p. 97-98

[129] Thomson, *Decline in history,* p. 105

[130] Braudel, *Civilization and Capitalism, 15th-18th century,* opus

[131] Braudel, *The Mediterranean and the Mediterranean World in the Age of Philip II, Vol. I,* p. 210

[132] Thomson, *Decline in history,* p. 120

[133] Huppert, *After the Black Death,* p. 75

[134] Fisher, *The Great Wave,* p. 79

[135] Braudel, *Civilization and Capitalism, 15th-18th century,* p. 134

[136] Braudel, *Civilization and Capitalism, 15th-18th century,* p. 196

[137] Fisher, *The Great Wave,* p. 72

[138] Beattie, *False Economy,* p. 81

[139] Fisher, *The Great Wave,* p. 77

[140] Fisher, *The Great Wave,* p. 77

[141] Fisher, *The Great Wave,* p. 80

[142] Fernandez-Armesto, *Millennium,* opus

[143] Hale, *War and Society in Renaissance Europe,* p. 93

[144] Fernandez-Armesto, *Millennium,* opus

[145] Huppert, *After the Black Death,* p. 55

[146] Cipolla, *Before the Industrial Revolution,* p. 12-13

[147] Hohenberg, Lees, *The Making of Urban Europe,* p. 26

[148] Hale, *War and Society in Renaissance Europe,* p. 83

[149] Gimpel, *Medieval Machine,* p. 143

[150] Hale, *War and Society in Renaissance Europe,* p. 84

[151] Hale, *War and Society in Renaissance Europe,* p. 84

[152] Hale, *War and Society in Renaissance Europe,* p. 16

[153] Thomson, *Decline in history,* p. 153

[154] Huffington, *Third World America,* p. 79

[155] Thomson, *Decline in history,* p. 108

[156] Huppert, *After the Black Death,* p. 74

[157] Fisher, *The Great Wave,* p. 86

[158] Fisher, *The Great Wave,* p. 87

[159] Braudel, *Civilization and Capitalism, 15th-18th century,* p. 484

[160] Fisher, *The Great Wave,* p. 68

161 Thomson, *Decline in history,* p. 126

162 Treasure, *The Making of Modern Europe,* opus

163 Thomson, *Decline in history,* p. 185

164 Kamen, *Spain 1469-1714,* p. 89

165 *Time* magazine, Dec. 13, 2010, p. 29

166 *Time* magazine, Dec. 13, 2010, p. 29

167 Lawrence Summers, The U.S. state will expand no matter the election result, *Financial Times,* Aug. 20, 2012, p. 7

168 Thomson, *Decline in history,* p. 185

169 Thomson, *Decline in history,* p. 174

170 Gibson, *Spain in America,* p. 150

171 Huppert, *After the Black Death,* p. 56

172 Hohenberg, Lees, *The Making of Urban Europe,* p. 146

173 Huppert, *After the Black Death,* p. 48

174 Kamen, *Spain 1469-1714,* p. 154

175 Kamen, *Spain 1469-1714,* p. 153

176 Gibson, *Spain in America,* p. 131-133

177 Hohenberg, Lees, *The Making of Urban Europe,* p. 117

178 Huppert, *After the Black Death,* opus

179 Huppert, *After the Black Death,* p. 81

180 Huppert, *After the Black Death,* p. 100

181 indybay.org, Jan. 18, 2004

182 Huppert, *After the Black Death,* p. 92

183 Huppert, *After the Black Death,* p. 98

184 Huppert, *After the Black Death,* p. 63

185 Braudel, *The Mediterranean and the Mediterranean World in the Age of Philip II,* opus

186 Kamen, *Spain 1469-1714,* opus

187 Fisher, *The Great Wave,* p. 95

188 Fisher, *The Great Wave,* p. 92

189 Braudel, *The Mediterranean and the Mediterranean World in the Age of Philip II, Vol. II,* p. 752

190 Rifkin, *The End of Work,* p. 239

191   Braudel, *The Mediterranean and the Mediterranean World in the Age of Philip II, Vol.II*, p. 753

192   Gibson, *Spain in America,* opus

193   Hohenberg, Lees, *The Making of Urban Europe*, p. 118-119, 152

194   Fisher, *The Great Wave*, p. 96

195   Gibson, *Spain in America*, p. 107-108

196   Boserup, *Environment, Population, and Technology*, p. 21-36

197   Fisher, *The Great Wave*, p. 93

198   Boserup, *Environment, Population, and Technology*, p. 21-36

199   Cipolla, *Before The Industrial Revolution*, p. 26

200   Martin Wolf's article in the *Financial Times*, quoted in Huffington, *Third World America*, p. 29

201   Huffington, *Third World America*, p. 20

202   Thomson, *Decline in history*, p. 132

203   Thomson, *Decline in history*, p. 57

204   Huffington, *Third World America*, p. 21

205   Thomson, *Decline in history*, p. 55

206   Thomson, *Decline in history*, p. 133

207   Hobsbawm, *The Age of Revolution*, p. 24

208   *Globe & Mail,* Mar. 27, 1989

209   Thomson, *Decline in history*, p. 135 and p. 174

210   Kamen, *Spain 1469-1714*, p. 216

211   Kamen, *Spain 1469-1714*, p. 235

212   Kamen, *Spain 1469-1714*, p. 215

213   Kamen, *Spain 1469-1714*, p. 218

214   Thomson, *Decline in history*, p. 169-171

215   Thomson, *Decline in history*, p. 126

216   Quoted by Thomson, *Decline in history*, p. 129

217   Treasure, *The Making of Modern Europe*, opus

218   Thomson, *Decline in history*, p. 120

219   Braudel, *The Mediterranean and the Mediterranean World in the Age of Philip II, Vol. II*, p. 755-756

220   *How America Can Withstand the Headwinds,* Financial Times, Nov. 2, 2010 p. 11

221 R. Kuttner, *Business Week*, Apr. 22, 1996

222 *Gulf News,* p. 33, Biggest Money Squeeze Since 1920s, Jan. 29, 2011

223 William A. Collins, *This Economy Stinks Worse than you think*, *MSN Money* website Apr. 26, 2012

224 *South China Morning Post,* June 19, 2006, p. A8

225 *The Economist*, June 17, 2006, p. 40

226 Reflected Glory, *Financial Times*, Jan.19, 2011, p. 9

227 China dims prospects for Silicon Valley jobs, *Financial Times*, Jan. 29, 2011, p. 4

228 Huffington, *Third World America*, p. 27

229 China dims prospects for Silicon Valley jobs, *Financial Times*, Jan. 29, 2011, p. 4

230 Nina Easton, Politicians need to face harsh realities about the U.S. jobs crisis, *Fortune magazine*, Sep. 5, 2011, p. 31

231 Thurow, *The Future of Capitalism*, p. 107

232 National Association of Realtors, *South China Morning Post*, Feb. 1, 2006, p. p3

233 www.ssa.gov/oact

234 www.ssa.gov/oact

235 healthpolitics.com, Dr.Magee

236 MarketWatch, Update: 4:51 PM ET Mar 10, 2006, *MSN Money*

237 U.S. National Center of Statistics 2002 data

238 *South China Morning Post*, Sep. 11, 2005, p. 12

239 Rifkin, *The End of Work,* p. 172

240 *Middle Class Areas Shrink as Income Gap Grows, New Report Finds.* http://www.nytimes/2011/11/16

241 Children Advocacy Institute website, Aug. 17/05: California Children Budget 2002-2003

242 Lucie Greene, Launch of the flagship armada, *Financial Times,* Sep. 29, 2011, p. 8

243 Rong Xiaoqing, *South China Morning Post*, Mar.19, 2005

244 Rong Xiaoqing, *South China Morning Post*, Mar.19, 2005

245 Forbes article from Mar. 2005, quoted in Mar.12, 2005, *South China Morning Post*

246 Forbes, *MSN Money*, March 10, 2006
247 Rifkin, *The End of Work*, p. 174
248 Editorial, *Financial Times*, Dec. 14, 2005
249 Rong Xiaoqing, *South China Morning Post*, Mar. 19, 2005
250 Rifkin, *The End of Work*, p. 174
251 Thurow, *The Future of Capitalism*, p. 22
252 Thurow, *The Future of Capitalism*, p. 24
253 S. Beck, *South China Morning Post*, Sep. 23, 1994
254 Rifkin, *The End of Work*, p. 77
255 National Law Center on Homelessness and Poverty, 2004
256 Rifkin, *The End of Work*, p. 180
257 Thurow, *The Future of Capitalism*, p. 105
258 Roger Cohen, *International Herald Tribune*, Sep. 10,11, 2005
259 City in Crisis, *Wall Street Journal*,1996
260 Lexington, *The Economist*, May 1, 2010, p. 38
261 America's 'near poor' at risk, *International Herald Tribune*, May 9, 2006, p. 4
262 *S. Beck, South China Morning Post*, Sep. 23, 1994
263 Rifkin, *The End of Work*, p. 176
264 Rifkin, *The End of Work*, p. 211
265 Rifkin, *The End of Work*, p. 212
266 Rifkin, *The End of Work*, p. 213
267 Rifkin, *The End of Work*, p. 177
268 Dieter Wermuth, *South China Morning Post*, Feb. 03, 2005
269 Martin Wolf, *The UK must escape its longest depression, Financial Times*, Sep. 2, 2011, p. 9
270 Thurow, *The Future of Capitalism*, p. 36
271 Thurow, *The Future of Capitalism*, p. 36
272 *South China Morning Post*, Feb. 26, 2005
273 Rifkin, *The End of Work*, p. 202
274 *Financial Times*, p. 7, A majority to accommodate, April 19, 2012
275 Bloomberg, *South China Morning Post*, Aug. 24, 2005, p. 5
276 *South China Morning Post*, Sep. 11, 2005, p. 14
277 *South China Morning Post*, Sep. 28, 2005, p. 5
278 *South China Morning Post*, Sep. 28, 2005, p. 5

[279]   *Business Week*, Apr. 22, 1996
[280]   *Business Week*, Apr. 22, 1996
[281]   Krugman, *The Great Unravelling*, p. 223
[282]   Krugman, *The Great Unravelling*, p. 108
[283]   *International Herald Tribune,* Apr. 11, 2006, p. 13
[284]   joehilldispatch.org, National Economic Trends, St. Louis Federal Reserve, June 18, 2005
[285]   Stiglitz, *The Roaring Nineties*, p. 123
[286]   Micheal Brush, *MSN Money*, Jan.18, 2006
[287]   Bob Herbert, *The New York Times,* Apr. 5, 2004
[288]   Sylvia Allegretto, Economic Policy Institute, *The State of Working America 2004/2005*
[289]   Michael Karp, Options Group, *South China Morning Post,* Sep. 27, 2005, p. B9
[290]   Dennis Cauchon, "Federal workers earning double their private counterparts", *USA Today,* Aug. 13, 2010
[291]   Laurence Brahm, *South China Morning Post,* Aug.2, 2005, p. A13
[292]   Brian Knowlton, *International Herald Tribune*, Jan.13, 2006, p. 5
[293]   Clients' rewards keep D.C. lobbyists thriving, Jeffrey H. Birnbaum, *Washington Post, MSNBC website* Updated: 11:16 p.m. ET Feb. 13, 2006
[294]   Brian Knowlton, *International Herald Tribune*, Jan. 13, 2006, p. 5
[295]   D.Stauton, Germans slip up on sleaze, *South China Morning Post*, Aug.12, 1995
[296]   *Financial Times Asia*, July 22, 2005
[297]   Briefing: The mood of Russia, *The Economist*, Sep. 10, 2011, p. 29
[298]   Editorial, *South China Morning Post*, Sep. 20, 2005, p. A13
[299]   Editorial, *South China Morning Post* (Bloomberg), Oct. 28, 2005, p. B11
[300]   MSN/NBC website, 7:13pmET, Mar. 3, 2006
[301]   Stiglitz, *The Roaring Nineties*, p. XII
[302]   *New York Times*, Nov.13, 2009, p. 7
[303]   Cipolla, *Before the Industrial Revolution*, p. 241
[304]   Ioan Grillo, Mexico Falls Victim to the China syndrome, *South China Morning Post*, Dec. 24, 2005, p. B5
[305]   Editorial, *New York Times*, May 12, 2006, p. 12

306 Rifkin, *The End of Work,* p. 201
307 Special Report: The Future of Jobs, *The Economist,* Sep. 10, 2011, p. 5
308 Editorial, *South China Morning Post,* Apr. 19, 2005
309 Stephen Roach, *Morgan Stanley website,* June 18, 2005
310 *washtech.org,* July 17, 2002
311 Special Report: The Future of Jobs, *The Economist,* Sep. 10, 2011, p. 11
312 Editorial, *South China Morning Post,* Mar. 25, 2006, p. E2
313 Rifkin, *The End of Work,* p.172
314 M.P. Dunleavey, *MSN Money,* April 8, 2006
315 Editorial, *The Economist,* June 17, 2006, p. 25/26
316 Editorial, *South China Morning Post,* Sep.6, 1995
317 Editorial, *South China Morning Post,* June 1, 2006, p. A19
318 Editorial, *South China Morning Post* (The Christian Science Monitor), Apr. 24, 2006, p. A16
319 Huppert, *After the Black Death,* p. 54-55
320 Erik Brynjolfsson, Shinkyu Yang, MIT, *Information Technology and Productivity: A Review of the Literature, Advances in Computers,* Academic Press, Vol. 43, p. 179-214, 1996
321 Snow, 1966, quoted in Tainter, *Collapse of Complex Societies,* opus
322 Rifkin, *The End of Work,* p. 75
323 Rifkin, *The End of Work,* p. 91
324 John B. Taylor, Stanford, *Wall Street Journal,* Oct. 18, 1996
325 Stephen Roach, quoted in Erik Brynjolfsson, Shinkyu Yang, MIT, *Information Technology and Productivity: A Review of the Literature, Advances in Computers,* Academic Press, Vol. 43, p. 179-214, 1996
326 M. Hodges, *Grandfather's Economic Report,* Sep. 21, 2005
327 M. Hodges, *Grandfather Economic Report,* Sep. 21, 2005
328 M. Hodges, *Grandfather Economic Report,* Oct. 30, 2010
329 Marilyn Gardner, *Christian Science Monitor, MSN Money,* March 5, 2006, based on the book *Green with Envy* by Shira Boss
330 Simon Read, Ditch the plastic before you are forced into distressed borrowing, *The Independent,* Nov. 5, 2011, p. 57
331 Rifkin, *The End of Work,* p. 35
332 Fisher, *The Great Wave,* p. 217

[333] *The Public Interest*, Issue #154, National Affairs, Inc., winter 2004

[334] Simon Read, Nine out of ten families will be forced to ration heat this winter, *The Independent*, Nov. 5, 2011, p. 58

[335] *South China Morning Post*, June 7, 2005

[336] *Nature*, British weekly science journal, quoted in *South China Morning Post*, March 10, 2005

[337] *South China Morning Post*, Feb.26, 2005

[338] *MEED*, October issue, 2008, p. 20

[339] *South China Morning Post*, Apr. 5, 2005

[340] *South China Morning Post*, Nov. 22, 2002, p. 18

[341] P. Kammerer, Modern Slavers Know No Borders, *South China Morning Post*, Feb. 27, 2005

[342] *The Straits Times*, Jan. 14, 2006, p. 38

[343] Irene Wang, *South China Morning Post*, Jan.24, 2006, p. A4

[344] *South China Morning Post*, Mar. 16, 2006, p. A7

[345] *South China Morning Post*, Mar.13, 2005

[346] *South China Morning Post*, Mar. 13, 2005

[347] *South China Morning Post*, Jan. 15, 2006, p. 12; 'Our 9 billion time bomb', (from Steve Connor, *The Independent*)

[348] *Financial Times*, Sep. 24, 2011, p. 20

[349] McMullen, *Corruption and the Decline of Rome*, opus, NOTE: Content of pages 285 through 295 is principally based on analysis and information contained in Mr. Ramsay McMullen's book and the author wishes to recognize with thanks this key source.

[350] McMullen, *Corruption and the Decline of Rome*, opus

[351] McMullen, *Corruption and the Decline of Rome*, opus

[352] McMullen, *Corruption and the Decline of Rome*, opus

[353] McMullen, *Corruption and the Decline of Rome*, opus

[354] Glencore reveals grain price bet, *Financial Times*, Apr. 25, 2011, p. 1

[355] Rifkin, *Entropy*, opus

[356] Rifkin, *The End of Work*, p. 53

[357] (*http://www.physorg.com/news4879.html*, July 1, 2005 article, accessed Sep. 20, 2011

[358] Tainter, *Collapse of Complex Societies*, opus

[359] Lanjouw, Shankerman, Mark, Patent Quality and Research Productivity, p. 441-465,

[360] Steve Lohr, Patent deals are the rage, but innovation might be the victim, *International Herald Tribune*, Aug. 18, 2011, p. 15

[361] East, *The Geography behind History,* opus

[362] Stiglitz, *The Roaring Nineties,* p. 18

[363] Peter Kammerer, Rich Pickings, *South China Morning Post,* Nov. 19, 2005

[364] McNeil, *Rise and Fall of Empires,* opus

[365] Cipolla, *Before the Industrial Revolution*, p. 249

[366] Fernandez-Armesto, *Millennium,* opus

[367] Johnson, *A History of the Modern World,* opus, NOTE: Content of pages 322 through 324 is principally based on "A History of the Modern World" by Paul Johnson and the author wishes to recognize with thanks this key source for the material.

[368] Johnson, *A History of the Modern World,* opus

[369] Fisher, *The Great Wave*, p. 197

[370] John Markoff, Highly efficient and no coffee breaks, *International Herald Tribune*, Aug. 20, 2012, p. 1

[371] Fernandez-Armesto, *Millennium,* opus

[372] Thomson, *Decline in History,* p. 122

BIBLIOGRAPHY

Aston, Margaret. *The Fifteenth Century: The Prospect of Europe.* WW Norton & Co, 1979

Beattie, Alan. *False Economy: A surprising Economic History of the World.* Penguin Books, London 2010

Boserup, Ester. *Environment: Population, and Technology in Primitive Societies.* Population and Development Review, 1976, book 2, 21-36

Braudel, Fernand. *Civilization and Capitalism: 15-18th Century.* Vol 1, The Structures of Everyday Life. Berkeley, University of California Press, 1992

Braudel, Fernand. *The Mediterranean and the Mediterranean World in the Age of Philip II, vol. II.* Berkeley & Los Angeles, University of California Press, 1995

Braudel, Fernand. *Civilization and Capitalism, 15th-18th century: The Perspective of the World.* Berkeley, University of California Press, 1992

Cipolla, Carlo M., *Before the Industrial Revolution*: *European Society and Economy, 1000-1700.* London, Routledge, 1993

Cole, G.D.H. and **Postgate**, Raymond: *The Common People 1746-1946.* London, Routledge, 1992

Cowen, Tyler. *The Great Stagnation: How America Ate All The Low-Hanging Fruit of Modern History, Got Sick, and Will (Eventually) Feel Better.* Penguin ebook, 2011

Domhoff, G.William. *Who Rules America?* New York, McGraw-Hill, 2006

Drexler, K. Eric. *Engines of Creation.* New York, Anchor Books, 1986

East, Gordon W., *The Geography behind History.* New York, WW Norton & Co, 1999

Elliott, Michael. *The Day Before Yesterday*: *Reconsidering America's Past, Rediscovering the Present.* New York, Simon & Schuster, 1999

Feather, Frank. *G-Forces: The 35 Global Forces Restructuring Our Future.* Toronto, Summerhill Press Ltd, 1989

Fernandez-Armesto, Felipe. *Millennium: A History of the Last Thousand Years.* New York, Free Press, 1996

Fisher, David Hackett. *The Great Wave,* New York/Oxford, Oxford University Press, 1996

Gibson, Charles. *Spain in America (New American Nation).* London, Harpercollins College, 1966

Gibbon, Edward. *Decline & Fall of the Roman Empire.* New York, Wildside Press, 2004

Gimpel, Jean. *Medieval Machine: The Industrial Revolution of the Middle Ages.* London, Penguin Books, 1977

Hale, J.R. *War and Society in Renaissance Europe, 1450-1620.* McGill-Queen's University Press, Montreal & Kingston, 1998

Hobsbawm, E.J., *The Age of Revolution: 1789-1848.* New York, Mentor Books, 1962

Hohenberg, Paul and **Lees**, Lynn Hollen. *The Making of Urban Europe, 1000-1994.* Harvard University Press, Cambridge, Ma. and London, 1996

Huppert, George. *After the Black Death: A Social History of Early Modern Europe.* Bloomington, Indiana University Press, 1998

Huffington, Arianna. *Third World America: How our Politicians are abandoning the Average Citizen.* London, HarperCollins Publishers, 2011

Johnson, Paul. *A History of the Modern World: From 1917 to the 1980s.* London, Weidenfeld & Nicolson, 1991

Kamen, Henry. *Spain 1469-1714: A Society of Conflict.* Longman, London, 1991

Krugman, Paul. *The Great Unravelling,* Penguin Books, London, 2004

Lilley, Sam. *Technological Progress and the Industrial Revolution 1700-1914: The Fontana economic history of Europe,* London, Collins, 1970

McMullen, Ramsay. *Corruption and the Decline of Rome.* Yale University Press, 1990

Newby, Howard, *Country Life: A Social History of England*, London, Cardinal Books, 1988

Pirenne, Henri. *Medieval Cities: Their Origins and the Revival of Trade*. Princeton University Press, 1969

Postan, Michael M. *The medieval Economy and Society: An economic History of Britain in the Middle Ages*. London, Weidenfeld and Nicolson, 1972

Rifkin, Jeremy. *The End of Work*, London, Penguin Books, 1995/2000

Rifkin, Jeremy. *Entropy: A New World View*, New York, Bantam Books, 1981

Schor, Juliet. *The Overworked American: The Unexpected Decline of Leisure*. New York, Basic Books, 1993

Stiglitz, Joseph, *The Roaring Nineties*, London, Penguin Books, 2004

Tainter, Joseph A. *The Collapse of Complex Societies (New Studies in Archaeology)*, Cambridge University Press, 1990

Thomson, J.K.J. *Decline in history: The European experience*. Cambridge, Polity Press, 1998

Thurow, Lester. *The Future of Capitalism*. London, Nicholas Brealy Publishing, 1996

Toffler, Alvin. *Future Shock*. New York, Random House Publishing, 1984.

Toffler, Alvin. *The Third Wave*. New York, Bantam Books, 1989.

Treasure, Geoffrey, *The Making of Modern Europe, 1648-1780*, London, Routledge, 1985

Zepezauer, Mark and **Naiman**, Arthur. *Take the Rich Off Welfare*. Tucson, Odonian Press, 1996

www.ingramcontent.com/pod-product-compliance
Lightning Source LLC
Chambersburg PA
CBHW051222050326
40689CB00007B/771